Under the Frontier Sky

Dewan Jagdish Dass Sehgal

Originals
(an imprint of Low Price Publications)
Delhi-110052

Distributed by
D.K. Publishers Distributors (P) Ltd.
4834/24, Ansari Road, Darya Ganj,
New Delhi-110002
Phones: 23278584, 23278368, 23261465,
e-mail: dkpd@del3.vsnl.net.in
visit us at: www.dkpd.com

ISBN 81-88629-01-4

Published by
Originals
(an imprint of Low Price Publications)
A-6, Nimri Commercial Centre,
Near Ashok Vihar Phase-IV,
Delhi-110052
Phones: 27401672, 27452453
e-mail: lpp@nde.vsnl.net.in
visit us at: www.lppindia.com

Printed at
D K Fine Art Press P Ltd.
Delhi-110052

PRINTED IN INDIA

Contents

To Shakti Sehgal, the wife, mother and eternal optimist, whose love, support and faith are like a rock that the family has always leaned on. Without her nothing would ever be possible.

Chapter One

Early Life

I was born on 16th May 1924 in a village in Kohat district. Kohat is in the North West Frontier Province of Pakistan, but until India was divided in 1947, it was part of India.

Tehri, my village, was the Headquarter of a tehsil, which bore its name. Tehri was one of the three tehsils in Kohat District. The Administrative control of the district was vested in a deputy commissioner and that of the tehsils (subdistricts) in tehsildars, who were responsible for land revenue collection and had magisterial powers. However, Tehri was a state with a Nawab. Though officially Tehri was the Headquarter of the Tehsil and the Nawab resided there, the factual headquarter was at Banda Daud Shah, an outpost about five miles from Tehri, on the main highway between Kohat and Banu. The Tehsildar held his court there. Apart from offices, the treasury, staff quarters and a couple of tea stalls, Banda had no other building. Of course, it also boasted of the only telegraph office in that area. Kohat was 30 miles from Banda and 62 miles from Banu.

N.W.F.P at that time had six districts: Hazara, Peshwar, Mardan, Kohat, Banu and Dera Ismael Khan. I believe it still remains the same. Kohat and Banda were connected by a good motorable road, to ensure the quick movement of troops between the northern parts of the province and the southern parts, but Banda and Tehri were connected by an unmetalled road. This road was further extended to connect it to Tal, a border town on Kohat Parachinar Frontier Agency Road, in the thirties for frontier defence, though normally it was never used. The Tehri Banda road was cut off when it rained heavily because of a flooded stream. This stream was normally placid but during the rains it became a raging torrent. This was because the drainage of this sub mountainous tract, ringed by mountains on the south, north and west, was based on this stream. While the mountain chain was not even a mile away to the south and was only about two miles to the north, it was quite far away on the western side. The terrain sloped towards the south and southeast, but the mountain chain here started at Banda Daud Shah, which was five miles from Tehri.

Toi (o pronounced as in broke, and i pronounced as in Thailand) which is the Pushto word for stream, came from the due west, but after passing Tehri on the south, swerved to the north, about a mile from the hillock, on which Tehri village was situated, and again took an easterly direction after a short distance. About three miles further down it turned towards the south, and thereafter cutting across the Tehri Banda Daud Shah Road, about a mile from Banda, it turned once again towards the east. It continued in that direction after passing under a bridge, on Banda Daud Shah Banu road, a few miles from Banda.

It frequently happened that a bus crossing the stream near Banda while going towards Tehri, had to rush back about a mile from Tehri, because the flood had made the stream impassable at that point. The bus then tried to reach Banda before the floodwater reached the stream where it cut across the road near Banda and made it impassable too. Normally bus passengers spent the night at Banda and tried the crossing the next morning or later, depending upon the flow of water. Occasionally a bus was taken to Amadi Banda, about two miles from Banda Daud Shah, towards Kohat. From there the passengers tramped down seven miles to Tehri on a detour, to the north of 'Toi', crossing a small rain water stream (called nala in Urdu and Hindi). The stream was usually dry but even in flood it did not pose much of a problem, as it dried up in two or three hours, the source of its water being very near. The mountain base from which it drew water was only about three miles from where it joined the Toi and less than two miles from where passengers usually crossed it.

Teri's population in the thirties was about 2000; about 500 being Hindus and the rest Muslims. The southeastern corner of the hillock was occupied by the Nawab's family and near relatives and the adjoining southern portion by his other relatives and hangers on. The market, 'bazaar', ran in a straight line in the centre, from south to north but did not occupy more than 150 yards. In width, it was not more than 15 yards. There were shops on both sides of the passage, which was about 12 feet wide. The Hindus had their houses behind the shops on the west, while the Muslim quarters were spread over the south, southwest and part of the eastern sector, wherever habitation was possible. Apart from the above population, which was enclosed within the perimeter walls, the majority of the Muslim population inhabited the western part of the hillock and the western and eastern slopes. The weavers' houses were further towards the east, on the road to Banda Daud Shah. The perimeter wall had three gates; in the southeast, southwest and northeast. Except at the extremities where the gates were situated, there was no free running perimeter wall: the outer walls of the houses at the periphery constituted the perimeter wall. At night the 'chowkidars' manned the northeastern and the southwestern gates. The southeastern gate was situated where the Nawab's quarters were located, and the security there was the responsibility of the Nawab's staff, but the salaries of the 'chowkidars' (sentries) were paid by the Hindus through monthly contributions for the purpose to their 'panchayat'. During the period, when there was a threat of attack by the Wazir Tribesmen, which was constant after 1938, the sentries were armed with 303 rifles, supplied by the Nawab. The Nawab also supplied rifles to a few Hindus who could handle them.

The boys' vernacular middle school, hospital (under the charge of a sub-assistant surgeon) and the police station (under a sub-inspector) were situated a little distance from the village, and were near each other, on a raised ground to the northwest. The girls' school, unto class four, was at the base of the village on the hillock. In both schools the medium of instruction was Urdu. In the girls' school only the Muslim girls of the lower middle class came to study, and that too from localities situated near the school. The Hindu girls took their lessons from a Brahmin lady in the Hindu locality, called the "Hindu Mohalla'. Their medium of instruction was Hindi.

Tehri was quite a large tehsil, and the Nawabs of Tehri had, not in the very distant past, exercised near full sway on this area of over 1000 kilometers. Khataks, the Pathans, who inhabited Tehri, were warlike people. They depended on agriculture and the earnings of those male members who were in the army. Agriculture was mostly rain fed, but the rainfall was not enough. The average rainfall in N.W.F.P. was 15 inches, and in Tehri it was even less. About two thirds of this rain came in the winter, from the northwest monsoon, and the rest came in the summer from the southwest monsoon. This brought in enough wheat for the relatively well-to-do, and bajra, millet, for the not well-to-do peasants. Around Tehri there were a number of wells where vegetables and corn were grown. Most of these belonged to the Hindus and a few were the property of the Nawab's relatives.

Tehri Tehsil had two salt mines: at Jatta and Bahadurkhel. In the Tehri tesil was Karak, which was really a town and had a high school with English as a subject upto matric.

Initially Nawabs could imprison people or immobilize them by putting one of their feet in a log of wood and locking it up by hammering in a thick iron nail. But gradually the British administration took away their powers. They brought in the police station and took away their powers of imprisonment. They then took away their magisterial and judicial functions. A tehsildar was brought in for that purpose. Before that the Nawabs had their own court (Kachery) building and a 'Kazi', the magistrate. In 1937, the Congress government of the province took away even the powers of the honorary magistrate, which were left with the Nawab. In lieu of the salt mining rights, instead of payment of a proper royalty, the British Indian Government gave the Nawab a grant of Rs. 10000/- per annum. Similarly in the mid-thirties, there was an agreement that instead of the payment of land revenue, the Nawab be paid a fixed amount of Rs. 50000/- per annum, irrespective of the yield.

To assist the Nawab in various matters of administration and other allied subjects there used to be a Dewan (minister), and he used to be from a group of families called Dewans. I do not know how the Dewans came to be called so: whether they all descended from a single progenitor who was a Dewan or they were known as such even before they came to Tehri. It is correct that the Dewans of Tehri descended from a single progenitor, but it cannot be stated with certainty that the Dewans were not called as such before they migrated to Tehri. Most probably, they were known by the same name before they came to Tehri, as at Kohat also there were Dewans, but not in the same number as in Tehri. It seemed a chance that some of the erstwhile Dewans became Dewans again. The Dewans claimed to be originally from Gujarat in West Punjab (now in Pakistan) and traced their descent from Raja Todar Mal, the Revenue Minister and a general of Emperor Akbar of the Mughal dynasty. A couple of Dewans had chronological charts to prove it but, unfortunately, I did not see them. But the belief that the ancestors of the Dewans came from Gujarat seems to be correct. In 1977, Mr. V. Sehgal, the then Deputy Director, Intelligence Bureau, once asked me in Srinagar, J & K, where we both were posted, what the Sehgals' original home town was. When I stated that according to our elders, it was Gujarat, Mr. Sehgal, who hailed from Jallandar, replied that the Sehgals in Jallandhar also believed that. He also replied in the same vein when I said that our people believed that we were descended from Raja Todar Mal.

I belonged to these Dewans. My father was the last Dewan of the last Nawab of Tehri. His name was Dewan Damodar Dass but when a khatak mentioned the word Dewan, it meant he was talking about my father, because in the case of all other Dewans, he would mention his name also. My grandfather's name was Dewan Gohar Dass. My great grandfather's name was Dewan Mehr Dass. He was a great Dewan. In the name of the Nawab he really ruled. Two brothers; Gorakh Nath and Shanti Ram started the two lines of Dewans in Tehri. My father was the descendant of the elder brother, Gorakh Nath, and my mother of Shanti Ram, the younger brother. This information is based on a chronicle chart, which covered the Dewans ancestory in Tehri.

I joined the vernacular middle school when I was four months short of seven years but the teacher judged my age as six, as was usual, on the date of joining, and so my date of birth officially became 15th January, 1925, instead of 16th May, 1924, which was my actual date of birth. I was good in studies, so, in a few months I had finished the preparatory (Quayda) and the first class and joined the second. The Nawab's son, Muzaffar Ali Khan, was my class fellow there. He, with his golden tresses, and large golden earrings was an attractive boy. He was stout, but, with his fresh rosy complexion, he cut a handsome figure. His elder brother, Mahoob Ali Khan, was taller and better built, and so was even more handsome. He was three years older and minus the tresses. Muzaffar Ali Khan was not doing well in class. He left within a few months. Later on I learned that the brothers had gone to Doon school. I met Mahboob Ali Khan occasionally in volleyball matches played between the Hindu youth and the Muslims, who were mostly from the Nawab's relatives and followers. My uncle, and occasionally my elder brother, played on the Hindu's side and Mahboob Ali Khan on the Muslims. I was very young then, but I still I refreed their games a number of times. Much later I saw Mahboob Ali Khan in Islamia College, Peshwar. We invited each other to our respective rooms, but none took advantage of the other's hospitality.

Amogst the Khans, the Nawab's family and near relatives, it was a custom to wear large earrings, 'murkies' in Urdu. Children upto a certain age did not cut their hair. In our family also we had the custom of wearing earrings, but our earrings were much smaller than those of the Khans. In the Hindus also it is a custom not to cut a child's hair until an elaborate mundan, hair cutting, ceremony takes place. I also wore earrings until I was nine years old. I wore a nose ring also from a very early age but it was removed when I was too young to remember it later on. It was removed, I understand, because it was a great nuisance and I had injured my nose by pulling at it.

I was very good in studies, and especially good in history and Urdu.I was known for my writing facility. At the age of 12, I could write on any subject, and speak to any audience, whether from a prepared text or extempore. In 1937, I was asked by the Headmaster of the school to address the middle classes (from the 5th to the 8th standard) on the India Act, 1935, which I did very well, as I had started reading books of various kinds from an early age. I do not know when I started readings books and newspapers, but it must have been from a very early age because as far as I remember I had always been reading books. Anyhow, on the conclusion of my speech, my Headmaster, Chaudhry Fakhr-I-Ali, paid me the highest accolade a teacher can pay a student. He said that he himself could not have spoken on the subject as well as I did.

In class, Krishan Chand or I used to come first. Krishan Chand was my mother's maternal uncle's son. As I have mentioned earlier, I was considered very good in Urdu. A new second master joined our school in 1936. In the parlance of those days, the second master was next to the Headmaster in authority. In a school gathering one day, the second master, Mr. Abdul Rehman, said that he had covered the whole province in his service but in no school had he met anybody who was as good in Urdu as myself. But the irony of the situation was that in the summer of 1938 when the result of the 8th class was declared by the Provincial Board, Krishan Chand came first in Urdu in the whole province and he was quite ahead of me in the total number of marks secured. However, my prestige did not suffer because everyone knew that I never crammed and, as my handwriting was very bad, it was concluded that I had lost many marks because of it. Actually my brother always said that one day someone would fail me. But my luck stayed with me and my examiners went through my paper, though some people always felt that they would not even bother to do so.

After I finished the vernacular middle, I joined the junior special class, which the school had started to teach English to all those who had passed the vernacular middle examination and wanted to continue their studies further. To make it possible for the entire school to begin English teaching by 1939, English was introduced in the 5th class in 1936, which was gradually extended every year, so that by 1939 there was English teaching from the 5th to the 8th standard. A junior special class was introduced in 1938 for teaching the 5th and 6th standard English to the students who had passed the vernacular middle examination that year, or even earlier. In 1939 a senior special class was introduced to teach English of the 7th and the 8th standard to those who had passed the junior special class.

When I was in the junior special classes, my teacher, who was new to the place and had recently come there, once asked me whether I was really as good in Urdu as my reputation made it out to be. I told him that I did not think so, as I was never satisfied with my writing. He said that he would test me, and asked me to write an essay on 'Taron Bhari Raat' ('A Star Studded Night'). I knew, then, that I had been caught. I was going to be exposed as a man without much substance, as I had never written on such a poetical subject. My little experience was limited to writing on something tangible or on subjects, which could be palpably described. Anyhow, I sat down and started thinking about the approach to be adopted. After some deliberation, I decided to extend my imagination as far as it went, rather than write on something prosaic. So, instead of learning English, which I was supposed to, I wrote Urdu prose that day, of the type Urdu writers wrote. My teacher liked it. He did not extravaganyly compliment me, but I knew I had made a new conquest.

I was good in the sports that we played in school. I was the best player of soccer and was equally good in volleyball. In other outdoor games also I was quite good. I think my advantage was that competition was poor. I was rather stout but, as I was always ready to play, I was reasonably fast in running.

My happiest day in school was the day of the Silver Jubilee celebration of the reign of King George the Fifth in 1936. The school had prepared for months to celebrate this day. The red brick building of the school was colour washed and the boundary stones were white washed. Boy scouts were drilled vigorously and students prepared a number of games to be staged before the VIPs. and the general audience.

On the big day, we got up early to be ready for the show in time. The celebrations were presided over by the Nawab. We, the members of the Boy Scout group, put up various demonstrations and paid many encomiums to the King Emperor and the Nawab. After that, the Nawab went away and my father presided over the celebrations. The last presentation had the drillmaster giving commands to a large number of boys in rapid succession, with the boys executing the orders promptly. Anyone failing to comply with an order or responding incorrectly to the order was to fall out, and was no longer in the game. Gradually the numbers decreased. Usually one boy remained, but sometimes none won a round as, at a given command, everyone went out for lack of concentration or more than one jointly won for persistingly not defaulting in carrying out orders. In my group, the number of participants gradually came down to ten, which included me. We were marching briskly when, suddenly, three or four commands came in quick succession. When I executed the last command, I saw I was marching alone in one direction while the others were marching in the opposite direction. I thought I was out, but suddenly I was surrounded by many of my schoolmates congratulating me. I was happy I had won, but my happiness was greater when I saw that I had carried out a command, which nine others had not been able to. This, however, was nothing in comparison to what pride and happiness I felt when I saw what was happening in the raised verandah where the VIPs were sitting. There, the headmaster and some teachers had surrounded my father and were praising my power of concentration and other merits, some real and some exaggerated.

At our passing out function, arranged to bid us farewell on our successful completion of the vernacular middle school course, I spoke fervently of our school days and the sadness we felt in our success, in leaving our comrades and childhood friends behind. I also read out an Urdu verse, which the Headmaster, Mr. Fateh Ali, had asked me to read, as he wanted to impress the invitees from outside. It was very good and appropriate. The Headmaster also spoke. Referring to me in his address, he said that one day I would be a great man.

Chapter Two

FAMILY AND VILLAGE

My father was a matriculate. I think, after his uncle, Dewan Bhagwan Dass, he was the second matriculate from Tehri. Dewan Bhagwan Dass was my paternal grandfather's younger brother. He was also my mother's uncle, having married her paternal aunt. My great grandfather, Dewan Mehr Dass, had seven sons and one daughter. The daughter had no issue, but the five sons had established their families and multiplied further. So, by the time I came on the scene and became conscious of things around me, I had quite a number of uncles and cousins. However, some had left for jobs in Kohat and other places. My three uncles were working in the Military Engineering Service (M.E.S.). Similarly, my grand uncle's (Dewan Bhagwan Dass) two sons-in-law were working in the M.E.S. The third was a dental surgeon, with a degree from U.K. My grand uncle's eldest grandson, the son of his eldest daughter, who was married to an overseer in M.E.S., had gone to U.K. to get a medical degree. When in five years he could not get a degree, his father asked him to come back, as his son was already married in India and he feared that the boy had already married or was to marry an English woman there. On his return, the father realized that he had committed a mistake, as the boy had not married in U.K. and in a short time he would have got his degree. He then thought of sending him back to U.K., but, before he could so, World War I, 1939-45, had started. The son then had to content himself with a chemist shop in Peshwar. My aim, in mentioning this, is to bring forward the fact, that among my relatives, the generation just before mine was drifting away from being feudal landlords into joining the professional middle class.

My great grandfather was a typical feudal lord. He owned vast stretches of land, over which he had absolute right. The peasants working on the land performed whatever additional services were asked of them and tended the cows, which had gone dry. As the Dewan of Tehri he had vast powers. The Nawabs in those days were simple and illiterate persons. They mostly followed the Dewan's advice.

Dewan Mehr Dass could immobilize any malefactor by locking a foot of his in a log of wood. Mehr Dass kept peace, helped the needy, and even gave money from his own pocket to those who were in dire need. He got the paths from the two city gates, in the southwest and the northeast, to their base paved with stones, as it was rather difficult to walk on a rocky steep surface. He spent his own money on this job. Later on, my paternal grandfather got the work done again on the northeastern path, and my maternal grandfather on the southwestern path. The third gate, near the Nawab's house, was not connected to the base by a stone paved path. The surface was rocky there, but only for a few feet. The rest of the path followed a gentle slope, on a spur, to the base. On this 'kachchi' (unpaved) road the Nawab's car could come right upto the Nawab's house. The other two paths were more motor able.

Tehri was connected with Kohat by bus. Lachi in Kohat District, at 18 miles, was the mid-point of the journey. Lachi was a large village. Every day about two buses ran either way between Tehri and Kohat. Buses touched Banda Daud Shah also, but one could go to Banda Daud Shah any time of the day on a tonga. Regular buses plied between Kohat and Banu. So, one could go to either of these places from Banda Daud Shah.

My grandfather was a very handsome man. He was very tall. He was more than 6 feet in height. I was very young when he died and whatever I am writing about him is from the memory of his image in a child's eyes. He concentrated his attention on the management of the land, including litigation in connection with land disputes. He was the eldest of seven brothers, and hence the responsibility of looking after the family property, at least a major part of it, devolved on him. He had two sons and three daughters. His second son, my uncle, was very much younger than my father. His mother died when he was very young. My mother raised him like a son. He did his matriculation in Jand, a small town in West Punjab. He obtained his engineering diploma from Lucknow (Utter Pradesh). He later joined M.E.S. as a work munshi and after sometime was promoted as an overseer.

My father was also a matriculate (as to where he did it from, I have no knowledge). His height, I think, was about 5 feet six inches. He started his career as an 'arzi navis' (a petition writer) in court. He, however, had no interest in it. I do not know how it happened, but he started working as a junior partner with some big contractors on some construction work. My father was a contractor in the construction of a bridge over the Indus at Sukhar, in Sindh province (now in Pakistan). That bridge was known to be the longest bridge in India at that time. Most of his working time he spent in Banu and Dehra Ismael Khan districts of N.W.F.P. The Razmak agency area in Banu district was being built as a large station for the concentration of troops, in the nineteen twenties, for dealing with the Wazir tribes insurgency. My father and his partners did quite a good amount of work there. He made a lot of money. A large number of persons (Hindus and Muslims both) from Tehri worked with him in Razmak. He got for two cousins of my mother the contract to run canteens in Razmak. They flourished there and extended their business further. I think, the money my father made and the rewards it brought, made my father reluctant to venture out again. Everyone who had worked with him claimed to be his faithful servant, and swore to give his life for him. Everywhere he went, people got up to honour him. In the Hindu panchayat his word was law.

He was the Nawab's friend as well as his Dewan. Actually, he was a friend of the Nawab's cousin, a powerful Khan, who was foully murdered. It was said that the murder was the result of intra-family jealousies. The murdered Khan was a popular figure. His death was widely mourned, especially by my father. The ruling Nawab was also on friendly terms with my father. He tried to bring my father near him. However, the Nawab died. The new Nawab, Bazgul Khan, the brother of the dead Nawab, also tried to befriend my father, and eventually they became good friends, as it suited them both: my father had money, popularity among both Muslims and Hindus, contacts in Kohat and an excellent brain to rely upon in making decisions. The Nawab had prestige, power and a name, which was known and admired in the whole Tehsil and certain circles outside. Father was the official Dewan but he did not receive any salary. He just could not bind himself to one chair. He was just an honorary Dewan for its glamour. In the beginning, it is possible, Father may have even helped the Nawab financially, and the Nawab may have helped out Father subsequently, but basically the arrangement was non-financial.

I remember, when I was young, everything was plentiful in our house. All seasonal fruits came in baskets. There was never any shortage of them. We were meat eaters and ate in plenty. It was common to have tikka kabab, shami kabab, 'tandoori chicken', Titar, 'pulao', besides curried lamb at meals. Another delicacy was 'Kaskar', the meat that remained after the sheep's fat was heated and the oil removed. My mother and sister were however vegetarians. In early winter, it was customary to make carrot 'halwa' and jam in sufficient quantities to last the winter, and in the summer, syrups of various flavours.

We used to live in a large mud plastered house, which we shared with at least one family. It was an old ancestral house, which belonged to my grandfather and two of his brothers. Ours was the portion to the west. The central portion belonged to Dewan Bhagwan Dass, my grand uncle. The eastern portion belonged to another brother of Dewan Bhagwan Dass, but his two sons had partitioned it. The elder brother had the ground floor and the other brother had built two rooms, one each on the first and the second floor. Except for this room of bricks and iron sheets, the house was two storied. As the younger brother was an overseer and posted outside, he kept his rooms locked. As Dewan Bhagwan Dass's only son was a practising lawyer in Kohat and he lived with him, we occupied two of his three rooms, one on the ground and the other on the first floor.

Father, however, had built a new brick house adjacent, and to the east of the old ancestral house. This one had a large living room, two bedrooms, a courtyard and a bathroom. The old house had no bathroom. Every family there had an open-air latrine in an enclosed place on the first or the second floor. Our new house looked nice with its cemented floor and a fireplace done in slated lime, which was so well done that it looked like marble. This new house, which we called as such, was meant for guests, but all of us, including my father, my uncle, my elder brother and myself, used it for parties and occasionally played cards with friends there.

I was not allowed to play cards, so I used to bring in my friends clandestinely. Whenever, my father and uncle were not in town, I used to get the key from its usual place and enter through the main door. Otherwise, we used to enter from the top through our old house. After reaching the roof of the new house, one of us used to jump upon the roof of a shop, the back of which formed the eastern wall of our courtyard, while its front opened onto the main 'bazaar', the market place. As its roof was about six feet lower than the roof of our house, it was easy to jump from the shop's roof into the courtyard of the house and remove the chain on the door of the stairs to admit the rest of us. We used to play sweep, rummy and bezique. Another game, which we used to play, was 'chaupat'. Chaupat is played on a piece of cloth so tailored that two strips of cloth are stitched together (each strip about three feet in length and about five inches in width) in such a way that they cross each other in the middle and thus form four arms of equal length. The game is played with 'gotis' (wooden pieces), which are moved on various chequered squares on the four arms, and the movement of the 'gotis' on the chequered cross is determined by the throw of cowries.

In December and January we used to have 'pukhar'. Pukhar was a whole night affair. It was a gala party for us. Stealing of firewood was permissible on a 'pukhar' night. So people in the adjacent houses to where 'pukhar' was to take place used to be wary of 'pukhar' thieves. We normally sang songs, played cards and told jokes. But we never consumed liquor for, otherwise also we did not drink. But when father and his friends had 'pukhar' they consumed liquor. We normally did not play cards for money, except at Diwali, when parents relaxed the tight reins. The men used to go out for picnics known as 'sohbat', meaning company, to irrigation wells, located within walking distance to the west and north of the village.

We had our own land and a well to the west. Normally vegetables and wheat were grown on the land. My cousins also had a well on that side, but not that conveniently situated. In the early thirties, my father purchased another piece of land with a well situated to the west but very near the village. This was a fertile piece of vast dimensions. Mud walls on all four sides enclosed a sizable portion of the land, near the well, and different types of fruit trees were planted along the inner sides of all the walls. The rest of the area within the walls and outside was left for growing vegetables, wheat and maize. Within the enclosure, large pathways and a grassy patch were left, with the aim of planting flowers all around them. Father intended to initiate my brother's marriage ceremonies (whenever the marriage took place; he was born on 17th, November, 1919) and start the marriage procession from there. The water in the wells was normally about 14 feet below the surface. This was not bad, considering that the area was dry and the rainfall scanty, but, perhaps, it was due to the 'toi' flowing from east to west on the south and to the northern part getting a lot of underground water from the nearby mountains during the rains. Water was lifted from the wells by a Persian wheel, which was operated by a buffalo going round and round and thus operating a shaft, which turned the wheel and consequently a chain of buckets carrying water over it.

Apart from 'sohbats' which I went to with my friends, I also went on many 'sohbats' with my brother, uncle and father. A couple of times I remember having gone for a 'sohbat' given by the Nawab. There for the Hindus in my father's party a Hindu prepared the 'pulao' and other dishes, while the dishes for the Muslims were prepared separately. Hindus or the Nawabs and his family had their parties, but it was very rare for the ordinary Muslims to have such pleasures. Some of my Hindu friends and myself used to play 'kabaddi' or 'konally' on the sand on the bank of the'toi' in the evening, before sunset, but it was really a rare sight to see Muslim boys playing like that. 'Konally' is a game well known in 'khataks' but I have not seen it being played anywhere else. In it a man runs and two of his opponents try to catch him. If the former manages to touch the chests of his opponents thrice without being caught, he wins the round. Each player from both the teams is given three chances. 'Konally' teams used to come from different places in the tehsil. The matches were played in a ploughed field, at some distance from Tehri. Quite a number of people used to track down the distance to watch these hotly contested matches between the villages. Most of the audience used to be composed of Muslims, but I tried never to miss such occasions. Hindus never played 'konally' like champions, being mainly a class of shopkeepers and being afraid to test their physical strength against the Muslims in Tehri or at other places, and this inspite of the fact that we boys played more and better 'konally' at our level.

I had a football, which, I think my brother had brought from Kohat, where he was studying in 'Bharatary' School, a school run by Hindus in 'Kohat'. He and his friends used to play soccer in the ground, which later on was brought under the plough by father to plant an orchard-cum-garden, during his vacations. My friends and I used to go often to that ground to play. When that ground was ploughed, I was the unhappiest man. We used to play soccer at school also but that ground was smaller and was stony. I was good in volleyball as well as in soccer. Actually, I was good in whatever game was played. In wrestling, I used to bring down contemporaries of my age group without much difficulty.

I had a great advantage. Not only was I the son of a very influential man, I had an uncle and a brother who were handsome, studied in places outside Tehri and were looked upto by their friends. I used to be with them in many of their outings. I accompanied my uncle many a time to gardens outside to shoot birds. Father had a double barrel gun, which was used for such purposes.

I had many fights with the boys in the Hindu 'Mohollah' during 'Holi', which was played rough. I still bear marks on my face of nail scratches inflicted by a boy from Lachi, whom I had cornered in 'Holi'. The Pathan spirit of revenge always burnt brightly in the most timid Hindu boy's breast. Many a time, I planned to waylay an adversary to avenge an insult. I did it to show my sense of honour to my colleagues, otherwise I did not have it in me to plan the beating of a person. Firstly, I was scared that my father would come to know of it; secondly, because I could not hit a weaker man. Thirdly, as I always won my battles alone, I never had partners, and so I was apprehensive that when I beat a person, he could also land some punches on me and thus my fair name would be besmirched. I, who was not afraid in a fight, was afraid of getting into a fight or of provoking a fight. So, I nearly always went either too late or too early when waylaying a person, and either I missed the person or he missed me, as there was always somebody to warn him in time about the waiting guy. I had a knife, 5 or 6 inches long, but not for use as I never carried it with me. I kept if for self- defence, but I wonder whether I could have used it, as I cannot see blood. Even now when I see a cockroach at home, I call my wife to deal with it. She sometimes laughingly says that she wonders what I was doing in the Indian Navy, which I joined in 1949. She does not know this, but I also wondered the same when I reported for duty and training at Cochin.

One day, the Commodore-in-Charge, Cochin, an Englishman, came to the Trainee Officers mess. Only a few of us were there at that time, and so he talked to us. He talked to us about his experiences during the war and naval life in general. In this context I asked him how could one kill a person face to face even during the war. I was afraid he might ridicule me, as that was my experience of Indian officers of the rank of Lt. Commander and above, but he appreciated my sensibilities and replied good humouredly that that was the advantage of the navy that we did not have to see what damage we caused to humans; we only pressed the trigger.

I think, I may mention an incident to illustrate the sort of danger a man like me, a leader who ventured to do things without thinking of the consequences, faced. In Tehri, the Hindus, especially the youngsters, bathed twice. In the morning invariably we went to the 'toi' to take a bath. In the evening, we usually went to the wells, when we were not playing, to bathe. One day, when I went to a well, a boy, who once used to be my friend, pointed out three boys to me and stated that they were planning to attack me on my way home. One of them was a classmate of mine. The second used to be classmate of mine and the third was a year junior to me in school. All three were well known to me and looked upto me as their leader. Individually, they were scared of me. Even united together they should normally have been scared of me, but maybe they saw me as weak at that time or without friends, so they got together to avenge a wrong or an assumed wrong. They followed me all the way to the base of the hillock, on which the village was situated, but did not attack me; presumably they were still scared of the consequences of an attack on me. At the base of the hillock, they stopped a little distance from me and the friend, who had warned me about their design earlier, came to me and informed that I should be ready as they were immediately going to attack me. Before leaving me, he left a stick with me as my weapon although I protested that I had never used a stick having always depended on my bare hands. I, in my pride, did not seek help from anybody at the well or from the people I met on the way back to the village, but just when one of my opponents picked up a stone to hit me, he was caught by an old class fellow of mine. Simultaneously, my second cousin, Gokal, who was passing on his way to the wells, intervened in the fight. So, an uneven fight had turned into a complete victory for me, as my opponents could not land a single punch while they took all the beating.

For a child to grow up normally is difficult in any village or small town, but more so in a village or town where the Pathan influence prevails because of the Pathans' prevailing spirit of revenge.

I did not spend all my time in playing or fighting; actually, my first love was reading. Urdu was the only language we were taught until I passed the vernacular middle school examination, and in that language I read whatever book I could get. Most of the books I read were novels as they were easily available. However, I also read also books like the Mahabharata, Ramayana, Geeta and even part of the

Bhagwata Puran. Though I was not allowed to read as my family thought I only read novels, I read them in hiding. But the reading of the Bhagwata they could not even contemplate as people considered its contents not suitable for children, because repeatedly it contains references to love affairs and love making. I read it in our new house in the evenings. It was kept there so that a religious man could read it daily, for an hour or so, to devout Hindus. It remained there for about 20 days. And every day after the departure of the 'kathak wachak' (the narrator of religious stories) and the listeners, I used to go and read it. From the school library also I issued many books I found interesting. I remember a book on Napoleon for after reading that I became a great admirer of him. In Urdu this book was in three thick volumes, but I read the same book in the English version later on in college and it was in only one volume.

Another book, which I read, was 'Fasana-I-Azad' by Ratan Nath Sarshar. I could not complete it for some reason, but it is a very interesting book. The story is so absorbing that once you start reading it you do not want to stop, but stop one must because it is too voluminous to finish in one sitting. However, this book was not given to me for the pleasure of its quaint fictional value by the English teacher who got impressed by my faculty in the Urdu language, but to improve my expression, vocabulary and knowledge of Urdu phraseology. Another book, I remember having read in those days was about the conquest of Spain by Alama Iqbal. Our school those days used to get two magazines every month. One was 'Rahnumai Talim' and the other a literary magazine, whose name I do not remember. Another magazine I used to read was 'Mastana Jogi' which my father used to get every month. It contained mostly religious and philosophical material.

One of my main sources of books was my fifth class teacher Mohommed Firdaus. He gave me a lot of material on Islam. I found the conquests of Imam Ummar and those of Khalid bin Valid very interesting. I used to go to his house to get the books. Like all Muslim ladies of the upper and middle classes, his wife kept 'parda' (remained in veil) but not from me, most probably because firstly, I was a young boy and secondly, I was a pupil of her husband. One day, when I was returning from his house, I met a Muslim classmate of mine. He asked me whether I knew why Firdaus gave me books. I replied that I did not. He then said it was because he wanted to convert me. On reflection I thought perhaps he was correct, because Firdaus must have seen in me an inquisitive student, who being very liberal and critical of the iniquities and idol worshipping in Hindu society, was an ideal candidate for conversion. Mohommed Firdaus was an Ahmedi, which is a branch of Quadianis who have their head office in Quadian in India. There are only slight differences in these two sects, but still they function independently of each other. The Ahmedis had their headquarter, those days, in Lahore and used to publish a weekly newspaper of their own. Firdaus used to give me that paper to me to read. Firdaus really had the appearance of a missionary, with his Turkish cap, dark bony figure with a dyed goatee and piercing eyes. He had the fervour of a zealot when he argued a point. One day I was walking with a classmate of mine in the dusk, discussing Firdaus, when somebody, who had passed us running without our noticing him, shouted from a distance 'Quadianis are dogs'. I then realised it was Nasir, the boy who had told me that Firdaus wanted to convert me. This was the feeling among Muslims which ultimately culminated in the Quadianis being declared non-Muslims, and persecuted in Pakistan for certain aberrations in their faith, inspite of the fact that Quadianis believed in the basic tenet of Islam. There is only one God and Muhammed is his prophet. Firdaus was, however, not liked by his students because of certain habits of his.

We had a second master, Hussain, who taught us in the seventh class. He believed and taught us that Imam Ali's sword was called 'Zulfiquar" because when he struck his enemies with the blade of his sword, forty blades actually struck them. When I asked how that was possible, he replied that it was because God had bestowed that boon on his sword. The same second master one day took a Hindu man who had converted to Islam to meet Mr. Gurdita Mal, a Hindu teacher who taught class six, and asked him to give some money to him as he was a newly converted Muslim. Mr. Mal's embarrassment one can well imagine! Firdaus, of course, when approached by Hussain for the purpose, blankly refused. Hussain got angry and stated that just because the person concerned had not become a Quadiani, Firdaus was not contributing any money, but if sometime Firdaus brought a convert to him, he would give a contribution because Islam would benefit even though he might be a Quadiani. Firdaus stuck to his point and said that it was not that the convert was a Suni or a Shia and not a Quadiani that mattered but that he, Firdaus, did not believe in converting people on payment of money. This all happened in our class, the fifth standard, which Firdaus was taking. I have narrated this incident to show the mediocrity and the insensitivity of the teaching staff of those days, though they took more pains with the students than the teachers of today. Firdaus came out well in this incident, but I do not know the true motive of Firdaus in not contributing the money. It could be due to his intrinsic miserliness, or due to the convert not belonging to his sect, or it could be due to the moral principle he had stated. But one thing I noticed was that the Quadianis, at least the Ahmedis, were an educated lot and argued about their faith with a certain amount of erudition.

It was not only in school that ignorance and bigotry prevailed. It had entered the village life as well. In about the mid-thirties the Hindus frequented two places of worship. All did not go to both the places. Some went to one place, and some to another, but worshippers at both the places swore by one name: Parmhans Maharajji, a sanyasi and a guru who shaped the spiritual life of the Hindus in the village. Parmhans is actually not a name but a person who achieves 'gyan', the supreme knowledge. Parmhans Maharajji was brought to Tehri from Sambhar (Rajasthan) by Dewan Bhagwan Dass, my grand uncle, where he was posted as Inspector, Salt, in the Central Government. Before Maharajji's coming, the Hindus in Tehri indulged in all sorts of moral vices. Drinking and gambling were quite common. He really gave a moral fiber to the people. Some of the citizens objected to the visit of ladies to him. Father was the leader of that group. Actually, father and a friend of his physically tried to stop the ladies. During this agitation, father and his friend suffered some grief, and consequently they were forced by their relatives to seek the pardon of Maharajji. This incident has been quoted in a biography of the Maharajji, written in Urdu by Babu Bhore Singh of Agra (Uttar Pradesh). In that book, certain other miracles, associated with Maharajji, have also been mentioned. Maharajji preached against ritualism and idol worshipping, but advised achieving gyan through a living guru.

After his death, his successor, Swami Swarupanand, who had been nominated by the Maharajji before his death, ascended the 'gaddi' and Maharajji's body was entombed at the place where he had lived and preached. Swami Swarupanand shifted his seat to another place, and this led to a division among the followers of the Maharajji. Some followed Swami Swarupanand as he was the rightful successor and the others stated that as the original power was vested in the Maharajji, his 'samadhi', tomb, was the most sacred place for the sect and as such should be the seat of operation for Swami

Swarupanand. Swami Swarupanand refused to shift, stating that it was the living guru that mattered for the spiritual guidance of the community and not the 'samadhi', and as such the proposal of making the 'samadhi' a spiritual headquarter had no relevance. This dispute split the community in the middle.

This split was superficial; the bonds of self interest, marriage ties and tribal loyalties could surpass any tangible divisive force, but, unfortunately, the deteriorating economic conditions of the people in general, the decline in the power of the Nawab and consequently, the diminished prestige of the Dewans, reduced the unifying force of the Hindu community. As a matter of interest, I may mention here that within a few years of his accession to the 'gaddi' Swami Swarupanand had greatly extended his territorial sphere of activities. Very early in his role as a guru he had established at Lakki (district Banu, N.W.F.P.) an alternate headquarter. Then he established an Ashram at Anandpur, near Shiv Puri (Madhya Pradesh). He shifted his headquarter there, from where he sent his orange robed disciples to various areas. By 1950, his successor had established his preaching posts at Delhi, Kanpur and Gwalior and other places. He died at the village named Nangli near Meerut (U.P.). That place is now a big religious centre. The sadhus there have disassociated themselves from the guru at Anandpur saying that they would recognize the current guru at Anandpur Saheb only if he established his Headquarter at Nangli, where the 'samadhi' of the Guru, who really started the sect, was located. So history repeated itself again.

Chapter Three

CHANGE IN FORTUNE

In the beginning the decline in the fortune of Tehri was gradual, but at the end it occurred with sudden acceleration, as is usual with people and civilization. Tehri was a prosperous place where agriculture was flourishing, business was good and the local aristocracy, the Khans and the Dewan had plenty to spend. The decline most probably started in about 1930. As usual, it started with agriculture. The landlords had plenty and started neglecting their agricultural lands. Tenants, who even in the best of times are far from being prosperous, started cheating the landlords. The landlords in turn started investing less and less in agriculture. The result was that the productivity of the land suffered. While on the one hand, the landlords (the Khans and the Dewans) gradually became nearly paupers, on the other hand, the land became less fertile and in some cases turned barren. The Nawab, who had other income besides the produce from the land survived, but just barely, as he started borrowing from Hindu moneylenders from Kohat. Most of the Dewans survived by taking jobs at Kohat and other places. The Hindu businessmen also suffered from having lesser income, and some, being marginal operators, became unemployed, along with some shop helpers. This introduced certain imbalances. While most of the local Hindu population was reduced to a hand and mouth existence, a number of Hindus from the smaller villagers moved in as they had brought in their accumulated money with them. They became successful businessmen and moneylenders. While the Dewans, Chaudhuries, Vasudevs and others languished for want of money resource, outsiders with money became the local leaders. But as they had neither the experience, nor the prestige of a noble ancestory or long established connections, their leadership was exercised in small disputes and back door maneuvers.

The real leadership remained with the Dewans, the chief of whom was my father. The situation, however, had changed. The Hindus' economic position was adversely affected, but worse was the feeling of insecurity in them. When the Nawabs were powerful, the Dewans were also powerful, and the Muslim population was docile. Refractory Muslim elements were kept contented by the munificence of persons like my father. But, with the gradual worsening of the all round economic situation, everything changed. The extent of decline in agriculture can be realized from one fact, and that is that in 1931 and 1932, there were five gardens around Tehri: four belonged to the Khans and one to a Dewan. They were beautiful gardens, with an abundance of luxuriant trees and a profusion of colourful flowers and a large number of birds. By 1937, only two were left, one belonging to the Nawab and the other to an insane Khan known to be a general of Aman-Ullah-Khan, the deposed king of Afghanistan. But their glory was gone, and the birds had vanished.

The poverty of the people was nearly universal. The common Muslim people had only 'bajra', millet, and jaggery or onions for meals. The Muslims generally took one bath in a month or months. They normally kept long hair, which came up to the neck, and which was full of lice. In school, we used to tease our Muslim friends about their lice and smelly bodies, but they used to retort good-humouredly that as the Hindus were dirty people they needed bathing.

As an indication of the general purchasing power of the people, it may not be out of place to mention that the maximum salary of a junior vernacular teacher those days used to be Rs. 35/- and that of a senior vernacular teacher Rs. 40/-. A local junior vernacular teacher used to get a salary of Rs. 33/- a month, and we used to wonder what he did with his money, because otherwise in Tehri a maximum salary of Rs. 20/- used to be the norm. We had a Muslim servant to do the odd jobs and we paid him Rs. 8/ as did the Hindu Panchayats to its 'chowkidars' (guards) who patrolled the streets and guarded the city gates at night. From 1936 onwards, the security of the Hindus was increasingly threatened. On one side, the intransigence of some Muslim bad characters increased and on the other, the danger of an attack by the Wazir tribesmen also augmented.

It seems my father's misfortune preceded that of the village. He was prosperous; the village was prosperous. His fortune started sliding down, the village's fortune followed suit. The trouble was, he and his partners lost money in the execution of a building contract, and his principal partner, because of it, did not even pay father what he owed him. This setback made him sit idle at home. After that, he did not make a serious effort to go back to work. Things were quite fine for a couple of years because of past earnings, but they began to tell upon the family's financial position after that. Things would have continued to be fine for a long time to come but for father's extravagant style of living. He spent lavishly on the running of his household; so lavishly, that sometime even now I wonder, how we could afford things then, which we could not do in much better times in the recent past. He spent exorbitantly on the entertainment of his friends, who occasionally visited from Kohat, and in the celebrations of festivals and any event of good fortune occurring in the family. He lived in the glory of being the leader of his community and the most popular person among the people of Tehri, among Muslims and Hindus both. His fame had spread beyond Tehri to the whole tehsil. The obvious reason for his popularity was his generosity. He employed a large number of men when he was working as a contractor. He took with him even those men who were not needed but wanted to make a living. He never refused to help people who approached him, even in his bad days.

It was a common joke among our relations that he did not get any financial benefit from his land holdings (actually he incurred a loss) because he could not be strict with his tenants. Whenever he approached a tenant for his share of the produce, which was seldom, the latter invariably brought up the precarious existence his family was leading and ended up getting some money from father. This was not slyness, but the real picture of the hard existence of the poor, hardworking and honest Khatak peasant. But the common landlord would never acknowledge that. He cursed the peasants, accused them of slyness and always managed to get something, even if it were a silver ornament of a peasant's wife. But the tragedy was that whosoever took money from father on loan, to set up a business or start an enterprise, never returned it. Usually it was a bad investment.

Father, for one term, was a member of the district board. His one achievement was the introduction of a primary school for girls, and the construction of its building. I remember once the contractor of the building left a small basket of fruit, as a gift, in father's absence, at our house. When father came home, he was very angry with us for accepting the basket. He sent for the contractor and returned the basket to him saying that he should not expect that by giving a basket of fruit he would get the building approved, and warned him not to do such things again.

However, as his finances declined, he started borrowing from his relatives and friends. In 1934, he married his daughter, when she was 14, to a scion of the Seth family of Kohat.The Seth family was one of the two richest families but the most influential family in Kohat. My sister was four years older than I was. The bridegroom's party was composed of hundreds of people. It was said that the Seths had kept a number of buses at the gate of the Hindu Mohollah of Kohat. Whosoever wanted to go to Tehri came along. When they reached Tehri, it seemed as if the whole Hindu population of Kohat had migrated to Tehri. The accommodation and the feeding of hundreds of people for two full days was a gigantic problem in Tehri, which had neither any hotel nor any spare accommodation. Every house, as it is, was overcrowded, because of the constraint of security. The fear of the Wazir tribesmen's raid and the possibility of attack by the local Muslim bad characters had confined the habitation of the Hindus to the Hindu Mohollah (enclave) on the hillock, within the perimeter walls. So, father got a large house of the descendents of Khani Dewan vacated, and obtained another from a friend of his. These two houses together with the 'dharmshala' and our new house, I think, sufficed.

Khani Dewan's house had a courtyard of the dimensions of a football field. This and the open space on the rooftop, together with its adjoining guest bungalow, a massive double storied bricked structure that had a number of large rooms, provided sufficient space to accommodate about three hundred persons. String cots, woven with the locally produced vegetable fibre, were procured from everywhere and spread in the above accommodation. As it was summer, people slept outside in the courtyards or on the rooftops. In winter, finding sleeping place, mattresses, quilts and blankets would have been really impossible for so many people. Quite a large number of beddings were obtained from the Nawab and the other Khans, who kept them in reserve for their guests.

The Hindus of Tehri did not hesitate to provide whatever was asked of them and gave of goods that were not even asked for. For example, every household, which could, delivered milk, in varying quantities at our house in the morning. Similarly ladies brought water in earthen pitches all through the marriage ceremonies, which lasted over five days, two days before the day of the marriage and one day after the departure of the bridegroom's party. For our relatives, who had come from Kohat for the marriage, left one to five days after the departure of the bridegroom's party. The supply of milk and water by the members of the Hindu community was not only a symbolic gesture, but a gesture which had its origin in necessity, born out of the scarcity of these items. Very few Hindus kept cows, as they needed looking after and it was difficult for hard pressed ladies to get fodder, dry fodder and concentrates and so the milk yield was meagre, about one to two litres a day. No work had been undertaken on our side to improve the breed, or for that matter even the varieties of seeds of vegetables and cereals. Coupled with the dependence on rain for crops and the absentee and ignorant landlords, poverty had become endemic.

The Hindu ladies, in Tehri, did the sweeping, cooking, washing of utensils and clothes at the'Toi'; prepared condiments and other delicacies such as'chatni'; 'phulwaries', 'carrot halwa' and fetched water from the'Toi' for the family. Some even ground flour on the 'chakki' (composed of two thick circular discs of stone, about 1 1/2 feet in diameter, of which the lower disc is fixed and the upper one is rotated with a wooden handle fixed in the centre, while grinding). The Muslim ladies worked even harder. Sometimes they worked with their husbands in the fields, or even fetched wood and carried weights. Actually, all the able bodied members of a peasant family worked. That was the one main reason for 100 per cent illiteracy amongst the peasants.

As Tehri was situated on a hillock, water was usually brought by the ladies in earthen pitchers, but brass pitchers were also used occasionally. A lady normally carried two pitchers on her head. Some would carry an additional pitcher on the hip, holding the upper part of the pitcher, its neck, by the elbow.

Milk was usually purchased from Muslim peasants, some of whom kept cows or goats. Goats fed themselves by grazing, while cows were fed the wheat straw and greens grown on the peasants' land. For a farmer, feeding of a bullock was more important than a cow, as it was needed for ploughing the land, while cows gave a negligible quantity of milk. For a poor farmer, the death of a bullock sometime meant starvation. Milk was in short supply, even though the Muslims did not drink it. The Hindus considered milk as a drink good for health and they drank it, but all could not do so because they did not have the purchasing power. People like father who had plenty of meat with their meals also did not like to drink milk.

Muslims, as a habit, did not like milk, but even otherwise the economic position of most of the Muslims was so bad that milk was their last priority. If they had limited money, they would buy meat rather than milk, while the Hindus' priority was the reverse of this. The Muslims liked meat above anything else, but still a common Hindu ate more meat than a Muslim. Actually, for a common Muslim, meat was far beyond his means, though the Khans and a few well-to-do Muslims ate it in plenty. The well-to-do Muslims were mostly pensioners or members of some families whose heads were working outside, mostly in Bombay, as chowkidars or in similar positions. The position of the Khans was also not very good. They were managing somehow on what they could mange to get from the tenants of their land, but they were mere obscure shadows in the thirties of what they had been in the days gone by. The common Muslims ate beef whenever they could manage, as no cattle were reared for beef. Only the useless cattle were killed for this purpose, and so it was much cheaper than lamb's meat.

As for the short supply of milk, to some extent, it was made up by the addition of water by the peasants who delivered it to the sweatmeat sellers or at the residences. Usually, sweatmeat sellers also added more water to the milk meant for sale to the customers. The sweatmeat sellers needed milk to make 'burfi', gulab jamuns' and 'carrot halwa'. The savoury prepared was 'tikki'. Lal mithai was prepared by frying flour and coating the piece with sugar, while boondi was small thin pieces, about one to two inches long, of gram flour, which were fried, and coated with sugar. Tikki was a disc shaped piece, about 2 1/2 inches in diameter, of flour fried in 'ghee' (clarified butter).

Water was normally brought by the ladies of the families, but people who could afford it paid some other women, poor widows and indigent ladies, to fetch water for them. On my sister's marriage, this usual method was used, but, in addition, asses were also used to bring water. Meals were prepared on a grand scale, as in addition to the bridegroom's party, most of the Hindus and quite a number of Muslims also ate at our place. Most of the people were involved in the preparation of the meals or looking after the guests. The meals for the marriage consisted of meat pulao, vegetable pulao, meat curry, vegetable curries, 'dal' (pulse) and a sweet dish, besides 'chutney' (an appetiser). Actually, the main dish was pulao (rice cooked with meat or vegetables and onions) as Khataks or for that matter all Pathans consider it foolish to touch anything else. As preparation of pulao involves more cost, people during marriages served only boiled rice and meat curry. The serving of pulao at my sister's marriage was a symbol of high rank. Meat curry was prepared just in case somebody wanted more meat. Vegetable dishes were prepared to cater to the taste of vegetarians. In Tehri, no male was vegetarian, but there were some Hindu ladies who were. For example, my mother and sister were vegetarians. My mother was a very good cook of meat dishes. She could prepare a variety of dishes, but did not eat meat herself, and used separate cooking places for meat and vegetable dishes. In Kohat, most of the women, but a lesser number of men, were vegetarians.

The bridegroom's party had brought dancing girls for entertainment. Father was very much against this idea, and he conveyed his feelings to the bridegroom's uncle, who was father's friend and who had helped arrange the match. But as the bridegroom's father and elder brother insisted that their family's honour was involved, he agreed to let the entertainment take place. I am sure that had it not been for the welfare of his daughter, he would not have agreed. However, he did not allow the dancing girls to come to his house with the bridegroom's party. The girls performed at night and in the morning at Khani Dewan's house, and the next morning at the 'kacheri's (court's) courtyard for all the people of Tehri. The bringing of dancing girls to Tehri where 'purdah' was strictly followed by the upper class women and where the lower class women were mostly rustic, and had never even heard of cosmetics, could cause great commotion, but that was avoided by father entrusting their looking after to a 'mirakhor' who was the strong member of his family and a friend of father. Mirakhors were the brothers of the Nawab's mother and their children. The word Mirakhor is derived from the Urdu word miraskhor, which means beneficiary of inheritance.

My sister was given a good dowry. Besides the bridegroom and his family, all his relatives, two paternal uncle's families, four maternal uncle's families and the maternal grandparents and even the servants were given presents. The bridegroom's immediate family, who lived in the same house, consisted of his parents, a sister, and his three brothers, the eldest of whom was married and had a daughter.

This marriage imposed a great strain on father's financial position. It rather crippled him financially. In 1935 or 1936, doctors diagnosed that he was passing albumin in his urine. He went to Lahore in 1936, the then capital of the Punjab state of India, for treatment, but got no relief. Meanwhile our financial position deteriorated further. Father's debts mounted to about sixteen thousand rupees, which was a staggering amount in those times. All creditors were friends and relatives, but they all charged interest, which formed a substantial part of the debt. My brother, Haridwar Dass, used to always grumble and wonder how we would be able to pay such a huge debt. But father always said that he unnecessarily worried, as he would pay back all the debts in one go when he landed a building contract. But that was to be seen. Meanwhile my brother was asked to discontinue his studies. He was studying in D.A.V. College, Lahore, for a degree in arts. By the end of the academic year in April 1936, he had passed the intermediate examination: the 12th class. He needed two years more to get a degree of the Bachelor of Arts. When father had asked my brother not to go in for further studies, it was meant as a temporary measure. He was told by father that he would be shortly sent back again, but that did not happen, as father's financial position did not improve and fate willed otherwise.

During those days I used to wear a discarded long jacket of my brother. I vehemently protested, but to no avail as money was scarce. I used to wear, as all others, an open necked shirt, a very loose 'salwar' and 'chaplis' (footwear resembling sandals). Normally, I used to have a brown pair of shoes. I also had a fur cap. But on important days I used to wear a turban from Mashhad (Iran), tied around a 'qula' (a sort of stiff cap round at the base and tapering, from three inches of the base), embroidered all around with gold thread in delicate needlework. My father and brother had Yazedi Turbans. This turban was also a silk turban, like the Mashhadi, but it was from Yazed (a city in Iran) and its silk was of a finer type. Haridwar, my brother, had trousers and suits, stitched in the western style, besides an overcoat and a sola hat. He wore these clothes on certain occasions. Ladies also wore 'salwars' and shirts, but of finer types. Father wore a 'quala' of a soft vegetable fibre and a long white shirt and a white salwar. He wore loafer shoes. Most of the elder Hindus wore the same type of shirt and salwar. The Nawab also wore the same type of dress, but most of the Muslims wore clothes of a dark grey colour because they needed less washing.

In 1936, I managed with an old jacket, but in 1937 I more or less managed without a jacket, by wearing sweaters.

On the night of 2nd December, father died of cerebral haemorrhage. He left behind a wife, three sons and a daughter. Father was 48 years old when he died. My mother at that time was 40 years old and my younger brother Ramesh, only a few months old.

A person was sent to Banda Daud Shah before sunrise to send a telegram to our relatives at Kohat about the death. By 11 o'clock two busloads of people had arrived for the funeral. Haridwar's and my hair was completely shorn off with a razor. Later on some of our relatives were sorry to see Haridwar's hair shorn. He was a very handsome man with fair skin, nice features and a very good physique. Once he deliberately missed his 'janev' (thread) ceremony to escape the shearing of his hair. At that time he was studying in the 10th class in Ferozpur (Punjab), where he was staying with a cousin of father's who was posted there as an overseer in the Military Engineering Service. He was supposed to reach Tehri on 11th April, after his qualifying examination, for the janev ceremony on the 13th. But he reached on the 14th, one day after the auspicious day. According to him, he went to Haridwar and had the Janev ceremony on the bank of the sacred river Ganges. Everybody was disappointed, as the guests from Kohat had come a couple of days earlier than the auspicious day, and quite an expenditure had been incurred on their entertainment. Haridwar, however, had got his thread but I missed it. Actually, I never got it. I grew up and everybody forgot about it.

At father's funeral nearly every Hindu (only males used to go with the funeral procession, probably because of a sort of purdah Hindu ladies observed in Muslim dominated N.W.F.P.) turned up. The market was closed. Even the Muslims, who were present at the village gate, when the funeral procession passed through it, expressed their wish to carry the wooden plank on which the body was lying. The cortege came down the hillock and wended its way to the cremation ground, a mile away, situated near the Tehri Banda Daud Shah Road, outside the once lush green garden, 'Darga'. There the body was consigned to the fire. Haridwar performed the last rites. On the fourth day, Haridwar went to immerse the ashes in the sacred river, Ganges, at Hardwar, and the responsibility of completing the rites fell on me. Every day in the afternoon, I used to go with a pundit to 'Toi' to consecrate 'pind' (a ball, of rice) to the Gods, for the feeding of the departed soul on its journey to purgatory. This lasted ten days.

These ten days were days of extreme mourning. Women came every morning and started a lament and at intervals did 'siapa' (ladies moved in a circle and beat their thighs, chests and forehead, in that order, and lamented in unison) This continued nearly the whole day.

People came the whole day, as if in tandem, to express their sympathy and demonstrate their solidarity with us in that hour of grief. A couple of hours before sunset the Garad Puran used to be recited. This lament and siapa was limited to woman only. Men used to sit quietly for some time and then went away enquiring whether they could do some jobs for us. At the recitation of the Garad, everyone, who could come, came. After the recitation, there was no siapa, as after dark no lament took place.

This expression of grief was a great strain for all of us in the family, but very much so for my mother, who had to participate in all the proceedings. The death of a man is a horrifying experience for his wife. She does not only lose her mate, breadwinner and protector, but also always has to be subjected to the public exposure of her grief, stress, fatigue and heightened tension. Her right to grieve in private is taken away. The Hindu society, during its development had acquired certain mores, which were very cruel to women. I am glad that our people have discarded those obnoxious practices and drifted away from that suffocating and confined atmosphere.

But, in all this grief and sympathy, the one person who was affected the most was forgotten. People came to offer words of solace to mother, Haridwar Dass and Shambu Dass, my uncle. I, who was less than fourteen years of age and faced the maximum deprivation, was there only to carry out the commands of the elders. No one knew of my hurt and my anguish. My brother, Ramesh, was too young to realize what had happened, but I knew I had become an orphan in the real and figurative sense. I had lost the powerful protection of my father: my future lay shattered before me, my aspirations for higher education were to remain only wishful thinking and my dream of doing something worthwhile in my life looked like remaining a dream.

On the tenth day was 'dha'. On that day the mourning period comes to an end. On the afternoon of that day people gathered to pay their last homage to the departed soul. The last paragraph of the'Garad Puran' was read by the pundit and a turban was tied round Haridwar's head to signify that he had assumed the place of the father in the family, as its head. Though the official mourning was over, the charities, to benefit father in his after life, had not ended. On the thirteenth day 'the kirya' ceremony was performed by the pandits at our house. 'Kirya' is a very essential ceremony to purify the household. Without this rite of purification the house is considered impure and no Brahmin or a person from a different subcaste than our own would have eaten or drunk in our house. Now-a-days our people are not that orthodox, but those days they were. A death in a family was supposed to make the family impure, and this impurity lasted for a fixed period of time. But still it did not go until the 'kirya' was performed and all the cotton clothes in the house were washed. On the fifteenth day the 'Brahman' ceremony was held, when all the pundits in Tehri (there were not that many) feasted at our house. They were served the best vegetable diet. They were served 'mah' pulse, fried potatoes, vegetable marrow, 'bhallas' (ground moong pulse made into a thick paste in water, fried in 'ghee' in circular shapes of 1 1/2 in diameter) 'kheer' (rice cooked in milk in 1:32 proportion for the best dish, otherwise the proportion can be reduced to 1:16 or even 1:8), 'puras' (wheat flour mixed in water with sugar or jaggery and then fried in ghee in circular shapes of 4" in diameter) which are like pan cakes but smaller in size and with a rougher texture, and 'puris' (dough spread like pan cakes to about 4" diameter and then cooked in 'ghee'). The pundits were also presented with some money and a garment each.

On the seventeenth day, a 'dagotra' came to our house from Kohat and he was given a cot, a quilt, a mattress, a pillow, some utensils, a pair of shoes, a shirt and a salwar. Actually all other goods were put on the cot, where the dagotra himself also sat down, and we carried the cot outside the gate of our house and sprinkled a little water to ward off the evil spirits. With that act, according to puranic traditions, the obligations of the family towards the dead ended. The Dagodra is a sort of degraded Pundit, who accepts goods meant for the dead, which a pandit does not expect. The Dagotra also normally presides over the ceremonies at the burning 'ghat'.

Immediately after the above ceremonies, the family's worries came to the surface. Besides the debts, survival was the immediately problem of the family. My brother was unemployed, but my uncle, Shambhu Dass, who had been working as an overseer in the M.E.S. somewhere near Kohat, had also become unemployed a couple of months before father's death. His job had not lasted for more than a few months. He had all along lived with father and mother. When he got married in 1930, his wife also came to live with us. They had a daughter of about three years at the time of father's death. So seven mouths had to be fed and there was no income and no cash. The first thing mother did was to send uncle to the Nawab for help. All our relatives thought that the Nawab would be enthusiastic in helping us in our hour of need in consideration of the friendship and helpfulness that father had extended to him. However, the Nawab gave only a thousand rupees instead of the five thousand expected. I do not blame the Nawab, as he might have believed that if in the past he had received favours, he had given favours also. In any case, his own financial position was not that good, and besides he had to feed so many mouths; his immediate family, his innumerable relations and a large retinue.

The Nawab's one thousand helped us to meet our household expenses for some time. Mother immediately initiated steps to pay back her husband's debts. With the help of a cousin of hers, she started a dialogue with the creditors. In a few months she had paid back the debts. The creditor to whom we owed the maximum amount, Rs. 8000/-, was given the prized land with a well in the north. The next was given the amount of Rs. 2500/-, which was received on account of father's insurance. The third was given Rs. 1800/- from the amount received from a building contract at Jatta salt mine which father had completed before his death. Another debtor was similarly paid. All these debts were paid after protracted meetings. In each case, the debt was scaled down, otherwise recovery would have been difficult, for all debts included a good amount of interest. Outwardly, one reason also could be that the debtors were all father's friends and relatives.

After the clearance of all the debts we were left with two houses, one four acre plot of land, with a well, to the west of Tehri, and one piece of land in Makori village, besides a share certificate of Rs. 1000/- for a forest generation project somewhere in New Zealand, which Haridwar sold for Rs. 600/- years later, and two flour grinding machines, one in Lachi and the other one in Tehri. Father had a third machine at Latamber, a village situated in an area known for the quality and the quantity of the wheat grown. Latamber was in Tehri Tehsil and situated near the salt mine, Bahadur Khel. This machine was managed by a relative of ours from Latamber. That person had looked it after himself but had passed on the losses to father. Ultimately, father sold it at a loss. Our oldest machine was in Tehri. It was not run efficiently but the person who operated it gave father a small steady income. The operator was a Muslim from Makhad (a town in Punjab). When father installed the machine later in Lachi, this operator ran that machine also. The operator had kept a relative of his there and used to rotate with his relative as and when he felt it was necessary. The machines at Lachi did not prove profitable for us. So, after father's death, uncle sold it to the operator, Sultan, for Rs. 900/-. In any case we needed the money. Even for the Tehri machine no accounts were being maintained and as Sultan's demands for money for oil, spare parts and repairs were persistent, uncle came to an agreement with Sultan that he would pay us a rupee a day and he would take the earnings from the machine and look after all its demands. A couple of years later we sold him the machine for about Rs. 1000/-.

The peculiar thing was that though Sultan cheated father, as there was no supervision, and he landed up with both the machines he managed, he was loyal to father and to his memory after his death. He always praised father after his death. Actually, he mentioned father's name with reverence. I know a couple of instances when I was in some difficulty and Sultan helped me each time in his own way. In N.W.F.P. there was a notion those days, which seems to still persist, that you cannot trust a Punjabi, but here was a Punjabi who was loyal to his benefactor even after his death, while dozens of others in Tehri, who had benefitted from his largess, had forsaken him even in his lifetime.

Father was very generous. Actually he was generous to a fault. He spent money freely. I think he believed that he would make more money when the time came. He did not believe in any rituals nor did he pray. He celebrated certain religious functions with gusto for the enjoyment of offering entertainment to others and seeing them happy. He visited Krishen Dwaar (temple) very occasionally, and that too on special occasions. He was liberal in thinking, but his record of voting was dismally pro-toadies, of British officials in India. However, during a lecture of Mrs. Amrit Kaur, a visiting Congress leader from Punjab at Kohat, an uncle of mine overheard father exclaiming 'we are going against our conscience'. However, he was so impressed by Mrs. Amrit Kaur, as were many other Hindus of Kohat, that he pressurized his cousin, Dewan Ram Swarup, son of Dewan Bhagwan Dass, who was a practising lawyer at Kohat and had stood for election for the Hindu seat of the Kohat district for the legislative Assembly of N.W.F.P. in 1937, to sit down in favour of the Congress candidate, which he did. Ram Swarup subsequently successfully competed and became a subjudge.

Father, even in those days preached against dowry and tried to persuade the 'panchayat' to prescribe a token dowry for the bride's parents to give their daughter at the time of marriage. But, at the time of his daughter's marriage, he gave a sumptuous dowry. He could have set an example for others, but he had to live up to his image for the sake of his reputation and for the welfare of his daughter. The problem was that he was a prisoner of the times. He was born and brought up at a time when prestige came from owning land and glory from the service of the British crown. In his limited atmosphere he achieved both. He earned money, remaining loyal to the British crown and got prestige by owning land. He was a leader of his community and had powerful friends in his own area. But in the years before his death, the feudal system around him was gradually crumbling away and the authority of the British Crown was being seriously challenged. He knew the trends had changed, but he was so enmeshed in the old system that socially, economically and traditionally he could not break away from his past. But, I know, before he died he realised that a new world was passing him by. He just could not leave his old habits. He had only one ailment and that was passing albumin in his urine, but he could not leave meat eating though doctors had told him to cut it out completely, as proteins were not good for his ailment. He died of cerebral haemorrhage, but he did not have blood pressure. Maybe he did have it, but we had never suspected it. During his last days, he was under the treatment of an unqualified, homeopathic doctor who used to give him high potency doses, which we thought brought about the haemorrhage, but perhaps we were wrong. Whatever be the cause, I feel on retrospection, he went away at the right time. He could not have adjusted to the changed circumstances and situations, which followed. He was a large man in every way. The tight situations we faced, the miserable accommodations we lived in and the small people we came across subsequently, could not have been borne by him.

My uncle got a job as a work munshi in the M.E.S. about eight months after father's death, and he shifted to Kohat. Haridwar went to Peshawar to learn typewriting and shorthand. He neither had the aptitude for secretarial work nor did he learn anything during the eight or ten months he spent in attending the classes. His heart was in getting a job as an officer. That seemed impossible, as recruitment was based on the proportionate representation of the two communities, Muslims and Hindus, as reflected by their numbers in the population of N.W.F.P. As Hindus comprised only five percent of the population, the chances of a Hindu getting a job were remote. On top of it, N.W.F.P. was a small province at the time I am writing about, and the population of the settled six districts was thirty lakhs and of the tribal areas also the same, but, as they were not settled and not administered by the provincial government, they did not count and consequently jobs were few and the Hindu share naturally a minor one. Hindus, being better educated, faced very tough competition among themselves to get a job. Haridwar, however, got selected as an excise inspector fortunately, but very unexpectedly. One Hindu, against seven posts, was to be selected, and this post was known to be earmarked for a cousin of the Hindu member of the legislative assembly from Kohat. This member was from Karak, in Tehri tehsil. This change in fortune occurred due to the intercession of the personal assistant of the Minister of Excise, Dewan Bhanju Ram Gandhi. The selection board was composed of Dr. Khan Sahed, Prime Minister of the Provinces, Mr. Ataullah Khan, Minister of Education and the second most important man in the Ministry and the Minister of Excise. It seems the selection of the Hindu candidate was left to the Hindu Minister and so Haridwar was in. The personal assistant to the Minister of Excise was known to a relative of ours.

Haridwar's problems, though, were not solved immediately. He was placed last in seniority, and did not get a posting for a considerable time, and even then in the beginning got posted against leave vacancies. Even by 1947, when he left the N.W.F.P. he had not become permanent. Until Haridwar's selection, no Hindu from Kohat seemed to have been appointed even in the subordinate civil services and the gazetted services were far beyond reach. But in the subsequent three years three sub judges (Hindus) from Kohat were selected on the basis of a competitive examination. They were Dewan Ram Swarup, Dewan Anand Parkash (from Kohat) and Seth Parmanand.

Mother and I remained at Tehri with Ramesh. At the time of my father's death, I was studying in the 8th class of the vernacular middle. In April 1938 after I passed the 8th class, I joined the junior special class at Tehri. Within a few months, my uncle's family and Haridwar moved away to Kohat and Peshawar respectively.

Meanwhile the situation of the Hindus progressively worsened. The Wazir tribes men had become bold enough to show their aggressiveness and evil intentions by passing remarks on Hindus. The menace of the Waziri's attack became so real that the Nawab distributed some breech loading rifles to a few Hindus. Two persons were issued magazine-loading rifles as well. To test the capabilities of people asking for rifles, the Nawab arranged a shooting demonstration. In this demonstration I also took part, although I had not asked for a rifle nor could I be given one because of my age, as I was only 14 years old. I was pushed into the shooting match by the insistence of the people present there. As luck would have it, I was the second best marksman there. I beat many who claimed to be good marksmen, among them my uncle, who had at that time not left for Kohat.

During 1938 and 1939, it was common to hear rifle shots every third or fourth night. They were fired by chowkidars (sentries), at the village gates, either at shadows or just to frighten the Hindus. This and the rumours kept tensions high. When we heard the shots, my cousin Gokal (who was four years older than I and lived within the same compound wall with his mother and father, but in the eastern corner) and I used to take our shot guns and stand on the sides overlooking our new house and the roofs of the shops in the bazaar, in order to prevent anyone coming over the low roofs of the shops from the bazaar. Gokal had a one-barrel gun while I had a two-barreled one, for which, after the death of father, Haridwar held the license. The first time when I took the gun for the defence of my home and my community, mother vehemently objected. But Gokal's father (my father's cousin) shouted down her protests by saying that I was a young man and should do whatever I had to do. Our bravado, however, was, based more on enthusiasm than on real strength. The fortification behind which we took our position was a wooden grill, and that too came up to our knees, as we could not have a proper view of the area while sitting. I am sure if the Waziris had come, they would have got us easily in the first two shots in our exposed position, as the Waziris were very good shots. They were reputed not to miss even a stick at 50 yards.

In April 1939 I got promoted to the senior special class (English of the 7th and 8th standard was taught in this class). In June, I went to Mansehra with my grandmother (maternal) to visit my maternal aunt. My mother had two younger sisters and no brother. My grandmother lived alone in her house. My aunt at Mansehra was the middle sister and married to an overseer, Mr. Hari Chand Vasudev from Tehri, of the Central Public Works Department, who was posted at that time at Mansehra. The occasion for the visit had arisen due to a theft that had taken place at my aunt's place. My grandmother was visiting them on a consolatory visit, as the theft was a heavy one. Besides, cash, clothes, ornaments, a sword with a golden hilt was also taken away. This sword was given to my uncle by my grandmother. When grandmother was leaving, Uncle Shambhu Dass suggested to my mother that he thought I should also go, and so I landed at Mansehra via Peshawar and Abbottabad.

Abbottabad was the capital of the Hazara district of N.W.F.P. While at Mansehra, I visited Abbottabad, Shinkiari, Oagi and Garhi Habibullah. I, subsequently, again visited Abbottabad three times, on separate occasions: twice to visit my aunt's family; once on the occasion of the wedding of my cousin sister and the second time to spend a part of my vacation there. The third time I accompanied my brother who had gone there to consult the civil surgeon of Abbottabad, Mr. Gupta, known to be a good surgeon, regarding a complication arisen from an arm fracture which he had sustained from a fall from a horse in Tonk in Dera Ismail Khan, which is the southern most district of N.W.F.P.

Abbottabad is a very fascinating and invigorating town, with its green hills and silvan surroundings. Abbottabad is situated in a small valley, at an altitude of about 4000 feet, with minor mountainous ranges five miles away to the east and the west, topped by pine trees. Kakool, the military cantonment is in Pakistan now. Hazara is the largest district of N.W.F.P. in area as well as in population. It is also the most beautiful part of N.W.F.P. Actually, the whole district of Hazara has been richly endowed with an enchanting landscape, with sub-mountainous tract and gently flowing streams and verdurous scenery. I have rarely seen such a beautiful landscape.

From Mansehra, I also visited 'Buddha Amarnath'. Amarnath is the famous cave in Kashmir, which is visited by Hindu pilgrims on a particular day very year to see a 'shivling' of ice, formed by the dripping water from a crevice. It can be seen only during a particular period, as earlier it is not formed and later it loses its shape. At Buddha Amarnath's cave there is a shivling, not of ice but only of stone. We visited it on a particular sacred day. I went there with my uncle, cousin and a servant. We came to Garhi Habibullah by car and then went on horses to Buddah Amarnath. The Nawab of Garhi Habibullah, whom Uncle knew, provided four horses. Enroute we crossed a quick flowing stream with some difficulty, as due to the rains the stream had gained more water and speed. The rest of the journey on the plains was easy. The mountainous journey was a bit difficult, as one would expect from a horse ride up the hill on a tortuous bridle path. The lingam was in a cave.

At the cave, when we were having lunch served to us by some people who had come earlier and were known to my uncle, we hard some shouting. When we came out we saw the horse, which my cousin had been riding, hanging over the valley below with his fore feet on the bridle path and the lower portion of its body hanging in the air. We all stood around watching helplessly, as none knew what to do except to shake his bridle occasionally in order to urge him to try to come up. I think I had rarely prayed as much as I did that day for the safety of that horse. When we had given up all hope, the horse suddenly gave a jerk and heaved himself on to the path. Everybody there was overjoyed. Only a horse, among the large animals, could perform that feat, even though it did it to save its own life, with its sleek body and strong legs and shoulders and with hooves, which unlike human hands cannot hold. Our return journey was uneventful. Our journey from Garhi Habibullah to Buddha Amarnath and back took us about ten hours. On return we spent the night in the resthouse of the Nawab of Garhi. At night instead of a proper dinner we had hot milk and 'jalebis', the syrupy sweet. Although it was the month of June, the night was cold. Garhi Habibullah's altitude was about 4000 feet, but being situated in the foothills it was cold at night. Garhi Habib Ullah is situated on the southern bank of Krishan Ganga, a small river. The road from Garhi, a few miles further on, curves up the mountains to the Muzaffarabad, and then on to Uri, Baramla and Srinagar. The old frontier state of Jammu and Kashmir started only a few miles from Garhi.

We spent a good night at Garhi at the Nawab's resthouse, as we were very tired and were provided with comfortable bedding and velvet quilts. The next morning we came back to Mansehra.

From Mansehra I visited Murree. Islamabad, the capital of Pakistan, is situated near Murree. From Mansehra, my cousin, Ganga Dhar and I went to a place near the foothills by road. From there we walked up the hill, along the motorable road to Nathagali, a distance of twenty miles. Nathagali was at that time the summer capital of the Governor of N.W.F.P. while Peshawar was the winter capital. At Nathagal we spent a very uncomfortable night in the public works department's rest house on hard mattresses and with inadequate covering. The next morning we covered the twenty miles to Murree by truck. After spending three days at Muree, we came back to Mansehra via Rawalpindi by bus. Rawalpindi is only forty miles from Murree.

While at Mansehra, we heard the news about the raid of the Waziris on Tehri. From various reports subsequently I learned that a party of about eighty Waziris (this figure is not reliable as the strength of Waziris could be less) raided the village at about 2100 hours, shouting and firing. The eastern gate of the village, located adjacent to the bazaar, was not yet closed. The Waziris entered the bazaar through that gate into the bazaar. The chowkidars, who had their position on a fortified position on top of the gate, did not fire. They either ran away or just remained quiet. Just about ten paces from the gate, a lane on the right led to the Hindu moholla. About thirty yards up the lane on the first floor of a house were sitting Dewan Sachdanand and Gyan Chand who loaded the rifles for him. This, while on one hand, prevented the Waziris from entering the mohollah, on the other, made their passage to the bazaar difficult. To cross the six feet width of the lane to reach the bazaar, the Waziris ran and jumped over it. The Waziris did not try to enter the Mohollah but set fire to two shops. Immediately after that the Waziris left. I do not think they looted much from these two shops. Immediately after their departure, the Hindus came out of their houses and extinguished the fire.

It was never determined why the Waziris left so soon. There could be two possible reasons. One was the expectation of the local Muslim population joining them, which came to naught, inspite of the general resentment prevailing against the Hindus. The second was that the Waziris were delayed while coming to Tehri and, so when they met resistance from the Hindus, they left after taking whatever they could from the shops and set fire to them as an act of bravado.

The border militia, based at the Hangu Tehsil headquarter of Kohat district, arrived in about an hour. If the Waziris had left a little later, they would have been entrapped. It was strange that the Waziris did not cut the telephone line connecting the police station with the outside world, as one would expect them to have donc before entering the bazaar. Perhaps they did not expect the police to inform the authorities outside, and nor did the Hindus, because of the general belief that Muslim policemen were communally inclined. Nevertheless a 'havaldar' (a rank less than that of a sergeant, but with two stripes like that of a corporal) heard the firing and the noise in the police station, situated about half a mile away on the other side of the village from the 'bazaar', and rang up the border militia, after correctly surmising that the village had been raided by the Waziris. On receiving the call, the intrepid commandant of the militia, D.W. Mehra, immediately left for Teri with his militia contingent. Hangu from Tehri is 61 miles. On finding on arrival that the Waziris had left, he left immediately in pursuit. I understand he caught up with them within a day or two, but the Waziris slipped away in the darkness.

W. D. Mehra had a tremendous reputation amongst the Hindus of the Kohat district and in the whole of N.W.F.P. I do not know whether he deserved it, as I am not aware of his exploits, but a man who commanded that esteem and respect from the men in the street must have deserved all the praise showered on him. His bravery was a legend, his honesty, a topic of household talk, and his concern for his men common knowledge. It must have been because of his reputation for honesty and capability that Pandit Nehru and Sardar Patel chose him to take charge of the Delhi police in September, 1947, when communal disturbances broke out in the aftermath of the partition of the country in August, inspite of his relative junior position among the available officers. He subsequently was posted as Inspector General of Police, Jammu and Kashmir, and retired from service there.

After a few days, I came back to Kohat, where I continued my studies, but memories of Abbottabad and Hazara have remained with me to cherish. Once I mentioned to someone that I had not seen a more beautiful area than Hazara till then. That was in 1945. The gentleman to whom I made that statement had replied that the Kaghan Valley was more beautiful. It might be correct as the gentleman concerned was widely travelled in the Frontier and had visited the Kaghan Valley. Since then, I have had a great desire to visit the Kaghan Valley but never found a chance to visit it. This desire has still not left me although nearly half a century has passed since then and I am now in my declining years. Since then, however, I have seen nearly all of India, including the hill areas of Uttar Pradesh and the North Eastern states, except those of Arunachal Pradesh, the Andamans and South India. Besides, I have visited nearly all areas of Australia, Christchurch and the tourist spots around it. I have been to the tourist spots of the Honshu Island of Japan, nearly all of Western Europe and Yugoslavia. I, however, did not visit Scotland. I also regret not visiting the Lugano area of Switzerland. I had got the opportunity to visit Lugano when I was posted at Frankfurt as Director, Tourist Office (Government of India) but did not avail of it, as the person who wanted to take me there had official dealings with our office, and I thought that this might be considered a corrupt practice, though the area was within my jurisdiction and I could have done some promotional but limited work there. I visited a few other places as well, but I have mentioned here only those places, which are, known for their natural beauty. South Germany, Switzerland and Kashmir Valley are beautiful areas in their own way, and so is Hazara.

This beautiful area, Hazara, was once part of the state of Jammu and Kashmir, but in the middle of the nineteenth century, the British authorities in India acquired it from Maharaja Gulab Singh on payment of two lakh rupees. This is a paltry amount from today's standard, but even considered from that day's standard, it is not much of a compensation for such a beautiful tract of land. Neither Hazara's people nor their speech and nor its scenery is similar to that of N.W.F.P. Its common village folk look like the 'Gujars' of Kashmir. 'Gujars' are the goatherds of Kashmir. In winter they graze their goats on the mountainous side of Jammu and in summer on the mountain of Kashmir. Both, the Gujars and the people of Hazara, are thin in build with lean, long, brown faces with sunken eyes. They both speak a dialect of Punjabi. They both wear beards invariably, with a style of their own. The beards are short and they are kept tidy by shaving the hair on the cheeks, and near the mouth and the lips. Hair is also shaven off below the cheekbone and the chin. They wear long shirts and 'salwars' like Pathans. While Pathans wear white shirts and salwars in towns and villages when they can afford them, the Gujars and Hazarvis invariably wear grey coloured clothes. People in towns are mostly Punjabi speaking. Even the Hindus were all Punjabis who had newly migrated. Before the partition of the country, the Gujars used to take their herds down to Hazare in the winters, and not to Jammu. This leads me to the belief that the Gujars and the common folk of Hazare are ethnically the same people.

The Pathans, in contrast to the Gujars and the Hazarvis, are robust in physique, florid in complexion and of full faces. The Pathans are Pushto speaking. Their normal occupation is agriculture. The Pathans are very sensitive, and can take offence even on small matters. The Pathans' honour is his most valuable possession. An insult or injury will not be forgotten even by succeeding generations. Even when an insult has been avenged, the matter is not forgotten, as now the other family is the aggrieved party, and is to be avenged, and so the family who has had their revenge after years of harbouring a sense of having been wronged, now has to be worried and guard against an attack of any sort. This sensitivity of the Pathans, with their taking offence even on a subtle or implied insult, does not make them ideal subordinates, though otherwise they make good friends. This sensitivity has rubbed off on many of us as well. Minus this, perhaps, I would have had better career prospects.

As for the scenery, while the rest of N.W.F.P. was mostly a dry land, Hazara was fertile and rich in vegetation. Peshawar and Mardan had some canal cultivation, but Hazara's greenery was something different. It looked more like a part of Kashmir than that of the Frontier.

Even, Hazara's politics was different. While in the elections, the rest of the Frontier voted for the Congress, Hazara voted for the Muslim League. This is the reason that the Red shirts leader Khan Abdul Ghafar Khan claimed that Hazara's representatives did not represent the public opinion of Frontier, but that of the Punjab. In 1937 the Congress had complete sway, but in the 1945 election, Hazara's representatives did make a strong impression in the legislative assembly, so much so that the Congress ministry, headed by Dr. Khan Sahed (the brother of Khan Abdul Ghafar Khan) had the support of only 19 members of the Muslim community in the legislative against 17 for the Muslim League. The point I am making here is that though the Congress did have the majority of the Muslims representatives, it was just that and not convincing. Hazara's 12 representatives out of a total strength of 50 in the assembly naturally contributed to the impression of the Congress seemingly having lost considerable influence with the Muslims.

The Muslim League was even able to form the Government in 1943, when the Congress members were in jail, with the help of three Sikh members. The Muslim League ministry, headed by Sardar Aurang Zeb, did not last beyond two years, but it gave a rude shock to the Hindus of the Frontier, as for the first time in the known history of the Frontier, the interests of the Hindus and the Sikhs had become separated. The worst part was that Sardar Ajit Singh, the Sikh minister in the cabinet, had obtained the blessings of Sardar Tara Singh, known as Master Tara Singh, the president of the Akali Dal. However, history was moving on its inexorable path. We know now what happened to this so called newly developed friendship between the Muslims and Sikhs once the partition came in 1947.

For us the people of Kohat the desertion of Ajit Singh was even a bigger shock, as he belonged to Kohat city, and his family was known to me. His brother and nephews were Hindus.

The Hindus and the Sikhs together sent the same number of members to the assembly as Hazara. Though the Hindus and the

Sikhs constituted about 8% of the population of the Frontier, they had 24% representative in the legislature. This was the result of the communal award announced on 16th April 1932 by the Prime Minister of Great Britain. Under this award, in the United Provinces, now Utter Pradesh, the Muslims got a representation of about 29% against a population of about 15% and in Bihar they got 24% against a population of about 11% in their legislatures.

So the Hindus in the Frontier, as long as they stayed together, were a political force when the two major political parties were nearly balanced in the assembly. As far as the Hindus were concerned, in the surcharged atmosphere of the forties, when the country was divided between the Congress and theMuslim League and the division of the country was a real issue, there was no alternative for them but to be with the Congress. So, the joining of three Sikh representatives with the Muslim league, at the most crucial moment of the history of that time, really hurt the Hindus badly.

Before I come back to write about Tehri and Kohat, I may state that I saw Mahatma Gandhi for the first time in Abbottabad in a public meeting in 1944. Khan Abdul Ghafar Khan was also present at the meeting. Mahatma Gandhi spoke for about 20 minutes at the meeting.

In the summer of 1942, I returned to Kohat from Mansehra and started studying there. My uncle, Dewan Shambhu Dass, meanwhile had brought my mother and Ramesh from Tehri, after the Waziris' raid, as Tehri was no longer safe. Before I write about my days in Kohat, I think, I must take the history of Tehri of those days to its conclusion.

After the raid, the plight of the Hindus in Tehri rapidly deteriorated. Some left immediately after the raid, as they felt Tehri was no longer a place where they could live honourably. But they were not many and were mostly younger people who could start life afresh. A few settled down in Kohat, but more went to Rawalpindi, Punjabi, and settled down there. The idea of the people who settled down at Rawalpindi was that if they had to leave, they should go to some place where there was scope for employment as well as security. They were right, as Kohat seemed a dead place for the Hindus even in 1939. It did not offer either employment or security. I will write about this later. However, the bulk of the people remained behind. These were shopkeepers and old people, many of them with their dependants, who could neither adapt themselves to a different environment, nor had any chance of earning their livelihood without government support and nor could they hope to maintain their social position.

The Hindus, who had once lorded over Tehri, led a life of bare existence after the raid. They tried to be on the best terms with all the Muslims and displayed meekness towards the leaders of the various sections of the Muslims as well as to the Muslim bad characters. So, even after the beating off of the raid, the Hindus suffered psychologically, and their confidence was shattered. So much so that when, in 1941, Dewan Remajk Chand, who was my uncle's father-in-law and kept accounts for the Nawab, was murdered, his sons did not want initially to prosecute the murderers for fear of reprisals. The Hindus at that juncture were in the real grip of fear psychosis, which a small minority suffers from when it has to face an aggressive majority of overwhelming proportions. Even when they beat off an attack, they fear another one; and when they have the law on their side in a dispute, they are afraid of reprisals.

The Hindus carried on like that, scared, but pulling on, with occasional deputations to the Nawab and the district authorities as the tension mounted due to the rumours of imminent Waziri attacks and communal strife in the country until March 1947, when the communal disturbances broke out at various places in the country, starting with Noakhali in East Bengal. After that the situation was disturbed everywhere in N.W.F.P. The Hindus in Tehri, for their safety, adopted Mussali Khan as their patron after presenting him gifts, as per the Pathan tradition. Mussalli Khan was from the ruling family to which the Nawab belonged. Mussali Khan, as it is, had influence as he had vast tracts of land and his immediate family had good muscle power. Besides, his much additional prestige came from his mother being a Wazir chief's daughter. The Hindus in Tehri itself did not come to any harm. But two Hindus, who were going in a tonga with Mussalli Khan, carrying with them a few thousands of rupees to Banda Daud Shah to catch a bus to Kohat enroute to Rawalpindi, were killed. Actually, Nihal Chand, a tailor, was migrating to Rawalpindi while Dwan Ram Chand was accompanying him for security reasons as Nihal Chand was carrying with him his life's savings. Mussalli Khan was accompanying them as a guard. Mussali Khan's presence itself was considered sufficient protection. However in the ford of 'Toi', just before Banda, they were waylaid by the tribesmen (waziris). Nihal Chand and Ram Chand were murdered and Mussalli Khan's hands and feet were bound by the tribemen. They also took away the money. It was never known who had warned the tribesmen about these two Hindus going to Banda with money. However, the Hindus suspected Ishaq Khan in this connection.

Ishaq Khan belonged to the same family as the Nawab. He was, however, different in many ways from the Khans. Firstly, he was a distant cousin of the Nawab, while the others were relatively near. Secondly, he did not own any land, unlike the other Khans. Thirdly, Ishaq Khan was dark in colour while the other Khans were fair and had florid complexions. Fourthly, he was in business while the Khans of those days considered it beneath their dignity to get into any business venture. Ishaq Khan was a man with meagre means. He had learnt driving and motor mechanics in some town. He came to Tehri, brought a new bus and ran it between Tehri and Kohat. Ultimately, he purchased another bus also and built up a garage for them in Tehri. He had competition as two Hindu brothers, Hari Chand and Dewan, ran another bus service. Father had also purchased a bus and ran it between Tehri and Kohat. While the others, who ran bus services, became rich, father lost money, because while the others operated their bus services themselves, father's was run by other people and besides, father was not a driver but the others were. He eventually sold his bus to Ishaq Khan, who was happy to purchase it to remove an influential competitor from his path.

Fifthly and lastly, Ishaq Khan became a politician while the other Khans never indulged in politics. The Nawab used to be a member of the district board, but always on an independent ticket. Later on, he used to be elected to the legislative assembly also on an independent ticket. In 1937, Saad-Ullah Khan, the president of the Muslim League of N.W.F.P. and their leader in the assembly, approached the Nawab with an offer to make him leader of his party, in case he joined their party, However, father dissuaded him from committing himself. He told him Saad-Ullah's party was in the minority then. He wanted to gain strength, and once he gained strength for his party by such an accretion, sufficient enough to form a government, he would throw him aside and himself become the Prime Minister. So, he should spurn such an offer, as this would not get him anything but the displeasure of the party in power then: the Congress party. The Nawab thankfully accepted father's advice and turned down the offer. In September 1947, Mussalli Khan and the Nawab arranged with the district authorities, under the new Government of Pakistan, to take the beleaguered Hindus to the refugee camp at Kohat for transfer to India, which eventually took place. This they did on the Hindus' request, as large-scale migrations were taking place between West Punjab and East Punjab, as the Hindus were going to India and the Muslims to Pakistan at the time of the partition of the country on 15th August 1947.This had convinced them that the time had come for them to leave their motherland for good.

However, many of the simple souls had thought that after the partition's turmoil was over they would come back to their native place. These were the people who knew they had no future except in their native land. One of them was a distant relative of mine. His name was Tara. He was a 'patwari', who kept the records of the land in his circle. He had buried his family's jewellery in his house, when he left the place for India, thinking that in his sojourn to India these may be lost, while they would be safe buried in his house. After a lapse of a few years, when things became normal, under mutual agreement of both the governments, visits of such persons were arranged so that they could visit their old houses. Tara Patwari, as he was called, found his jewellery intact on digging the spot where he had buried it. According to him, many houses of the Hindus had collapsed, as they should have, for lack of care; after all they were mud houses. However, my grand uncle, Dewan Bhagwan Dass's house was occupied by a sub-inspector incharge of the police station. My own aunt had left her jewellery buried in her house at Kohat, but she never went back to retrieve it. Tehri's Hindus are now a much happier lot than their fathers or for that matter their forefathers had ever been. They say they had no future there. They now feel that in Tehri they were like prisoners sealed in a compartment. Being enterprising, they flourished in a free India. They are now in any profession one can name such as engineering, medicine, services, business, construction works, academics.

In concluding this important chapter of my life I must say, the Muslims of Tehri were not bad, on the contrary they were good people. There were tensions in the late thirties and forties, but to some extent I blame the Hindus for them. Until 1924, there were no grounds for tension. People were simple and their wants were few, while the land was productive. The Dewans were the only educated among multitudes of ignorant and illiterate people, and they looked after the people well, under the overall charge of the Nawab. Earlier my great grandfather (paternal) Dewan Mehr Dass earlier and later my maternal grandfather, Dewan Hem Raj, had kept things under control. They were both capable men with courage. In the mid-twenties there was a lot of tension in Northern India, so much so that Afridi tribesmen from 'Dara' raided Kohat in 1924. 'Dara' is only seven miles from Kohat. 'Dara' in Urdu means a mountain pass. A minor mountain range lies athwart, about a couple of miles from Kohat town, on the road from Kohat to Peshawar.

The road ascends the mountain in its zigzag course on the left side of a small valley, formed between two parts of the mountain. It goes up five miles up to 'Dara' a mountain pass, lying in a depression of the mountain ridge, above the narrow and the northern end of the valley. From 'Dara' the road goes down relatively in a gentle slope to a level surface, three or four miles away. From there the road goes to Peshawar on a nearly level surface.

The Dara's Afridis live in the valley below Dara or on the mountainside round about Dara. According to an agreement between the British Authorities and the Afridis, the road alone was under the jurisdiction of the Afridis themselves. The area occupied by the Afridis was also called Dara and the Afridis occupying that area were called Dara Afridis. They manufactured their own small arms. They even now do so, but their arms are now much more sophisticated and they have imported machinery.

The raid on Kohat was incited by the local Muslims, because of strained relations between the Hindu and the Muslims. The raid continued for three days. Ultimately the military beat them back. The Hindus suffered a great loss due to the looting, and that is why the Hindus of Kohat call this incident 'loti'. Most of the Hindus had run away to Rawalpindi, which was 110 miles away, but not to Peshawar, though Peshawar was the capital of the province and was only 40 miles away. This had been always the case. In case of trouble, the Hindus of Kohat district always looked towards far away Rawalpindi, but not at nearby Peshawar. The main reason was that Rawalpindi was predominantly a Hindu city and they found succour there, while Peshawar was predominantly a Muslim city, and there was no hope of help there. Another factor, though a minor one, could be that there was no direct link between Kohat and Peshawar, but it was there between Kohat and Rawalpindi. As a matter of interest, I may mention here that Bannu was the only town in N.W.F.P. where the Hindus were in a majority, constituting about 80% of the population.

As for Tehri, father's fortune was already at its Zenith by 1924, and people looked upto him for advice, monetary help and employment. His munificence was proverbial. There was nobody to take over from him when his financial position became weak or when he passed away. So, until 1937, there had been no trouble in Tehri, but the selfishness of the Hindu shopkeepers and the usury of a couple of moneylenders, as well as the relative prosperity of the Hindus in contrast to the poverty of the common Muslim folks had brought about a sort of alienation of the Muslims from the Hindus. Added to this was the pernicious influence of the Muslim League, which became perceptible in 1937 due to the elections of the legislative assembly, and it gradually increased, but at a slow speed. But the Muslim League was never a factor in Tehri.The little influence that it had was only on the surface and that too because of Ishaq Khan, its president. The Hindus of Tehri were not rich. The only thing was that they were managing, with a slightly better standard of living. Some Hindus were well off, but some were poor also. However, if the Hindus had collectively made an effort to help the very poor Muslims, the sting of envy from which the Muslims suffered, because of the Hindu's better dress and food, would have been removed. Some Muslims also were rich, but they did not incite that much envy as the Hindus, because they were after all their co-religionists. The Khataks were good Muslims but they were not fanatics. They were simple, courageous and hospitable people; I have not heard a single instance where a Hindu might have been hurt on visits to smaller villages for grain collection (share of crop) or otherwise. Dewan Remal Chand was killed, but in Tehri, and that too by hired assassins, over a property dispute and in bad times. These bad characters are parasites living on the periphery of a society. These were the few bad characters who had spoilt the atmosphere of Tehri in the late thirties and early forties, but they were a threat to both the Muslims and the Hindus. Actually, the poor Muslims suffered at their hands even more. What better testimony can there be for the Khataks than that they did not harm the Hindus when they were isolated? On the contrary, when the Hindus wanted to leave, they arranged to send them to a safe place for expatriation to India.

I remember the early thirties when the 'Surakh Posh' (red shirt) movement was very popular and Mahatma Gandhi and Frontier Gandhi were household names. The name Frontier Gandhi was given to Khan Abdul Ghafar Khan, as he lived an austere life and was as popular in the Frontier as Mahatma Gandhi was in the whole of India. I still have a vivid recollection of the visit of Jawahar Lal

Nehru to Ahmedi Banda, enroute to Bannu by car. Thousands of people had come from surrounding villages to have a glimpse of the crownless king of India, as Jawahar Lal Nehru was called during those days. He was Panditji to the people who individually and affectionately referred to him as such. At that time I was six or seven years old, so, the year would be 1930 or 1931. An attendant, who was more like a family member, had carried me on his shoulders to the destination and back, a distance, which was more than fourteen miles. As Pandit Nehru was passing Ahmedi Banda in the morning, my brother, some relatives, my brothers' friends and I left early in the morning, as we had to cover seven miles to Ahmedi Banda. Enroute we met hundreds of people from other villages who were going on the same mission as our own. On the roadside rope barriers had been erected to control the crowds. Ahmedi Banda was chosen as a stop as it was the home place of Aslam Khan Khattak, or Aslam Khattak as he was called, and Aslam Khattak was the chief Salar of the 'Surakh Posh' organisation.

Panditji came along with Khan Abdul Ghafar Khan, dressed as he usually was in those days in a 'khaddar' 'Kurta, 'churidar pajama' and jacket, Aslam Khan himself was in command of his 'Surakh Poshes'. On Panditji's arrival, he was presented a guard of honour by the Surakh Poshes. After which he delivered a short speech and went on his way to Bannu. But that glimpse of the great man meant a great deal to the boy of six years, whatever it may have meant to thousands of others.

Aslam Khattak was an intense, honest and loyal leader of the surakh poshes. He did not succeed in beating the Nawab of Tehri, Baz Gul Khan, in elections, except once, I think, because of the old feudal loyalties of the people of Tehsil and the Nawab's money power. But he was a very popular man from the early thirties to the mid-forties. During elections, thousands of people came to Tehri to cast their votes. The Nawab, who used to keep a herd of camels, on such occasions provided a couple of old camels to feed those people. Many old leaders had deserted the Congress in 1945 and 1946, sensing the direction in which the wind was blowing, but Aslam Khattak had remained steadfast right upto the time the partition of the country took place.

Before I conclude this important chapter in my life, I would like to mention something about the cultural peculiarities of the Khattaks.

The Popular dance of the Khattak is 'balbala' in which the men, not women, dance in a circle, alternately bending and clapping and straightening and clapping their hands overhead in unison. This dance is very similar to what ladies in the Gujarat state perform. Similarly, the 'gatkare' performed by the Hindu men in N.W.F.P. is the same dance which the Gujarati men and women perform, though in Gujarat, variation and sophistication have been introduced in it. In the playing of 'gatkare', men dance in a circle with a wooden rod, about two feet long and about one inch in diameter. In 'gatkare' a man strikes the 'gatkare' of the man on one side on the first beat of the 'dhol' (drum), on the second beat he makes the dance movement in his own way, and on the third beat he strikes the 'gatkare' of the man on the other side, and these movements are repeated, in tandem, again and again. I am mentioning these two instances of similarities between the dances of N.W.F.P. and Gujarat to show the cultural unity underlying all artistic forms. N.W.F.P, even otherwise did not have, like most of the Islamic countries, much variety in dance and music. The music instruments most commonly seen, in pre-independence N.W.F.P. were 'dhol' and a wind instrument like 'shehnai', but cruder in form and smaller in size. However, like the 'shehnai' it was played in marriages, accompanied by a 'dhol'. The 'dhol' played by 'Khattaks' is smaller than what accompanies the 'Bhangra' in Punjab, but it was played with a greater verve.

The 'sarangi' is a string instrument played with a bow. One came across it at shops or at functions arranged by the Nawab.The harmonium was another instrument, which had become common by the thirties. On it one could hear 'pashto' songs set to 'Urdu' tunes. However, the typically 'Pashto' song sounded like an Urdu 'ghazal'.

As for the dance form, the only dance one could come across was by a 'nacha', a male dancer. It was actually a 'Khattak' dance by a male, in which the dancer danced in a long skirt, in mostly circular movements. The swirling skirt, accompanying the circular motion of the body, the beating of the feet, the gestures of the hands and the flailing of the neck and the long hair of the dancer, along with the accompanying dhol beat, provided the rhythm and the vigour of a solo Khattak dance.

I once had the opportunity to witness a Khattak sword dance. I had not even heard of such a dance earlier. The Governor of N.W.F.P., George Cunningham, once visited Tehri (it was sometime in the mid thirties) and camped in the school compound for a couple of days. The school was closed for the Governor's visit. The Nawab was the host, and as such he paid for all the lavish hospitality provided on the occasion. The last night of the Governor's visit was a gala affair. The Nawab had provided a lavish feast. All the 'maliks' of the tehsil had been invited; and to suit the martial spirit of the 'Khattaks', a sword dance was arranged for the occasion. I think my father was the only man from Tehri proper, besides the Nawab, present on this occasion. He had taken me along with him. The dance was performed by thirty or forty men standing in a circle. It was not the type of dance one sees in a movie or on the stage; a dance of fast wielding swords by handsome, smart and beautifully attired men: but a dance of slow movements of the rugged 'Khattaks' in their usual dress of gray long shirts and heavy 'salwars', with a 'cummerbund' at the waist. The dancers went round and in a circle, dipping their swords, in one movement, to the ground and, in the second, taking a turn and bringing their swords high in the air above their right shoulder, at an angle; and in another turn the swords were dipped again. And so, it went on like this again and again.

What surprised me most was where these thirty odd swords had come from. Most probably, the Nawab had provided them from his armoury. They must have been leftovers from the old days, as we had one in our house and my maternal grand father had one with a gold hilt, for otherwise I had never seen any sword in public.

Chapter Four

Schooling in Kohat

Getting admission in a school in Kohat proved to be a real problem. Three of us, who had migrated together from Tehri, approached the Headmaster of the Bharatary School, founded by the Hindus of Kohat, to arrange for our schooling, but he flatly refused, as, according to him, he could not provide a special senior special class for us. We then approached the Headmaster of the Government High School, and he immediately agreed to start a special class for four students as one more had joined us from another village, Shakar Dara. However, when we had successfully completed education upto the 8th class in English and wanted to migrate to Bharatary School, Mr. Hazarat Gul, the Headmaster of the Government School, refused to give us the discharge certificate. Inspite of our best efforts, he remained adamant and did not give us the certificate, stating that he had run a special class for for the four of us, but after our problem period was over we wanted to leave the school, which had helped us in our difficulty. So, we enrolled for the 9th class in the Government High School in Kohat, in April 1940, and that proved to be a blessing.

My family circumstances, to begin with, were precarious. Mother, Ramcsh, my elder brother Haridwar Dass (who had left his shorthand and typing class at Peshawar after he was selected as an Excise Inspector) and I lived with my uncle Dewan Shambhu Dass at Kohat in one large room. The room was on the first floor of a small house in the Hindu Mohollah of Kohat. The house belonged to a pandit overseer in the M.E.S. In the room besides the four of us, lived my uncle, my aunt, their two daughters of 6 and 4 years of age and their two-year-old son. We were very happy there as the room was large and quite long, and we all were very nicely accommodated there. The overseer, in whose house we were living, was posted out of station, and he very occasionally came for a day or two. His family lived in a room across our room, and it comprised of his wife, two teen-age daughters and a son of about 5 years. They were nice people, and our relationship with them was very good. We used to draw the water for our use from a narrow well whose narrow interior was bricked. The kitchen was situated adjacent to our room and in such a position that when one came out two steps and turned sharply to the left, the next two steps found him in the kitchen. A few feet from the door of our room and that of the kitchen stood a revolving wooden drum with a sisal rope wound round it and mounted over the well hole. The mouth of the well was just below on the ground floor. We used to draw water with a bucket for drinking as well as washing. There was a small common bathroom where we used to carry water in buckets for bathing and washing. The house was centrally situated near the small shopping area of the Hindu Mohollah, and so we were all very happy.

An additional advantage was that on the northern side, the wide side, there was a large window with a 'chique'. The 'chique' was always closed except when we wanted to get something from the street as vendors of vegetables, savouries like 'samosas' and 'gulgulas' and various sweet delicacies were commonly seen going around in the Mohollah. We quite often used to purchase vegetables from these vendors and occasionally other eatables for the evening tea. We used to throw down one end of a rope from our room and the vendors used to tie the goods with it and we used to pull the rope up. The agreed price then used to be thrown down to them. We ourselves also, when we went shopping, used to send up by rope certain articles, which were rather bulky or heavy and that we did not feel like carrying up ourselves. We only had to shout for the rope or the basket from below. Only one rope was thrown down for articles that could be tied to a rope, but for others, which were in paper packages or were loose, a basket tied to the rope end was sent down. My first year in Kohat passed happily. Our neighbours were good and we were together, for after all we were one family. My uncle had lived with father and mother since his childhood, and my aunt had been with them since her marriage, and the same joint family continued in Kohat.

Around the middle of the next year we shifted to another house, as our landlady wanted us to leave for her husband was coming back on transfer, and we wanted to shift, as we had started to find the accommodation a bit tight. The house we shifted to was a fort like large house. It was situated just outside the Hindu Mohollah. It was a new house constructed just for renting out. The entrance door led into a 'deodi', a small entrance room. This in turn, after stepping out and walking a couple of steps to the left, led to a large courtyard which was of an irregular shape, as it followed the shape of the house. The building was two storeyed. On the ground floor were about twelve rooms. Eleven rooms were located along the circumference on three sides; north, east and south. One room was located on the west side just adjacent to and to the left of the entrance passage which led to the courtyard. The door of this room opened directly into the courtyard to the east. All other rooms opened into a verandah, about eight feet in width, which ran along all the three sides in front of the rooms. A common bathroom, with a single tap, was located adjacent to the inner wall of the room situated adjacent to the entrance passage. The door of the bathroom was on the northern side. The eastern and western sides of the quadrangle were the longer sides and the northern and the southern sides the shorter. On the first floor there were fewer rooms and no verandah.

On the first floor, in the northern wing lived the owner of the house, Dewan Naunehal, with his two married sons and their families. This wing had a good open space for the use of the owner's family. On the second floor, the roof of the rooms on the first floor was partitioned in such a way that each tenant with two rooms had some privacy in the enclosed open space allotted to him as the night quarters and a clothes drying place in the summer. As for latrines, one or two enclosed places had been provided on the roof for the purpose. In this accommodation lived some of the specimens of the respected members of the middle class of Kohat.

We had taken three rooms in the southeast corner for Rs.9, at Rs.3 for a room per month. We wanted only two rooms but had to take three, as two rooms were relatively well lighted but the one in the corner received no light. This dark room was the last room in the wing containing the rooms on the southern side and one on the eastern side. The two wings were formed by the ramp of the staircase to the first floor. Had we not taken this dark room on the east side, someone else would have taken that room. On the one hand this would have deprived us of whatever little privacy we had. On the other, we would have been deprived of the precious space for the kitchen. As no separate kitchens had been provided to the families, every family had to use the space outside their rooms, in the verandah, for the purpose. So, by occupying the dark room, we not only had the space in the verandah outside the three rooms, but also the additional space in the corner adjacent to the staircase. So, we could use the additional space in the corner as a kitchen, and the rest of the space in the verandah as a sitting room.

In the summer, we used to carry our beddings to the terrace in the evenings, in order to sleep in the open at night. If there was rain, one could hear noises of rapid talking and hurried shuffling of feet at night, as everyone on the roof assembled his or her bedding and ran for cover to their quarters on the first or the ground floor.

We had two enclosures on the second floor, as we had three rooms for which we paid rent. Even otherwise, the owners were our relatives. Mother's cousin, the daughter of her maternal uncle, was married to the younger son of Dewan Naunehal. Dewan Naunehal was a Dewan from Kohat. Father's name commanded respect from him. In the evenings, we carried our dinner to the second floor and had our dinner there in our enclosure. Nearly everybody, or more correctly every family, ate their dinner upstairs, as downstairs it was very warm and stuffy in the summer. It was really like a community picnic. One could hear others talking in their enclosures. Many a time people talked to each other across the waist high brick walls, which were the enclosures' barriers. On moonlit nights the atmosphere really used to be gay, enchanting and convivial. Everyone seemed to forget their dreary lives and the suffocating atmosphere.

Indians like sleeping in the open in the summer, and the poverty of the masses and the relative security of those days had made sleeping on rooftops or even in the streets for the very poor a common occurrence. However, for us all at Kohat or at Tehri, sleeping on the rooftops was necessary for the simple reason that there was no electric supply either at Kohat or at Tehri. But I am sure that even if there had been electricity, people would have slept in the open, as people those days were too fond of open air to exchange it for stale air in a closed room. However, those who could afford it would have used a table fan in the open to ensure circulation of air. However, it is seldom that there is cool air in the summers in northern India. And only in the stillness of the rainy season, can the fan provide cool air. When it is raining, the air is cool, as it is the wind, which brings the clouds. So in N.W.F.P. and Punjab in May and June, there is so much heat that even the fan does not give you any relief.

In Delhi the 'loo', a hotwind with particles of sand and dirt used to blow with such ferocity until at least four decades ago that one had to close down the windows and the doors at the hottest time of the day to escape the searing and suffocating particles of dirt and sand. I had this experience in June of 1947 when I was staying in a hostel room on Anand Parbat in New Delhi. Now Delhi does not have that terrible loo, at least the people of Delhi do not feel it as much because of the planting of hundred and thousands of trees in and around Delhi and the huge construction work undertaken. Delhi is situated on the verge of a desert, and so people in Delhi still get some taste of it, but the intensity of the yesteryears was something different. Even now one sometimes sees a red sky in the summer months. The falling of dirt from above is still sometimes witnessed. Occasionally, for days the red dirt continues to rain.

In Delhi now the rich use air conditioners day and night to keep cool. Their not so fortunate cousins use air coolers, which are contraptions in which water is poured over 'khas khas' grass through the use of water pump, and the cool air is pushed into the room, through the window or door to which this contraption is fitted, by an exhaust fan fitted on the inside of the "khas khas' mats but facing towards the room. As coolers are based on the principle of cooling the air by saturating the air with water, they are not effective in the rainy season. The lower middle class use fans and the poor depend upon the bounty of the nature to keep them cool and comfortable. Our fate in Kohat was the same, in this respect, as that of the poorest of the poor today, but only a mile from us the 'bada sahebs' the representatives of the British Government, white as well as brown, and their henchman had all the comforts, which electric power provided to the Cantonment.

Every morning, one had to take one's turn to go to the latrine and stand in a queue to a take a bath. Ladies used to wash the clothes after the menfolk had gone for work. One gets used to any life one is confronted with. I used to take up the beddings of all the family members to the terrace on the second floor. The beddings were not necessarily full beddings, as mattresses added to the discomfort from the heat of the atmosphere. The essential parts of the bedding were a pillow, a sheet to cover oneself with in case there were mosquitoes or to safeguard oneself from the unexpected cold in the predrawn period or a' durree', a thick but tightly woven cotton sheet, stylishly coloured. Some needed a bedsheet to cover the durree. Of course, there were always some who cared more to relax the body than to reduce the scope of excess heat, and so they needed mattresses too. There was some justification for it, as all the cots were stringed, and flimsy as they were exposed to the weather all the year round. The cots in the rooms below were also of the stringed type, but of a slightly better quality.

The Hindu Mohollah of Kohat was very congested and some portions of it were very dingy. It suffered from nearly all the ills of overcrowding, except in some vital aspects. Overcrowding was the result of the desire of the Hindus to live in one place for the sake of security. This is how a normal ghetto mentality works. However, some Hindus who came from Punjab for work lived in various lanes, branching off from the main bazaar. Actually Kohat had only one long bazaar enclosed within two iron barred gates. One was situated near the Hindu Mohollah and the other demarcated the limits of the city and the cantonment, in the east west direction. The eastern gate was located just outside where the cantonment started, and the western gate was near the Hindu Mohollah. A few houses of the Punjabi Hindus were in an enclosure near the bus station as well. Some rich Hindus like Sardar Makhan Singh had property in the cantonment, and they lived there. My cousin sister was married to one of the sons of Sardar Makhan Singh and she and her husband lived there. Some others who were working in canteens or such establishments catering to military personnel and gazetted civilian officers also lived in the Cantonment. A few like us lived just outside the Mohollah to the south or at a short distance from the Mohollah at a slightly higher level, to the southeast, near the civil hospital.

The vital aspects, which made the Mohollah livable, were: one, its lighting system. At short intervals in the streets, lamps were fixed on poles, on the pattern of old time London.These kept the streets lit all through the night. I never saw this lighting system fail, as one sees in Delhi as the streetlights are quite often off.

Secondly, the seweage was very efficient. The sewage from the houses was led into underground sewers through open drains. The sewers ran in the middle of the streets, which were mainly quite wide. However, faecal matter from the latrines was mostly carried away by sweepers. The sewers were cleaned very often. The sewers could be entered easily as wide openings were situated near them and they were guarded by two heavy steel plates, of four feet by one and a half feet at each opening. All streets were bricked and were dirt free. Water was freely available. The Municipality's taps were available everywhere at convenient distances.

Water was no problem, as Kohat had been gifted with a number of springs and as underground water was available in plenty, many houses had wells as, most probably, they were dug up before piped water was made available by the municipal committee. Perhaps, the easy availability of ground water prompted the Municipality to provide piped water free of charge. The first time I saw Kohat's springs I was amazed, as I had never seen such clear water before. It was absolutely transparent. Even if the proverbial needle were dropped, one could have seen it at the bottom. The springs were about a mile to the north of the Hindu Mohollah. The Hindus came to these springs at least once a day in the summer. Many boys who had nothing to do spent the whole day at the springs. Watermelons were a common sight at the springs. People kept them in the springs for hours, as the water in the spring was comfortably cold, and ate them at leisure. Muslims normally were not fond of daily baths, nor did many of them patronise the springs.

Kohat's cantonment one of the best kept cantonments, with large green grounds, lawns, well topped roads, green hedges on the roadside, large bungalows with large lawns, running water channels and luxurious vegetation. It really looked like a large garden from a distance. The English officers found it very peaceful. I remember having read a book by an English man in the mid-forties, when sentiments ran high about the issue of Pakistan's formation. He was pro-Muslim and pro-Pakistan, which actually meant the same thing. To show the superiority of the Muslims, he tried to prove it by comparing two towns, one in India and one in the area claimed for the proposed state of Pakistan. The places he chose for comparison were respectively, Meerut and Kohat. He stated that he had served during his career at Meerut and Kohat, and stayed in the cantonments of both the places. While he found the Meerut cantonment ill kept and rather dirty, he found Kohat's cantonment a delight to live in. Of course, there is no doubt that Kohat's cantonment was pleasing to see, but the main reasons for it were abundance of greenery, its water channels and less population. Meerut's cantonment is by no means dirty. It is larger in area and has more people living there, and so some areas of it are not that clean. Kohat's cantonment was definitely a gem. Kohat had another distinction, as it had the largest military airport after Karachi.

Kohat's citizens, Hindus and Muslims both, spoke Punjabi. Muslims, however, spoke it with a delightful accent. In a word of two syllables ending with 'r' if the alphabet 'a' came before the 'r', they would pronounce it as 'u' as in put. They had some other substitutes of their own for a few words. However, the language of the villages round about was Pushto. Jungle Khel was the nearest village; it was just across the springs. Gadi was another village a little distance away to the west, across a rain water stream (called 'Toi' in Pushto'), but the distance to Gadi was only a couple of miles while that to Jungle Khel was not much, as it more or less adjoined the town.

In Kohat, there were three high schools for boys. These were the Government High School, Islamia School and Bharatary High School. The Muslim boys of the city studied in Islamia School. It had about five hundred students. In Bharatary School, three to four hundred Hindu students studied. In the Government School, students were mainly from Jungle Khel. A few came from Gadi as well. A few Hindu students like myself were also there. Out of a total of one hundred and fifty students, the Hindu students were not more than twenty.

Neither the Hindus nor the Muslims in Kohat had much character. But the people from the villages and especially from Jungle Khel had character. They were simple, brave, honest men one could trust, but unfortunately one cannot say the same about the people from the town. The Hindus were in general afraid of all Muslims, but even the city's Muslims were afraid of people from Jungle Khel. In Islamia School, there were five hundreds students but they were scared to face the students of the Government High School, as they were mostly from Jungle Khel.

I found that the boys from the Hindu Mohollah had not developed with time. One could not find in them any patriotism or any intellectualism. They were aggressive in packs but cowards individually. Actually, I did not see any sign of cultural development in Kohat in general nor in the Hindus particularly. As for their religion, the Hindus of Kohat were through and through materialistic. Religion did not mean anything to them spiritually. Quite a number of the ladies went in the morning to a 'Krishandwara' (literally meaning house of Krishan), but more for gossip than in pursuit of any spiritual development. On certain occasions like Janamashtami (the day of the birth of Krishan) a large number of Hindus went to the main 'mandir (which had a large enclosure). In the Hindu Mohollah there was a large Shiv Mandir, called 'Devithan'. Shivism had been quite popular in Kohat about a generation earlier, but when we came to Kohat in 1939, the Devithan used to be deserted. Sikhs, of course, celebrated all their religious occasions with enthusiasm. As for Muslim religious occasions, I remember only Moharram. It was observed with great solemnity and the procession taken out by the Shia community used to be very impressive and largely attended.

My brother Haridwar got married on 16th May 1940 to a girl of the Dewan family. Her father was an overseer at Peshawar. He belonged to the public service department of N.W.F.P. The marriage was fixed through negotiations, but my brother had long before indicated his choice and had refused many good offers received earlier. He was at that time posted on a short-term assignment at Mardan. The marriage took place at Tehri. In this connection, I had approached the extra assistant commissioner, civil supplies, Mr. Khaled Khan, for a quota of sugar for the marriage, as food was rationed and the supply of sugar in the quota was meagre. For our day-to-day consumption we had to obtain sugar in the black market. For marriages or other such functions separate quotas were given. But Mr. Khaled Khan refused the special quota. Even asking for a special quota was an act of foolishness, as it was known that such quotas were only allotted to people with connections. However, I used to be very confident those days, believing in justice and equality, and so was never afraid to see anybody. After the marriage, my sister-in-law lived with us at Kohat, as Haridwar knew that his tenure at Mandam was very temporary.

I started my stay at Kohat on a good note. I was good in studies and used to take part in debates in Urdu. My headmaster in the school was very happy with me. I made good friends in the class and outside. I started to improve my physique as well. I had been an outdoor person from childhood, but then I thought of developing some muscles as well. I used to get up much before dawn, when it used to be pitch dark. In our dark room I used to do sit-ups and push-ups and then used to go running to the cantonment. After running there for some distance I used to come back home. By that time, the house used to be buzzing with the morning activities. I used to be off to school after a hurried bath and breakfast. The school was only a ten-minute walk from the house. In the evenings I used to go again for a long walk. On my return, I used to visit the townhall, which subscribed to a number of daily papers, in English and Urdu. The papers used to be spread over a large oblong table.

The papers were the Milap, Pratap, Zamindar and Shahbaz in Urdu. The English papers were the Tribune and the Civil Military Gazette. Milap and Pratap were published by two Arya Samaj leaders Mahasha Khushal Chand and Mahasha Krishan. Both were nationalistic and both were leaders of two different groups of Arya Samajists. Mahasha Khushal Chand led the Arya Prithinadhi Sabha, which was the group, which controlled colleges run by the Arya Samaj and believed in the spread of education through colleges, while

Mahasha Krishan was the leader of the Arya Sarvadeshak Sabha which believed in the spread of education through traditional norms and thus promoted 'gurukuls'. Ultimately another paper had come up, called 'Parbhat'. Its editor was Nanak Chand Naz. He was the person who first established the Pratap and then the Milap and then established his own paper, Parbhat. He was the stormy petrel of the Urdu press of Punjab. He successively left two papers because of disputes but each paper had been made into a premier paper by him. When he established his own paper, it had the largest circulation among the Urdu press. He was a trendsetter. Later on, the Sanatan Dharam Sabha Punjab also set up its own paper, Vir Bharat, but its circulation did not catch up with the three Arya Samajist papers.

Shahbaz, Zamindar and another paper, which I think came up later, Nawai Haq, were run by Muslim publishers, but these papers were conservative in outlook and mostly supported the government in the beginning and later on the Muslim League when it became popular.

Mahasha Kushal Chand and Mahasha Krishan became the dictators of the two 'jathas' which were successively sent by the Arya Samaj to Hyderabad to perform 'Satyagrah' there in protest of certain restrictions placed by the Nizam's government on observance of certain rites by the Hindus. Khushal Chand ultimately took 'sanyas' (became a recluse) and his sons ran the paper. After Mahasha Krishan's death his sons ran his paper. After the partition, they published the Hindi editions as well. These papers together with the Hind Samachar and Tribune continued to play an important part in the politics of the Indian Punjab. I did not hear anything after the partition about Vir Bharat and Parbhat. The Tribune was a national paper, but a sedate one, and enjoyed greater popularity than the Civil and Military gazette, which was a pro-government paper.

I have mentioned about these papers here, because these papers played a great part in the political and the social life of Punjab and the Frontier. The Frontier did not have a newspaper worth mentioning here. And, so, Punjab's papers were as important to the Frontier as to Punjab. Kohat had a paper 'Hamdam' in Urdu. It was, I think, published every week, but it had nothing of substance. It was run on advertisements and subventions of corrupt government servants, a breed which was as common then as it is now, but which was not that rich.

The Hindu Urdu press and the Muslim Urdu press were always at loggerhead then over one issue or the other. However, the main issue of contention used to be politics. The Hindu press was generally nationalistic and liberal while the Muslim press was pro-British government and sectarian. However, the period I am writing about witnessed a strange transformation in the Hindu Urdu press. During those days, the Unionist Government of Punjab, headed by Sir Sikandar Hyat Khan, passed various laws, imposing certain restrictions on shopkeepers. I do not remember the exact provisions of the laws passed by the legislative assembly of Punjab, but the Hindus greatly resented it. The laws were justified, but as previously there had been no laws to restrict the malpractices of the shopkeepers, they took the new laws as measures by the government representing the rich land owning classes, to repress them. And as the shopkeepers were mostly Hindus, the Hindus in West Punjab, under the influence of the Hindu Urdu press, took it as an onslaught on the Hindus. Similarly, some laws were passed affecting the moneylenders, and as the money lenders in rural areas were Hindus, so the Hindu press came out in full throttle, against the bills originally, and the laws later on, when the legislature passed the bills. The bills were called black bills by the press and the announcements regarding them were black lined. Actually for a considerable time, the front pages of Hindu newspapers were black bordered.

Agitations were launched and many strikes were declared, but the Unionist Government did not yield, as it had an overwhelming majority in the legislative assembly. The Union Government introduced many other bills also relating to landholdings and foodgrain markets. In the debates a prominent figure emerged; that of Sir Chhotu Ram, a Jat leader from East Punjab. He was a senior cabinet minister and a staunch protagonist of farm legislation, but a strong baiter of 'banias' (shop keepers). The Punjabi Hindus hated him. The Punjabi Hindu press gave him many pejorative names, but he rejoiced in them all. However, he objected to the writing of one paper and that was the Arya Gazette.

I, normally, after looking at the papers, used to go to the Arya Samaj from the Town Hall.The Arya Samaj also had a library and it had a couple of papers which the Town Hall reading room did not have and the distance between the Town Hall and Arya Smaj was not much. TheTown Hall was situated in an open space, about a hundred yards from the northern perimeter wall of the inner city. A gate facing the town hall led into a lane fifty feet in length. This lane led into the main long 'bazaar'. However, on the left side of the lane, about twenty yards from the gate was the door of the Arya Samaj. One day I read in the Arya Gazette, at the Arya Samaj, a letter from Sir Chhotu Ram, addressed to the editor, complaning against the policy of the Arya Gazette in criticising the 'black legislation', which, according to Sir Chhotu Rama and the Unionist Government, was progressive legislation. He stated in the letter that the Arya Gazette was the official organ of the Arya Samaj, and so it did not behove the Arya Gazette to take sides in matters, which affected the economy of different sections of the community differently. The argument went home and the Arya Gazette stopped taking sides in the matter. Sir Chhotu Ram was of course right in his contention, but the trouble was that the Hindus in Western Punjab were mainly 'banias', and any act of the Government which was to the disadvantage of the 'banias' was taken as an attack on the Hindus by the Hindus, for even a Hindu Government servant also belonged to the community of the 'banias'. Similarly, Hindu press barons who also controlled the Arya Gazette were 'banias'. Otherwise the Arya Gazette would not have criticised a leader like Sir Chhotu Ram who himself was an Arya Samaji, and a pre-eminent Jat leader. Today Jats are mostly followers of Arya Samaj and Sir Chhotu Ram's name is the most respected in Haryana.

The Unionist party was not a progressive but a conservative, zamindar (big landlord) and pro-British party. It was also the representative of the soldier's lobby, as the British Indian Army's largest numbers and the better soldiers came from the agriculturist classes of Punjab.

However, any conflict in the interests of the land owning classes and the traders was bound to become a Hindu and Muslim question and the same was the case in respect of agiculturists and moneylenders. Jawahar Lal Nehru had written in his biography, which came out in 1936,that India's total rural debt was about Rs.900 crores, and of that the Punjab's share was Rs.135 crores. He had pointed out in his biography that in Punjab as the agriculturists were mostly Muslims and the moneylenders Hindus, any conflict between them would become a Hindu Muslim conflict. This was the one main reason that while the Congress swept the polls in the rest of the states, in Punjab it lost heavily to a party, which represented the land owning classes. The Unionist Government was not a socialist government and so it did not bring out revoltionary changes to distribute land or remit all loans.

The winning of the elections by the Unionists in 1937 was only a harbinger of the things to come. The coming of the Muslim League to power in Punjab subsequently and the formation of Pakistan consequently, perhaps, would not have taken place, but for this inherent cleavage of Hindus and Muslims on economic basis; the exploiters and the exploited. If Punjab had not been lost, N.W.F.P would not have been lost either, as it was only the loss of Punjab to the Muslim League that N.W.F.P was lost as Punjab's press and conditions always had their effect in N.W.F.P in the long run.

Outside the town hall, a loudspeaker had been fixed. I used to hear news there. It was there that I heard one day in the Urdu broadcast, in October 1941, that Lord Wavel had stated that Generals December, January and February were coming and they would help the Soviet army against the German army.

In school, I continued to make progress. I made a number of friends. I was considered very good in studies. I was a very good speaker in Urdu. In debates when I spoke I could control my audience. If I wanted them to laugh they laughed, and when I wanted them to clap, they clapped. On the suggestion of the Headmaster, I wrote and addressed the audience in English. I played and was good in football and vollyball. I do not know how it came about, but it did, that I enjoyed great prestige in the school and had won my fellow students' respect. The Headmaster, in the school meetings, while referring to my speech, called me his intelligent, knowledgeable and erudite friend. I was the unchallenged leader and spokesman of the students and the Headmaster and other teachers accepted me as such.

When I passed my senior special class, I chose to take Science, Hygiene and Physiology as additional subjects. English, Mathmatics and General Knowledge (History and Geography) were compulsory. I had always intended to be a lawyer, but when the time came to choose the subjects for my chosen career, I chose science subjects, as being dependent upon my uncle I wanted a career to support myself as early as possible, and wanted to be sure of getting a job as soon as I discontinued my education. My Headmaster told me that I was a person whose inclination was towards humanities and so I should choose Persian and Urdu and not Science. He kept after me to change my subjects all through the year, but I did not listen to him. Even after the summer vacation in 1941, he asked me to change my subjects, and my Urdu and Persian teacher told my Headmaster that he would normally have never agreed to accept a student so late in the academic period, but in my case he would agree. The Headmaster was keen on my taking the art subjects because of my proficiency in Urdu and English, my debating ability and my general knowledge. Because of my reading habit and tendency to read books of all kinds, I had acquired a store of knowledge, which boys of my age and academic standard usually did not possess.

It happened many a time, in the history class, or otherwise, that the Headmaster, while discussing the causes of the decline of Hinduism and the ascendency of Buddhism in India, had stated that the decline of Hinduism was natural, as no religion which preached that one man was superior to another because of reason of one's birth could have adherents for long. I saw great force in this argument. I had earlier read books on religion and history of Islam in Tehri, and was greatly impressed by the brotherhood of all Muslims. But I saw only one flaw in this principle and that was that this brotherhood was limited to people of the Muslim faith only; why could not it be extended to people of other faiths also. The Hindus extended the brotherhood principle to the people in one caste and the Muslims only to their co-religionsts. So while I agreed with the arguments of the Headmaster, I had doubts in my mind about many things. My friend, Dayanand, was of a revolutionary temperament. He gave me many tracts and books about revolutionary personalities and movements in India and abroad. This coupled with what I read myself independently, (one day I even got hold of a copy of Satyarath Prakash, a book written by Swami Dayanand, founder of the Arya Samaj) had put me in a revolutionary frame of mind and convinced me of the brotherhood of all men, irrespective of their religion.

I was a boy scout in Tehri, but had not joined the organization at Kohat. At Kohat, however I had done two short courses in first aid and hygiene and sanitation of The St. John Ambulance Association. These courses though were too inadequate to be of much use. As a boy Scout, I had come to Kohat once or twice to attend a scout camp. I used to be part of a patrol from our school. Many schools in the district used to participate. The camp used to be for three days and it coincided with the agricultural fair held every year. We used to be busy throughout the day. We used to get up early in the morning, in the dark, when reveille was sounded. After the morning ablutions, breakfast and tidying of the tents, our work started and it lasted until 10'o clock at night, with intervals for meals. In the mornings we did our drill and prepared for the demonstration we had to present at the fair. In the afternoons we did our duty at the fair or watched the various shows arranged in connection with the fair.

There used to be all types of competitions, such as competitive performances by various scouts groups, horse riding, running, rope pulling and spear marksmanship. We liked the competition between the spearmen. A piece of wood, about ¾ thick, about 8 inch in length and sharpened at one end was driven about 2 inches into the ground with the sharpened end up, with a view to fixing a target for the spearmen. These pieces of woods were immersed a few days before the competition in water so that they were not too hard for the spearmen to pierce.

This competition is a test of the horsemanship as well as of the dexterity of the spearmen competing. Every spearman comes in turn to spear the piece of wood fixed for him and takes it away. Horsemen come at high speed and aim at the piece of wood. The successful one takes the piece away on the point of the spear. Great dexterity is required from the spearmen. If he does not hit at the right time, he misses the target or does not do it cleanly. If he hits hard, he might leave his spear behind, and if he hits lightly he might leave the target behind. At the fair, every spearman was given three chances before the placings for prizes could be determined.

Besides these competitions, there used to be a market for selling goods or eatables. And, of course, there were animals in different enclosures to be judged for that was the purpose the fair was held. One could see Mr. John Malcolm, the deputy commissioner, with his sola hat on, going round the animal enclosures nearly every day of the fair, along with others, for grading the various types of animals. Mr. Malcom, a tall and thin man had a nice disposition. He did not seem to care about the clothes he wore while our inspector of schools, Mr. Azri, was a tall, dark, haughty dandy. In camp at night after dinner, around the fire, every contingent presented a skit. At least one night Mr. Azri also came to watch.

I was a popular student in school, and I had made a number of close friends among the Jugle Khel students. These were Nisar, Gulrehman and Qadar Khan. Another good friend I had made was Johandad Khan. Nisar, a son of a subedar major in the army, was a handsome and an active man. He had a good physique and had a jovial temperament. He laughed a lot, and his laughter was pleasant to one's ear, never raucous or malicious.

Gulrahman's uncle was a doctor in London (I do not know what his father did). He was a serious man and we always talked about serious matters. According to him I was one of the two sincere persons he had met till then in his life. He told me that he would show me the other person some day.

Qadar Khan, unlike Nisar and Gulrahman, was a bit darker in complexion. He was thin in built when I first met him, but gradually he developed into a tough muscular personalty due to daily strenuous exercises.

Jahandad Khan was a short and stocky person. He used to be immaculately dressed. One could recognize him from a distance from the starched plume of his turban. Qadar Khan was my desk mate. We used to sit at the back of one of the central rows. Ours was a strange combination. He was considered at the bottom of the class in studies while I was first. I always sat at the back in my school and college days, the reason being that I felt suffocated having the attention of the teacher as well as of all the boys sitting behind me, while sitting at the back I could throw things at the students in front and shout at them. I could also talk to students sitting near me without attracting the attention of the teacher. The problem was I could not always keep my full attention on the teacher. Either I knew what he was teaching or he was teaching so badly that I thought there was no use paying attention to him and it would be better to read from the book at home. Jahandad Khan was not from Jungle Khel. At Kohat he was staying with his sister. His brother-in-law was prosecuting inspector in the police and Jahandad was very proud of him because of his influence. I used to torment Qadar Khan quite a lot. When a teacher asked a question of Qadar Khan and he got up to reply, he fumbled and gave an incorrect reply. I added to his confusion by pinching him or whispering inanities. His answer used to be to press my right hand in the iron grasp of his right hand whenever he got a chance.

Nisar had started going to a secluded spot on the channel down stream of the springs for massage and exercise, after school hours. Actually, Qadar was the one who had first started going there. After I discovered Nisar's after hours exercises, Gulrehman and I also started going there. So, we four, including Qadar, started going to that spot for exercise. There was a place prepared for wrestling; a dug up place with fine and smooth dirt, prepared by pulverizing the lumps of dirt into fine dust and mixing it with a small quantity of oil, but only Qadar wrestled there, while the rest of us did other exercises. Even before going there, I used to go to a 'toi' beyond and to the east of the cantonment every Sunday for massage and exercise. Many a time we first played soccer with others and afterwards went for exercise. Toi had running water in the rainy season, but, otherwise, it was mostly a dry bed of stones with pools at some places and a trickle of water flowing in one corner.

In the winter of 1940, my brother, Ramesh, died of diptheria. For two days and nights he breathed with difficulty, and lay unconscious on the cot. Mother remained with him all through. Earlier on the doctor had made a wrong diagnosis, in the absence of tests. He had diagnosed cough or whooping cough, I think, from the symptoms, but two days later when Ramesh's breathing became laborious and he lost consciousness, the doctor knew it was diptheria, but it was already too late. In any case what were the chances of a cure those days. However, we all prayed. But, prayer, as is usual, could not save him. Mother was already a wreck after keeping a continuous watch over him for so many days, but Ramesh's death really hit her hard. She was a very confident woman, but after Ramesh's death she she lost her confidence, and was suddenly conscious that she was vulnerable, and that the unknown could hurt her, and suddenly. Haridwar, who was at that time in Kohat after a tenure or short-term employment as excise inspector somewhere, and I suffered a great deal too. Actually he was more attached to Haridwar than to me, but I did not love him less. The only thing was that Haridwar took him out quite often, which I seldom did. Ramesh was a very lovely child. He was so charming and friendly that everyone who came across him became fond of him.

The memory of my young brother has remained with me all my life. I still mourn him in the solitude of my heart, though the routine of my life has run on as before. This pain only those can realize who have lost a young one. The pain is more when the tragedy occurs at an age when one is not a child but neither an adult. That is the age when one is growing up and is impressionable. I feel young ones should not be allowed to die. Any society that is indifferent to the welfare of the children is, I believe, uncivilized and barbaric. In Hindu mythology there are stories that whenever a child or a young man died in that mythological period, people believed that the king had gone astray from the path of 'dharma' (true path, duty), as in those days, parents never had to face the pangs of grief of the passing away of their children. I always grieve in my heart with the parents of the young ones who die early.

In school, I continued to remain in the good books of the Headmaster. In every school, run by the government, the Headmaster had the authority to award scholarships to a few students, whose parents were not well off financially, or to remit tuition fees in those cases who were more deserving. In the case of our school, the Headmaster had entrusted the work of awarding scholarships or remission of fees to Hindu students, from out of the quota assigned for Hindu students on basis of some formula, to the Hindi teacher, Gyan Prakash, and myself. It was a great honour for a student to decide the award of scholarships and the remission of fees to his colleagues. Gyan Prakash, though a teacher, was more like a friend to me. He was a nice gentleman and always cheerful.

As I mentioned earlier, whenever ancient India was discussed in the History class or otherwise, I always accepted the reasoning of the Headmaster in the interpretation of Hinduism, its concepts and the inherent weaknesses of these concepts. However, in my quest for knowledge, one day, I borrowed a copy of 'Satyarath Prakash', a commentary of Hindu scripture and a critical study of various religious books written in the post Vedic period and of books of other religions, written by Swami Dayanand. Swami Dayanand discarded all the Hindu religious books written in the post Vedic period. He particularly rejected the Puranas, written in 8th century A.D., which, according to him were written by the Brahmins for their selfish ends. He wrote in 'Satya Prakash' that idol worship was repugnant to the teachings of the Vedas and the Upanishads. I think he was the first Indian to declare that a bad self-rule was preferable to a good foreign rule. He established the Arya Samaj to launch a reform movement in the Hindus. The Arya Samaj succeeded a great deal in Punjab and Haryana in making the Hindus look at their religion with a different insight than they had been doing earlier. I remember having read in the late thirties that Gandhiji had written in the 'Harijan' that the Hindus were even then practising casteism inspite of his and many others' efforts. Goswami Ganesh Dutt had written to Gandhji in this respect stating that the Hindus of Punjab were not exercising any discrimination on caste basis. Gandhji, mentioning Goswami Ji's letter, again wrote in the Harijan that when he had earlier written on that subject, he did not have Punjab in mind, as the Hindus of Punjab were greatly influenced by the Arya Samaj. Though the Arya Samaj's adherents are not many, but it has influenced a great many people in northern India.

There was a time when the Hindus believed in idol worship unabashedly, but today, in Northern India at least, the idol worshippers justify their this practice by pretending that their idea is only to worship God by concentrating on the image of a God, because all Gods are in the image of the one God. That is nonsense as the Hindu God is imageless, but it is everywhere. The urban Hindus of today are hypocrites. This is not an original saying. Nirad C. Chaudhri has stated it earlier. A person who lacks in material wealth or the intellectual insight of his religion, but wants to maintain his position in these days of fast development in all fields, when peoples' fortunes are changing rapidly, has to pretend to be something which he is not, either by spending a lot on customs like giving sumptuous dowries to his daughter or indulging in unnecessary rituals to impress his peers. India is not unique in this respect. Victorian England was no different. In India this phenomenon has been accentuated because of the impoverishment of people in recent times. When I read Nirad C. Chaudhri's 'Autography of an Unknown Indian' a few years ago, I mentioned to some of my relatives and friends the passage where he has written that Hindus go to temples not to worship but to, ask the deity concerned for some favour. They were all angry, stating that Nirad C. Chaudhr was defaming Hindus and that he was too much of an Anglophile. However, I agreed with his observation instantly. The present craze of Devis', especially of Vaishno Devi, or for 'Sai Baba' in yesteryears is the manifestation of the same phenomenon. One could discern this from the songs being sung in praise of Vaishno Devi or from the miracles performed by Sai Baba, especially his production of watches from nowhere. Now the Sai Baba of Shirdi is in vogue because, inspite of his being no more in this world, his name is associated with miracles.

Spiritual values have been discarded in favour of materialistic gains from personalities or deities, although the teachings of Hindu religion are otherwise. Good conduct is the only religion Hindus have. Only an individual's karma can determine one's fate. So, when good deeds only determine fate, where is the need to go to the so-called messengers of God for favours. Swami Dayanand's interpretation of the scriptures is that God is just. He is not kind to one and angry to the other or generous to another. He is beyond these emotions. God is eternal, the soul is eternal and so is the matter. Swami Dayanand died of poison administered in his food by his cook, allegedly at the instance of certain Brahmins, in 1985. It is said, when he felt that he had been poisoned, he asked the cook about it. The cook confessed his crime. After learning the background about the poisoning, Swamiji made him run away before the police arrived.

Swami Dayanand's slogan was "Back to Vedas" as he believed that subsequent to the Vedic days 'dharma' (religion) was subverted by the addition of spurious books by the Brahmins for personal gains.

That is why Arya Samajis call their teaching Vedic Dharmanand History books, and the subsequent period is referred to as Brahminism.

Hindu religion actually is a result of the thinking and meditation of the sages of old. Its philosphical doctrine was built up in hundreds of years. The basic principle of its religion is that every person's life is governed by the law of karma. If a person does good deeds in one's life, he would get the reward for them in the next birth. As for evil deeds, there would be punishment, proportionate to the crime, in the next birth. The belief in the transmigration of souls is an essential concomitant of the belief in the law of karma. When a person becomes absolutely free from evil, he becomes free from the cycle of birth and death, and his soul joins the universal soul. Implicit in this belief is that life is full of suffering. All Hindus believe in this doctrine, whether they are Buddhists, Jains or Sikhs. Rituals may be different, but rituals do not constitute religion. Rituals are accretions acquired over the years for convenience or as an adornment. Whether Buddhists are agnostic or Jains atheists is immaterial as life is governed by the law of karma alone and the God of the Vedas is not an autocrat. Some scholars see the germ of enquiry contained in the Vedas themselves. Hinduism is a religion, which is universal, not bound by anything but human reasoning, and based solely on the welfare of living beings.

Not being a religious scholar, I will not dwell on this topic any longer; I will quote a scholar here, who is well versed with Hindu religious books. My only aim in writing about this subject here is to give a background to my thinking. In the introduction to the Bhagwad Gita, translated by him in English, Juan Mascaro has quoted the 'Song of Creation' in the Rig Veda x.129. I quote below the last verse of it to illustrate my point:

'Only that God who sees in highest heaven: he only knows whence comes this universe, or perhaps he knows not.'

I quote his interpretation of this verse:

'In the last verse of this poem we have the beginning of philosophical inquiry: the poet of the Vedas states that for the progress of the mind, man requires doubt and faith.'

I believe a faith based on philosophical reasoning is open to enquiry and leaves scope for different interpretations. The law of karma remains the cardinal principle of Hinduism. Buddhism was a forward movement, as it preached certain home truths, which were easily understood by the common people. Buddha laid before the people a simple path of piety, non-violence, service and good neighbourliness for the attainment of salvation. He also preached renunciation of desire, as it brings sorrow in its wake. Renunciation of desire is being preached by Hindu 'Rishis' from time immorial. This principle is behind people renouncing the material world and changing into saffron coloured clothes. Buddhism remained supreme in India for many centuries, but, unfortunately, it developed idolatory and certain other ills, the result of which was that while on the one hand people became dissatisfied with it, on the other they lost the will to defend their country and themselves, because of people having discarded arms in favour of introspection. Buddha got enlightenment through introspection and so did the rishis of yore who compiled the Vedas and the Upanishads. This of course was unavoidable to some extent as, after all, Hindu thought is the product of metaphysics. The Hindu faith, as I have mentioned earlier, encourages the search for truth. However under Buddhism, this process was taken to an extreme so much so that in the search for truth, they forgot their duty. Civilizations rise, follow a faith, decline and fall, either because the path they follow had an inherent weakness, which was not obvious because of the vigour and determination of the founders; but in subsequent generations this weakness came to the surface due to the complacency and weakness of the rulers. Such civilizations are not able to change in changed circumstances. The result is that another civilization or even backward community, which is vigorous and more innovative, overthrows it or incorporates it in its own civilization.

In the case of India, stress only on introspection destroyed initiative, spirit of innovation and vigour, but the Buddhists universal preaching of non-violence had completely destroyed the martial spirit of the people as well. The result was that when Mir Qasim attacked Sindh, he took over the whole province without much resistance, inspite of the fact that he had come with only a few hundred soldiers. The Arabs took over even Multan in 713, having taken over Sindh in 712.

Buddhism gradually declined and nearly vanished from the land of its birth. Brahmins took over from Buddhism, and with that came all the ills from which Hinduism is suffering now.

With the coming of Brahminism came the Puranas. The Puranas brought myths, idolatory, casteism, corruption in the temples, the belief in paradise or hell after death and the belief that whatever one gives to Brahmins at an appropriate time reaches one's dead ancestors (of course, the Brahmins do not know the whereabouts of the concerned dead). But the worst damage the Brahminism did to Hindus was that they killed the spirit of enquiry that gave birth to Hinduism and nourished it. Instead of enquiry came dogmas and obscurantism.

When the Muslims first came to India, the Hindus became conscious of the need to create some mechanism of defence, as Indians had lost their fighting class, the Kshatrias, during the preceding generations, due to their involvement with the matter of spirit only. Buddhists, in pursuit of their spiritual happiness, had forgotten their duty to defend themselves, which is part of dharma, according to the Upanishads. The Gita, written before the time of Buddha, preached that the duty of a Kshatria was to fight even his kith and kin if required. Swami Dayanand wrote in the Satyarath Prakash that a Hindu was not to touch meat but if during fighting no vegetarian diet was available, then he should cut his left arm and eat it and fight with his right arm as that was the dharma of a Kshatria.

Instead of the Kshatrias of old, Brahmins raised a new class of Kshatrias, as per tradition, or they rose themselves to become the ruling class. This was the Rajput class.

However, after the 7th century A.D., India was lying prone. When Mahmud Ghaznavi attacked India, he met no serious opposition. He first came in 1008 A.D. but then he came nearly every year. He came to India seventeen times. His most famous attack was on the rich Somnath temple, on the west coast of India. This was a remarkable feat at that time as Mahmud Ghaznavi went with his army that far through the desert. It was another matter that he came to loot the wealth of the temples and cause their destruction, otherwise he could have established an empire here easily. He confined his attacks to the north, except once when he attacked the Somnath temple in the west.

When Shahabuddin Ghori attacked India, the only serious resistance he met was from Prithvi Raj Chauhan, a Rajput, the king of Delhi and Ajmer. He defeated Ghori in 1191 but in 1192, when Ghori attacked again, Prithvi Raj was defeated, taken prisoner and then later slain. Ghori's Viceroy, Qutab-Uddin-Aiback laid the foundation for a 500 hundred rule of India. Then gradually northern India was subjugated. All the Rajput princes fought lonely battles, instead of putting up a concerted fight together. Bakhtiar Khilji took Bengal with only a couple of hundred soldiers, by removing the Buddhist king from the throne. It was only Alauddin Khilji(1296-1316), whose general went down to the South.

In 550 years of Muslim kings and foreign dynasties, no progress for Hindus was possible. Hindus remained subjugated. Foreign rule is bad but when it is opressive and discriminatory, it is the worst type of tragedy for a nation. Iran's old civilization vanished from the face of the earth against Arab onslaught, but Hinduism survived and so did India's languages, some old books and architectures and sculptures in far off and out of the way places. I recently read an article of a Muslim writer (I do not recollect the name) who stated that the reason Iran's old civilization ended completely was that Iran was invaded by Arabs, and Arabs were zealots. They did not spare anyone unless he was converted to Islam, while in India came the Turks, who were not that fanatic to kill or convert when they could make money. According to him, it was more important for them to make money through the Jezia and other means and live a life of pleasure.

That seems correct to some extent but, I think, India's size and the inherent resilience of the people against aggression and their implicit conviction in their faith, also played a great part in the survival of the indigenous civilization. Where there was more aggression, the survival rate was higher. Similarly, where there was Buddhist predominance, submission was higher. It is pertinent to note that round about Delhi and Agra, the Hindus retained their overwhelming majorities, and so did they in Maharashtra, Andhra and Karnataka, which were mostly under the four sultanates of the Deccan. Even in Punjab, the Hindus were able to save themselves to a considerable extent, though Lahore had been in occupation of the Afghan kings much before Mohammad Ghori's attack on Delhi. And it was in these areas that the invaders met with resistance. At first, the Rajputs in Rajasthan, near Delhi, put up resistance against the Afghan kings and then against the Mughal kings.

Later on in the second half of the17th century, the Marhattas rose in the Deccan. They had become so strong that by 1750 their empire extended from Punjab to the Deccan. Had the Marhattas under Bhao not been defeated by Ahmed Shah Abdali in the third battle of Panipat in 1761, perhaps the fate of India would have taken a different course than what it ultimately did. As before, the third battle also proved decisive and opened the way for the British to the throne of India. More or less simultaneously with the rise of the Marhattas, the Jats had risen in the Mathura-Bharatpur area, very near Agra, (with Mathura 30 miles and Bahartpur about 20 miles away) and the Sikhs had risen in Punjab. Under Maharaja Ranjit Singh, the Sikhs had taken all Punjab beyond Sutlej, and also driven away the Afghan rulers from

N.W.F.P. Their one general had reached even Kabul, and brought back the gate of Somnath temple, which Mahmood Ghaznavi had taken away in 1024.

In History, the Afghan rulers of India who came after Muhmmad Ghori and before the Mughals emperors are termed as Afghans. Actually, the slave kings were Turks, as was Mahmud Ghaznavi, even though he had established a kingdom at Ghazni in Afghanistan. The Saiyads were also not Afghans. The Khiljis, the Tughlaqs and the Lodhis ruled from 1290 to 1527. The Saiyads came after the Khiljis and the Tuglaqs and they ruled from 1414 to 1451 and so this period is to be noted to arrive at the correct period of the rule of those three tribes. All those three tribes are tribes of Afghanistan.

The Mughal rule lasted from 1526 till about the middle of the 18th century with a slight interlude of about 15 years of Afghan rule of the Suri dynasty. Actually, Mughal rule had collapsed within a few years of Aurangzeb's death in 1707, but the Mughal ruler remained in Delhi upto 1857, when the last ruler was finally deposed. But historians count the East Indian Company's rule in India from 1757, the year it won the Battle of Plassey, otherwise the Mughal rulers of Delhi had become irrelevant long before from the Indian point of view.

This long rule of foreign potentates, which was autocratic and based on fundamental religion, affected the Hindus badly. Not only did they lose a good proportion of their population to an alien faith and the greater part of their literature and nearly all the old architectural and sculptural wealth in the north, but they also suffered the worst damage to their psyche. The Hindus had mostly switched over to Brahmanism before the invasion of the Muslim kings, and had fallen from the sublime to the mundane. During the period of consolidation and expansion of the Muslim rule, they became resentful and hostile and put up piecemeal resistance wherever they could, but they soon realized that they were no match for the foreigners. The use of horses and the mobility they provided to the foreigners was entirely a new concept to them. The Hindus concept of war was static in character, being based on elephants. The Muslim foreigners were better in command and structure and their social order was also much superior. Apart from this, the Muslims were much more vigorous and ruthless in battle and otherwise. The Hindus had not seen such fanatic fighters before. They, having chosen the path of introspection even before the time of Alexander, had become so soft that they had lost even their Kshatrias before the Muslims came, and were not prepared for the type of fighting the Muslims imposed upon them.

So, by the beginning of the 14th century A.D., the Hindus had decided upon the path of submission and co-existence, instead of confrontation, with the Muslims. The Hindu preachers spread this message all over India. This process continued right up to the beginning of the 17th century. This must have been one of the rarest occasions in history, when an overwhelming majority preached sermons of submission and co-existence with a small minority constituting the ruling class. The Hindus did it for self-preservation. They tigtened their family bonds to ensure the family's survival and to ensure racial purity, made the caste system rigid. To avoid the tyranny of the rulers, they lay low, but they lay so low, and for so long, that when the people rose, they rose only at a limited number of places, and that also because there was more oppression there.

The Marhattas rose against the oppression of the Sultanates of the Deccan and then fought against Aurangzeb and others. The Sikhs rebelled against the tyranny of the lesser Mughals like Farrukh Siyar and their Subedars (governors) and ultimately the Sikh generals carved out small separate states for themselves. Maharaja Ranjit Singh brought all these states under him, strengthened his empire and then expanded it considerably.

The Jats carved out a kingdom in the Bharatpur Deeg area near Delhi, in the middle of the 18th century. Theirs was not an act of large-scale rebellion, but that of opportunity. The weak Mughal kings could not prevent them from wresting an area in the environs of Delhi.

The result of prolonged foreign rule, spread over 500 to 550 years, was the loss of the Hindus true indentity. They were no longer a nation. They were not even Hindus. They believed Hinduism was the worship of idols, observance of ridiculous rituals, and belief in casteism, supernatural beings, mythology, and other similar things.

They forgot the law of karma and the concept of duty, the true bases of Hinduism. Dialectic is the lifeblood of Hinduism, and they had to shun it to save their religion. They believed what the Brahmins preached. That pleased every one and so a very civilized people gradually became a backward and ignorant race.

Many foreign writers ascribed the Indian attitude of resignation and indifference to a long foreign rule and many invasions. Long foreign rule yes, but not invasions. People like the Punjabis, the Jats and the Marhattas, who suffered the maximum oppression, were not the ones who could be blamed for resignation and total submission or indifference. Even the south, which faced the invasion of Alauddin Khilji's generals, in pursuit of his aim to extend his empire, and which suffered the atrocities of Malik Kafoor, Alauddin Khilji's commander-in-chief on this campaign, saw the emergence of the Vijaynagar Empire in 1336, when the empire of the Khiljis had fallen soon after Alauddin Khilji's death in 1316 and the Tughlaq empire had weakened in the reign of Mohammad Bin Tughlaq. The Hindu empire of Vijaynagar flourished up to 1565, when it was thrown out by the combined onslaught of the Sultanates of the Deccan.

The climate could be responsible for the apathy of the people to some extent, but it could not be the reason.

Long alien domination is the worst thing that can happen to a people. It saps people's energy, makes them lose confidence and become fatalistic and as they are not invested with any responsibility of any worth, they gradually lose the capacity to manage their affairs.

When the British came to India, the people were in a sorry state of affairs. They were poor in all respects. They had forgotten their heritage, lost their spiritual wealth, were mostly uneducated and the common people did not have much in material goods.

I remember having read a book by Abbe Dubois, a French priest who came to India in 1784, titled, I believe, 'Hindu Customs, Manners and Religion'. I read this book when I was very young, about forty years ago and therefore cannot recall everything written in this book. Actually, I only recall that he condemned everything about the Hindus. He condemned their religion, their indifference, their fatalistic attitude, their insane rituals, their filthiness and their poverty. He was, of course, ignorant of the Hindu philosophical thought or how people of a land, where milk and honey flowed, had come to that end. But neither did the Hindus know this themselves.

It was only after the Britishers and others foreigners dug up the Hindu past from the land and books that they came to know that they had a civilization which dated back to at least 15th century B.C. and that Sanskrit was the oldest Aryan language and was the key to their religion, philosophical thought, cultural wealth, past history and the arts and sciences of old. Many people in the 19th century contributed to the unravelling of the Hindu thought. Notable among when was Max Mueller, a German scholar. But, I think, Swami Dayanand was the true apostle of the Vedic dharma and the most reliable interpreter of the Vedic scriptures, because of his single minded devotion to clear the Vedic dharma of all the dross, the beliefs, rituals, myths, ficititious literature and specious interpretations it had acquired through the misguided zeal of its followers or the machinations of persons motivated by self- interest.

I believe, as Hinduism is based on the fundamentals of karma and dharma and they cannot be determined or measured except by one's own conscience, so if anybody says he is a Hindu he is definitely a Hindu. Codification of Hindu religion is, therefore, neither desirable nor possible. It may be said that the conscience of the ignorant may be different from that of a wise person or that the concept of evil or virtue may change with the distance in time. As for an ignorant person, if he cannot understand, how can he be judged? Is a child responsible for his actions?

As for the concept of evil and virtue, theoretically it may change from age to age, but does it really change?

Have the truths on which Hinduism is based changed? They are illustrated by the four noble truths as preached by Buddha. They are: The world is full of suffering; suffering is caused by human desires; the renunciation of desires is the path to salvation; this salvation is possible through the eight fold path. The eight fold path is right views, right resolves, right speech, right conduct, right livelihood, right effort, right recollection and meditation.

All the above principles of actions are as valid today as they were 2500 years ago or even earlier when the Upanishads were compiled. So, observance of the right principles is as important for spiritual progress as for the physical well-being.

It follows from above, that Hinduism does not differentiate on basis of birth, caste, status and faith to determine the real value of an individual as karma alone is the criterion. For a Hindu, a Muslim or Christian is as good a brother as is another Hindu, irrespective of past History or any bickering.

During the British rule the Hindus lost another portion of their population to Christianity (but proportionately a smaller portion than they lost to the Muslims) due to the vigorous missionary activities under state patronage and allurements of food, jobs and cash doles.

Under British rule the whole population suffered, but the Hindus were the worst sufferers as they were already the deprived ones, due to the systematic exploitation of the Indian people through the export of raw materials at cheaper rates and import of finished products at higher rates. Connected with this move was the artefact of detroying the flourishing cotton industry by exorbinant levies which the Britsih employed to pave the way for the products of Lancashire to sell here. The monopolies of growing poppy, indigo and tea were kept with the Britishers so that they could make their fortunes at the cost of cheap indentured labourers and the fertility of the soil.

Further, instead of the introduction of land reforms and industrialization of the country to feed the growing population of India and better the economic conditions of the poor, the British kept the people poor and dependent on agriculture for the twin objectives of having a vast market for the British Industrial goods and a huge reserve of manpower for providing cheap cannon fodder to fight its imperialistic wars. The consequences were as to be expected. Millions died in famine and more in dire or slow starvation. To the shame of the British, they left India poorer than they had found it. Still they could send Catheryn Mayo to lament over the dirtiness and the unhygienic conditions in which the common people of India lived. Of course, what could one do with people who did not help themselves. The British were too busy to bother about such matters. Many in the hue of Catheryn Mayo wrote in the same vein. The last one to write in the same vein was a product of British education but an African of British domicile, Ronald Segal.

None of them thought for a moment how a people who are the cleanest in the world, as written by Lapierre about the Hindus in his book,' A City of Joy' about a slum area in Calcutta, came to be filthy and miserable. I have already written the cause for it. My argument is even more applicable to British times; poverty and the deprivation of people were no less in British times, only the methods were different. The common man's oppression was even more deep and extensive, as the Government was more efficient and the means of communication much better.

Ronald Segal blamed the resignation of the people, which according to him was the product of the Hindu religion. Unfortunately, Segal does not know the Hindu religion; otherwise he would not have stated it. Resignation is inactivity and that is contrary to the Hindu doctrine of action (dharma).

Segal is not even an historian, as otherwise he would have known what an effect prolonged oppression has on a civilized people. In this case, the civilized suffer more than the uncivilized. Even a zoologist would be able to tell him that in captivity animals become listless, lethargic and lose their skill for survival.

Coming to my school days, in 1941 I founded a society, 'Young Mens' Moral Society'. The aim of the society was to inculcate in young men the virtues of good morals and thus help in the creation of straightforward youth of good moral character, but in those days of 1941, every party or society was bound to be looked at with suspicion and our society did not prove to be an exception. We had only a few members, and all of them belonged to Tehri and Karak (in Tehri Tehsil). We used to meet at odd places, where Dayanand, a friend of my childhood, and myself spoke about French and Russian revolutions and the heroes of the past such as Maznini, Bhagat Singh and George Washington. I compiled material for a tract and gave it to a boy to get it printed for general distribution. Next day in the afternoon, while I was having a siesta after eating my lunch, the tracts were delivered at our house. I got up a bit late, as I had come late from school. When I got up, I saw my uncle and brother, Haridwar, sitting glumly. Nobody talked to me. I immediately guessed the situation and did not say anything. After a while, Haridwar produced a tract and asked me about it. I told him all about the society. He had burnt all the other copies of the tract. He told me to resign my presidentship of the society, as otherwise I would endanger their jobs (uncle's and his).

Uncle also spoke on the same lines but there was acerbity in his voice. He was short tempered and of an irritable nature. He was a good-natured person, but the only defect in him was that he believed everything my aunt told him. Without my knowing the cause of his displeasure, he would not speak to me for days.

Mother later on told me about the whole incident. She stated that while I was asleep, a boy had delivered the bundle of tracts. As Uncle was at home at that time, he read a tract. On reading the tract, he got very angry, and said that I would make him lose his job because of my activities. While he was speaking like this, Haridwar arrived from Thal where he had been posted as a land customs officer some time back. Haridwar, on hearing what uncle was saying, burnt all the tracts.

My uncle's and Haridwar's apprehensions were not baseless. In those days the British Indian government was very apprehensive of the subversive activities of the Congress and other organizations allied to it.

At that time, the Deputy Commissioner of Kohat was a notorious person, Mahboob Ali Khan. He was enormously fat. His trousers were stitched very loose to accommodate his large belly and hips. He was the first Indian Deputy Commissioner of Kohat, as was Sikander Mirza of Peshawar. Both were offsprings of the political service.

It was rumoured that Mahboob Ali was posted at Kabul when Aman Ullah Khan was overthrown, and he was instrumental in inciting the tribesmen to rebel against Aman Ullah Khan. Aman Ullah Khan was an educated man, with a sincere mind to convert Afghanistan from a backward country into a modern state. He had removed the restriction of pardah for women, but before he could achieve some worthwhile results, he had to flee the country because of a British engineered rebellion.

The British were apprehensive of Aman Ullah Khan, as they wanted Afghanistan to remain a backward country under British protection and not a modern country on which they could not exert any influence. A modern Afghanistan was dangerous to the hegemonic position of the British in India, as it could enter into agreements with Russia and other western countries with consequent disadvantages to Britain.

Sikander Mirza was shrewd but Mahboob Ali was cunning and so more treacherous and more dangerous. The British Deputy Commissioners looked liked other people and were humane, but Mahboob Ali moved like a Mughal potentate and talked as if everything ran according to his whims. Even during the Congress rule in the province, he did not care for the Congress Ministry. His belief in the invincibility of the British was absolute.

In 1941, or for that matter later on in 1942 and 1943, after the Quit India Resolution of Congress, Mahboob Ali did not allow any dissent in the district. It was said that anybody found indulging in Congress agitation was hanged upside down from the ceiling and flogged. He was not taken off the hook until he apologised.

I accordingly resigned my position as president and in my place Hardayal Shad was elected president. But before that the news about the formation of the society under my presidency had already appeared in the Urdu weekly paper, 'Hamdam'! A nephew of the Hamdam's editor used to chat with us whenever he met us in the street or bazaar. He had got this news published. Some days later, in the assembly of schoolboys I spoke on a topic, in connection with which the assembly had been organized. After my speech the Headmaster also spoke. While commending me on my speech, the Headmaster mentioned that the Deputy Commissioner had enquired about my background. He said that he had informed the Deputy Commissioner that I would definitely come into public life, but that I would not be a Gandhi but a Sarvarkar. I immediately knew the basis of his assumption. He later told me about it personally, and enquired about the society. He advised me that if I wanted to I could join politics, but only after the completion of my studies. I had, however, already made this resolution independently on my own.

I was always conscious of the fact that until I started earning myself, I was a burden on my brother, and that the sooner I started earning, the sooner this imposition would end. This feeling circumscribed my whole approach to the actions in the next few years of my life.

Normally, I am aggressive. I do not keep quiet when something happens that affects me. I always react, but that day I did not react at all when my brother burnt the tracts and asked me to desist from the line of action I had taken. When we were younger, I sometimes had terrible fights with him, but that day I immediately surrendered. The reason was that I had completely collapsed. I suddenly realized that I had nothing of my own; what I owned belonged to these two. That day something in me died. I had read such a phrase earlier many times, but today when I recapitulate my feelings on that day, I realize what authors mean when they write a similar phrase. I have sometimes wondered whether my reactions would have been the same had it been my father instead of my brother. I do not think it would have been the same. I would have rather fumed, cried, shouted and sulked before yielding. This is the reason I suffer inside when a breadwinner dies I always think of the source of the dependants economic survival, but besides it, of their development as human beings. Socio-economic conditions of the dependants definitely suffer greatly, in case the breadwinner of the family does not leave behind resources sufficient for the dependants to live a normal life, but in such cases cultural deprivation is total. In my career as an administrator, if there was any failing, it was never to deprive anybody of his job, inspite of great provocation, for where would that unforunate man go. By punishing him, one does not punish him alone, but also his whole family, which may consist of not only his wife and children but also his parents, brothers and sisters as well.

As for the Headmaster's assumption that I would be a Savarkar, he was very much off the mark. In my life, I have never thought of myself as a follower of the Hindu Mahasabha, let alone think of joining it. Hazrat Gul had a sharp mind, with a good bit of study to back it, but in this case he was wrong, because he misinterpreted my defence of Hinduism, which I could adequately do after reading the Satyarath Prakash. Previously in a discussion I could not argue with him, as most of the things he found fault with in Hinduism were really indefensible, but after reading the Satyarath Prakash I could tell him what was true Hinduism. In order to show him my erudition, I even went into the Philosophical doctrines. As Hazrat Gul had discussions with me on an intellectual level, and not as a detractor of Hinduism, he could not beat my by logic, due to my newly acquired wisdom, and he took my defensive mechanism as an assertion of my resolve to defend whatever Hinduism stood for. I, on the contrary, am against obscurantism, hypocrisy, superstition, inequality and political parties. I was rather trying to tell him that Hinduism was based on dharma and karma and not on any predestined belief. So, a Hindu could be a member of a Hindu Mahasabha or a communist group, as long as he was working for equality and against the exploitation of the weak by the strong. As for myself, even if my religion did not preach the same, I would still stand for equality and against the exploitation of the weak.

In the spring of 1941, we shifted into another house, which was dark but at least was independent. The house was in the Hindu Mohollah, in the market area, and its rent was Rs. 15/- per month. It had a room and another covered but open space on the rooftop. This was useful, for while sleeping in the open on the roof, in the summer, one could move to the covered place, instead of coming down, in case of rain.

In the summer, I started having low temperature of 99 to 99.5 degrees farenheit. It persisted, but I went on working. When it persisted for a couple of months, I went to a doctor named Gulati.Gulati was a mass scale doctor. He used to charge Rs. 2/- per visit. In his clinic, he used to charge for his medicine only. His medicine used to be only a mixture or a few tablets or both. Dr. Gulati's clinic medicine did not help me.

I did not know what to do, as I had nobody whom I could consult or who could take me to a good doctor. My uncle remained busy with his job. He never talked to us. My brother-in-law, my sister's husband was there but he was of no use to me, as his was a joint family with his parents and three brothers, all of whom lived in one house and this family and his chemist's shop in the cantonment, which he ran with his one brother, left him no time for us. We did not even see my sister for months, as she mainly looked after the cooking of the entire family, inspite of suffering from asthma.

So, I went to see a doctor called Jaggi who did not have a clinic, but saw his patients in somebody's shop. He did not examine patients but prescribed medicine, his diagnosis being based on symptoms. He was known to be an eccentric but a good doctor, but people had avoided going to him and his clientele over the years had greatly diminished, as it was stated that in order to make money he diagnosed every patient's ailment as tuberculosis. I knew about his reputation, but in the absence of a better choice I went to him. He asked me whether I had lost weight. I told him that I had, but that it was deliberate, as I had the tendency to put on weight, and at that time being overweight, I was trying to lose weight. He, however, said I was suffering from T.B. I told him that I should have an x-ray. He, however, said that it was so minor that it would not show up in an x-ray. He then gave me a diet chart and asked me to follow it and see him after ten days. I paid him his fee of Rs. 10/- and went home, fully knowing that he had hooked me for a long time. His diet did not help me at all. On the contrary, with that relatively rich diet I felt more uncomfortable.

However, a few days after that something happened which aggravated my ailment. Our school had a football ground near the Town Hall. The Muncipal Committee, which owned the ground, refused to leave it with us. They allotted the ground to the Islamia School, I think. This ground had been with the government school for so long that nobody knew that it really belonged to the Muncipal Committee. Naturally, this high-handed act of the Muncipal Committee greatly perturbed all of us. We met the Headmaster. The Headmaster said that he himself was very angry at that unjustifiable act of the committee, but he could not do anything himself. After some deliberation, he said a committee of students should meet Malik-Ur-Rehman, a member of the provincial assembly from Garhi, for the purpose. He nominated five members to the delegation to meet Malik- Ur-Rehman. I naturally was one of them. We got the appointment for the next day through Mahboob-Ur-Rehman, the son of Malik-Ur-Rehman, who was studying in the 9th class of our school. We went to Garhi the next afternoon. It was quite far off, approximately five kilometers one-way. We reached there after going through the dry bed of a stream (toi). Being the chief spokeman, I did the bulk of the talking in the meeting with Malik-Ur-Rehman.

On the way back, I knew my temperature was high. When I reached home it was very high. It was 103 or 104 F. I think it was the next day or one day later that my uncle called Dr. Gulati. He, as usual, gave some mixture. Here I was lying on the bed, with nobody knowing what I was suffering from, with mother sitting with me all the time, and there my sister's-in-laws wanted mother to be at their place to nurse her daughter as she was expecting her baby. But mother was sick with worry about whether I would survive. When mother did not go, her son-in-law used the utmost pressure on her, but she went on pleading her helplessness. I still recollect mother's anguish, which I observed from my bed, where I was lying feverish. I was really very worried, even in my feverish state, about mother's health. I did not sleep at nights because of the discomfort of fever and aches, but she did not sleep either. Even if I moaned slightly, she was up, asking me where I had pain or what she could do for me. I saw that uncle and aunt, who had not taken my illness seriously earlier, were also worried when the fever persisted. I heard them one day saying to each other that my mother was not conscious of anything else anymore except my illness.

In the above paragraph, I mentioned my sister and her in-laws only to show the pressures on a daughter-in-law in a joint family. Even her parents are not immune from these pressures. In my sister's case, her in-laws were rich people, and they could easily hire any service they wanted, and they were nice people. My brother-in-law was a simple man and arrogance and anger never touched him. Still, under the pressure of his parents, he pressurized mother. One can visualize the pressure on the daughter-in-law when the in-laws are not nice people. The joint family system is breaking up amongst the educated Hindus for the simple reason that no daughter-in-law wants to live in a joint family now. With the increase in education and affluence, the joint family system will vanish from this land. It deserves extinction in its present shape, but many changes will have to be introduced in it if this system is to survive even in a limited sense. This system has served the Hindus admirably so far in keeping its traditions alive, its orphans and not so well-to-do provided and kept the tribe or society united, besides providing a sense of security to its members. In a poor country like India where there are neither proper institutions nor any social security system, the joint family system has still to play an important part, at least for the time to come. When India becomes prosperous, it will be immaterial whether the joint family exists or or not, but the main thing is that the family feeling should remain intact, and I personally feel that even when the nuclear family becomes the norm, the mutual love between brothers, sisters and parents will not vanish. This assessment I am making on observing nuclear families, which exist now. In a joint family nowadays one observes quarrels, but not between the members of related nuclear families; rather there is a lot of affection, which exists there.

One day, during my illness, Haridwar came from Thal. He became very perturbed and asked our brother-in-law, Nand Ram, whether he could suggest some doctor, as being a chemist he was familiar with nearly all the doctors in Kohat. He brought Dr. Rashid, the assistant surgeon of the civil hospital the next day. Dr. Rashid, on examination, said that I had malaria. He ruled out tuberculosis altogether. He prescribed a mixture of quinine and magnesium sulphate.

Inspite of the doctor having stated that I did not have tuberculosis, my brother and mother were very worried. One day I spied them, in a corner, weeping. I could understand their anguish. In our family we had lost, in a few years, my father and my younger brother, and now they thought that I was also going. I knew nothing would happen to me, but in my ailment I could not assure them.

My fever came down to normal in about twelve days of my starting on a mixture of quinine and magnesium sulphate. However, as I was quite weak, I had to remain in my bed for quite some time. While in convalescene for a few days, I again had fever of 102 F. Dr. Rashid was called, but he said that he did not understand the recurrence of fever. He said I that should be admitted into a hospial, and only after I had undergone tests, would he prescribe medicine.

Mother would not agree to this, as admission to the hospital was admission of the fact that her son was seriously ill. Similarly, I would have been taken in a cot, carried by four persons, to the hospital, as cars could not come to our house, Even if a car driver could have managed to reach our house, we did not have a car and nor did any relative of ours own a car, but as carrying somebody on a cot had a different connotation, it was not acceptable to mother. I knew mother was catching at straws for support to reassure herself that her son was not seriously ill. With her being in that condition I could not tell her that it was in my interest to be admitted to the civil hospital, and so I went along with her.

Having decided not to be admitted to the hospital, I started taking medicine from a homeopath, at the instance of my uncle. My aunt had been under treatment of that homeopath for quite sometime. She was suffering from a peculiar disease She felt that her heart was sinking, and this feeling was relieved by eating. This cycle of sinking feeling and eating made her fat. Even earlier she did not do any work because of this feeling, but once she put on excessive weight, the aversion to work greatly increased. She had gone to Lahore also with Haridwar, for treatment, to a homeopath, who did not charge a fee, which was all right as he was inexpensive and charged for medicines only. However, could a physician who was satisfactory for a patient with a minor ailment, be suitable for a patient whose need was immediate and whose disease had not been diagnosed? Naturally not, but it was an easy option for a person, who had refused to accept the only other option available to him. I was fortunate that my fever gradually started coming down; .5 degree every day, after a few days, so that on the 13th or 14th day it was completely normal. It was I, myself, who diagnosed my ailment the third day since my temperature commenced coming down gradually by .5 degree each day. I told mother that the second attack of fever was typhoid and not recurrence of the old fever, which was chronic malaria. I was again fortunate that this attack of typhoid lasted for 13 days and not 21 days or 90 days, as typhoid lasted those days of prechloromycetin. If the fever had lasted for long, there would have been serious complications for me in the absence of an attending qualified doctor. I, however, remained in convalescene for quite sometime, as I had become weak during my illness.

I used to have a bout of malaria every year, without interruption, from my childhood, but since my last attack in 1941, I have not suffered from malaria. When I did not suffer an attack for 12 years, I thought I had become immune to malaria, as I had read somewhere that once one is afflicted with this malady, the causal germs live in the liver and periodically attack the host, but if a person does not have an attack of it for twelve years, one becomes immune to it. However, recently somebody told me that I was correct in the assumption that I was immune to it, but only to the attack of one strain; other strains of malaria could still attack me. I hope he is wrong.

However the after effect of malaria and the heavy dosage of quinine and magnesium sulphate took its toll and left me with severe constipation. So, parafine liquid eventually became became my normal intake after I had tried various remedies, especially ayurvedic. I think it was after a couple of months of my convalescence that I came across

Haridwar and his friend, Seth Parmanand, in the cantonment, while on a walk. Parmanand asked me what he was hearing of my suffering from constipation and said that a person like me should be able to cure myself of such an affliction by sheer will power. I do not know whether he said this in jest or whether he meant it seriously, but I got the message, knowing he must have known about my forming 'The Young Mens Moral Society'. After that, I stopped taking medicines, and gradually I was able to overcome this handicap.

Seth Parmanand was a young lawyer without any worthwhile practice. Luckily, in 1942 or thereabouts, he got selected in the competition for the subordinate judicial service as a sub-judge.He later on, after the partition of the country, got absorbed in the Rajastan Administrative Service and later on was promoted to the I.A.S in the promotion quota.

During my convalescence, a chance came to shift to a better house, and we did. My uncle, Diwan Ram Swarup, was transferred to Peshawar as a sub-judge and we took his house .The rent for that house was Rs. 25/- per month, but still we shifted, as all thought that the house we lived in was unhealthy, and otherwise also the house we were shifting to was much better. The new house had two bedrooms with a verandha facing the east, forming the western front of a well-lit courtyard during the day. To the south of the courtyard was a covered space for the kitchen (open towards the courtyard) and a well for water. Towards the east of the courtyard was a 'tandoor' for making 'roti' (bread) and a small bathroom with a watertap with very good water pressure. On the north was the wall of the adjoining house and an alcove, for sitting in the sun in the winters. The house was originally built to meet the requirements of purdah, as adjoining the above inner enclosure was the outer part, enlosing a 'bethak' (drawing room) where the men sat and adjacent to it was a servant room. Both these rooms opened into a large 'deodi' (recepetion area). The entrance to the deodi, or for that matter the house, from outside was through two doors. One was a very large and thick wooden door, which normally remained closed. There was a small door to the north, which remained open during the day for the normal going in and coming out of the first floor. Stairs led from the deodi to an enlosed terrace on the first floor with an independent latrine. The inner enclosure had a separate terrace with a covered space, but open on one side (to sleep in, in case of rain at night) and a latrine. Both latrines were dry. Between the inner enclosure and the outer enclosure was a door, which was bolted at night. Facing this door, on the inner side, was a seven feet high wall with a passage on one side for people to use as entry or exit. If a person from outside came to this door, even when it was open, he could not see into the interior.

The owner of the house, who lived next door, was a sub-divisonal officer of the M.E.S. His wife was Dewan Ram Swarup's sister, and hence a cousin of my father as well as of my mother.

The day we shifted to the new house was the first day I stepped out onto the street after my illness. I had put on my fur cap to protect myself from the cold, if any. In my hand I carried a stick for support.

While I was resting at home, I learnt that my name had not been sent for the matriculation examination, which was held in February or March, as my attendance was short of the required limit. Although I could not go to the school at that time, I was keen to appear in the examination that year. As it was I had lost three years; one year at the time of the first admission into school and later on two years in doing junior and senior special classes, and I did not want to lose any more. I asked mother to talk to uncle to see the Headmaster to recommend waiving off the requirement of minimum attendance in my case. She talked to uncle about it, but he, however, brushed her off, saying I was not in a fit condition to sit for the examination. A few days later, my brother-in-law came to see me. He stated that it was no use sitting for an examination, which I had no hope of passing. I pleaded which him stating that passing the matriculation examination was no problem for me. He, however, did not listen. Fortunately, during those days Haridwar came to Kohat. He met the Headmaster.The Headmaster told him he would be glad to recommend my case, as even now I would get a first division. He talked highly of me to Haridwar, stating that in the last examination in English, he had awarded me 97 marks out of 100 marks though I deserved 100 percent, as he did not think one could be awarded 100 marks. I wrote to Uncle Diwan Ram Swarup at Peshawar, to meet the registrar in the office of the Director of Education to ensure that he agreed to the waiver. The examination for matriculation for Punjab, N.W.F.P and Baluchistan was conducted by a board of the Punjab Government, but the administrative details were looked after by the respective governments. The waiver from the registrar was received within a few days.

I attended school for a few days before we had preparatory holidays. Nisar also had some ailment the year I was sick. He became ill earlier than me and reported back earlier also. Nearly everybody in the school commented on this coincidence, as both the leaders in the school fell ill more or less simultaneously, and remained absent for a prolonged period. I was still weak when I started attending school. At night when I read for more than an hour or so, I felt slightly feverish. The worst was talking. Whenever I talked more than necessary, and that was quite common, I felt feverish. However, I gradually gathered strength and shed my fever and weakness. I have since then never suffered from malaria.

During my high school days, a communal militant party had acquired a considerable following in the Punjab and N.W.F.P. This was the Khaksar Party. The founder of this party was Inayatullah Mashriqui. He was the Head of the Department of Mathematics in Islamia College, Peshawar. He had acquired a tremendous reputation there of being a mathematician of a very high calibre. He later on went away to the Punjab University. He founded the Khaksar Party, I think, sometime in the late thirties. This party spread rapidly, as they were supposed to be the soldiers of Islam. The party's name in Persian means 'like dust'. They were supposed to serve the people. In the beginning, they did some social work like the clearance of rubbish from the road. However, as they grew in strength, the underlying intent of the party became more obvious. They used to carry spades, which were ostensibly for service but were actually weapons of offence. They were light, sharp edged and clean, unlike service blades, which are heavy, dull edged and without any shine. The blades had slings to hang them from the shoulders in case of a long march. For the parades, they had translated all the words of command in English into Persian.

We Hindus found ourselves very insecure when we heard the tread of their marching feet. As I mentioned earlier, I used to go for a walk regularly in the evening or even at night after dinner to the cantonment. One tall constable always used to look at me with his malevolent eyes. I always got the feeling that the man would try to harm me sometime. Either it could be fanaticism on his part as I was a Hindu and he Muslim, or just a resentment on his part on seeing me daily with my friends, chattering gaily among ourselves and ignoring the all important policeman altogether. I think the real reason constituted both the above elements. The more I think about it, the more I am convinced that he resented us Hindu boys having a good time. One night, when six or seven of us were leisurely walking on a road, deserted except for us, in the cantonment, we came across this constable. We would have passed him unnoticed, but as we came near him he shouted for us to stop and ran towards us. The boys on the periphery ran away but he caught hold of four of us who did not run away. He took us to the police station, saying that he would teach us a lesson. I thought he had caught us because we were not supposed to walk on those roads in the cantonment at night, but that action, I thought, warranted a warning and not an arrest. However, when we reached the police station, he made us sit by a wall. In a few minutes the head constable came in putting on his belt. We knew the head constable was not properly dressed. He only hurriedly dressed up when the constable called him. While in the process of entering the room, the head constable asked him what the matter was. The constable said that we all were 'Khaksars', but before he could explain further, the head constable asked us to go away. While we were leaving the premises of the police station, we heard the head constable shouting at the constable. The stupid constable in his fanaticism had become so blind not to realize that Hindu boys could not be Khaksars.

My friend in the school, Gul Rehman, used to always tell me that he had met only two sincere persons in his life (though he was only about 18 then). One was myself and the other was a middle rank holder in Kohat's Khaksar organization. One day he showed me that person, when we passed a Khaksar detachment parading. He did have an honest face. According to Gul Rehman that person always helped others and sincerely did the meanest of jobs entrusted to him.

The Khaksars had acquired considerable strength in Punjab and the Frontier, and they looked very menacing in the early forties. It was felt that the British India Government could not control them, being afraid of the bloodshed and the strength of their following among the Muslims. But they met their match one day. In the Anarkali Bazaaar, Lahore, there was a Sikh gurudwara, which the Muslims claimed as a mosque. This dispute had been lingering on for a long time. Anayatullah Mashiqui led the movement for taking possession of the so-called mosque. He thought that the agitation in this connection would greatly increase his following among the Muslims. The Khaksar volunteers courted arrest every day by infringing the ban imposed by the state government for entry into a specified area. When the excitement was built up and the tempo of the movement had risen to a high pitch, Anayatullah Mashriqui announced a date when the Khasars would occupy the mosque. Everybody felt that the government would give in, as the Khaksars were considered strong enough to generate large disturbances, which were expected to culminate in the downfall of the Unionist Government. But the Khaksars had underestimated Sir Sikandar Hayat Khan, the Premier of Punjab and the leader of the Unionist party, which principally was the representative of the landowners of Punjab. On the date indicated by Mashriqui, the Khaksar contingent advanced in Anarkali Bazaar towards the Shahid Ganj Masque, in an organized manner, with their spades. The police, at a specified point, asked them to stop, but they still advanced with spades in their hands and then the police fired. Their front ranks fell or fled. The ranks at the back came forward and also fell or fled. This continued for a minute or so, and then they broke rank and ran. With their collapse in Anarkali, the Khaksars brought down their organization for good. I believe the Khaksars must have thought that in Anarkali, the police would either yield to them or join them in their pursuit. They did not realize that even had the police contingent in Anarkali joined them, nothing much would have happened, as an organized state is too comprehensive and complex an organization to be brought down or deterred from its course of law enforcement because of a setback in one particular place.

In the matriculation examination, I got a first division, scoring over 60% marks. I do not recollect the exact marks but most probably they were not more than 63% marks, which were not that high. My old rival, Krishan Chand, of Tehri got about 70% marks. However my schoolmates did not give him any credit for it. They stated that if I could get over 60% marks without studying for about six months, I would have beaten him hollow if I had not been ill. However, one day, I told him when he came to see me at my place, that even if I had not missed the studies, I would not have got more marks than I had obtained, as in any case, I would not have studied anymore than I did. He said he felt the same, though everyone else was saying I would have got more marks.

During my school days, I always stood first in three subjects, English, General Knowledge (History and Geography) and Hygiene Physiology. In the remaining two subjects, Mathematics and Science, I used to come first occasionally. I was considered good in all the subjects. In mathematics, there used to be a tussle between Krishna Chand and me and in science between Mohammed Jana, a fair coloured, thin, short youngish looking boy and me. In high school there used to be five subjects: three which were compulsory; English, Mathematics and General Knowledge and two additional subjects which depended upon whether one took Science or Arts. For Arts, the additional subjects were Persian and Urdu and for science the additional subjects were Science and Hygiene Physiology.

After the examination I visited my brother and sister-in-law, Padma Vati, at Thal. It was a frontier-trading centre, where merchandise like almonds, walnut, goats, sheepskins and 'ghee' (purified butter) from Afghanistan were sold and sent to the other centres in India. That was the main market of the Parachinar Frontier agency about 58 miles away. In the winters, tribesmen from Afghanistan brought herds of goats and sheep to graze between the grassy land between Thal and Hangu. They used to carry permits from the office of the political agent, Parachinar, for the number of animals they could bring into India, but they usually brought in many more. They also brought in clandestinely other items such as almonds and walnuts. Haridwar's job was to prevent the clandestine trade and unauthorized animals, but the tribesmen could always bring in more of everything, as the border was very thinly guarded and bribes could shut any eye. Dry fruit at Thal was therefore much cheaper and so was Khilji ghee because of regular and clandestine imports. The ghee was called Khiljee ghee because, most probably, the Khiljee tribesmen brought it. The Thal post was manned by the Excise Department of the N.W.F.P government unlike other major customs posts, which were managed by the customs and excise department of the central government. The custom post's irregular soldiers were sometimes fired upon by the tribesmen who carried weapons clandestinely. In the summers the tribesmen used to go back with their herds carrying with them items of daily use such as cloth, sugar, kerosene and oil. The tribesmen were cheated both ways by the traders. Items were weighed generously while purchasing goods from the tribesmen but were underweighed while selling goods to them. The Tribesmen were also quite cunning in their dealings. They mixed inferior grade almonds or walnuts with superior grade items. Similarly ghee contained whey.

Nights in the open in the summer were pleasant as Thal was situated in a submountainous area at an altitude of about 2100 feet above sea level. One could see scattered all over the area surrounding Thal tanks obstacles as a measure of protection in case Thal was attacked through Afghanistan. Perhaps originally these obstacles and other protective works were meant against possible Russian attack, and later after Germany's invasion of U.S.S.R, against Germany's attack.

Thal, I do not think, had any fruit trees but Parachinar was famous for its peaches, commonly known as shalils. I have never seen such large and juicy peaches anywhere else. It was in Thal for the first time that I tasted chocolates. Haridwar used to go for inspection of the military canteen at the Thal fort, as they used to sell imported liquor. There Haridwar took a slab of chocolate, and gave me a piece to taste. I never thought that anything could be as delicious as chocolate. Haridwar gave me a couple of chocolates and after this episode I never lost the taste for them. I ate pastries for the first time in Kohat. Pastries were sold in the Kohat cantonment in a canteen. I think it occurred to the contractor running the canteen one day that he could make money by selling them outside also. So while I was were living there, he started sending a glass case, mounted on wheels and propelled by a salesman mounted on a cycle in front. I do not know whether it was because this was the first taste of pastries or otherwise, but I found them very delicious. They used to be sugar coated and were of different flavours. I do not like the taste of pastries that much now because they are coated with cream and are not well baked. I had tasted cakes earlier. Father used to bring them home occasionally when he went to Kohat, especially at Christmas time. I remember once he brought a rasin cake, but the one I liked best had sugar icing.

I visited Thal at least once again when I was in the college. I will relate one incident here, which created a very favourable impression on me about British officials. One day, in the morning, we got a telegram stating that my maternal grandmother had died of a fall from the roof. She was living alone at Tehri. My grandparents had three daughters but no son. When I told mother about it, she said she would immediately go to Tehri.

The roads were closed those days and no public vehicles were plying as the Wazir tribesmen had robbed some vehicles and it was known that they were active in the area through which the Kohat Banu Road passed. I told her about it. She, however, was not prepared to listen to any argument. She was determined to go to her mother's funeral. I think it was the guilt complex in not being with her mother in her hour of need and the feeling that had she been with her she would not have died in the circumstances she did. She asked me to do something, not knowing what her 18-year-old boy without influence could do. I knew how difficult it was to talk to an official. No official bothered about any ordinary citizen, let alone do something for an 18-year-old boy.

I went to a police office in the cantonment, which I thought to be the office of the Superintendent of Police. There I learnt that the Superintendent of Police was at his bungalow. I took the bungalow's address and went there, which was more than a mile in another corner of the cantonment. There was a sentry in the passage leading to the bungalow. When I told him that I wanted to see the Superintendent of Police, he let me go. The Superintendent's office was right in front of the passage opening into a verandah. The Superintendent was a Britisher, and he seemed to be between 35 to 40 years of age. I narrated to him my problem and asked him if he could provide us with some protection. He said a road patrol was leaving at 1200 hrs, and so our vehicle should be at the octroy post, exactly at 1200 hours and when the patrol vehicle passed, us we should follow it. He said that the patrol car however was going straight on towards Banu and therefore from Banda Daud Shah to Tehri we would be on our own. I then went to the bus stand and asked a gentleman from Tehri, who was working there, to arrange a bus for me. My mother and some other relatives were just in time to reach the cremation ground at Tehri, due to the kindness of an English Superintendent of Police. The cremation place was situated about a mile from Tehri, a small distance away from the Tehri Banda Road. As those were distrubed days, the Hindus in Tehri did not want to be out of Tehri proper late in the afternoon, so they had brought my grandmother's body early to the cremation ground, and waited there for the arrival of my mother, but when by 1600 hours she did not arrive, they decided to light the pyre. But at that moment they heard the sound of a vehicle approaching and so they held back and mother made her tryst. Mother's vehicle was delayed enroute as the patrol vehicle had met with an accident.

Chapter Five

COLLEGE

In May or June of 1942, my mother's cousin, Lakhpat Raj, and I went to Rawalpindi and sought admission in Gordon College. On getting admission, we joined immediately and that was my biggest mistake. Schools were to close for the summer vacation in about fifteen days and we could have joined after the vacation of two months, as most of the other boys did. In our innocence we joined earlier in order not to waste fifteen days of education. There was no education of any sort, but we were ragged terribly in the hostel. There were very few first year students in the hostel, and they all were considerably ragged, but I think, I was ragged the most. Perhaps they saw in me a source of potential danger. I have been told since then by people that I have a strong personality, so that people who meet me the first time start taking sides, for me or against me.

The ragging mostly consisted in asking us to do exercise or sing, but I never sang as I do not sing at all. It was the frequency of the visits and the dread of numbers, with seven or eight people visiting us in a group that was frightening. Actually all the members of the group that ragged us were Muslims from West Punjab, the area around Jhelum.The worst part was that they did not rag Muslim students and this did not do much for communal harmony. This I learnt from a couple of second year Hindu students from Banu.They were not happy about this group ragging us. They told us that only Hindu and Sikh students were being ragged. I knew that one student, Bahadur Singh, from Parachinar had also been badly ragged. But these students from Banu did not help us at all. Most probably they were scared of the group's reputation. They told us that some members of the group had committed murders and their gang leader and other students carried revolvers with them. In the forties communalism in West Punjab was rampant. This nefarious group, I think, thought that I carried a knife, because one day they came in the afternoon and searched all my belongings. Later on I heard that they were boasting that I had taken out a knife, which they snatched from me. This ragging gradually died down. After the vacation there was no ragging at all.

In Rawalpindi there were two colleges. One was the Dayanand Ayurvedic Degree College for Arts and the other was Gordon College, run by a Christian mission. It was a degree college for bith arts and science. Its principal was a foreigner (a European) and most of its faculty members were Indian Christians.

I, unfortunately, did not do well in studies. I had no habit of studying text books for hours and in college, in the beginning at least, there was no alternative to that, as firstly the level of studies was much higher in college than in school; it was not a gradual progression. Secondly, I had taken science (non-medical group). To be sure, I could get a job in engineering or barring that switch over to the medical side, as chemistry and physics are common subjects for both the lines, and it was possible to get admission in Medical colleges, even without taking zoology in the intermediate (12th class). And one had to mug fundamentals like valencies in Inorganic Chemistry; in trignommetry one had the same problem with sins, cosine, and tangents. Similarly in Mathematics or Physics my problem was aggravated by a thin, dark, short and middle aged lecturer who took an intense dislike to me. When I knew that he disliked me, I provided him with more opportunities to increase his displeasure with me.

One day, when all the students were seated at their respective places and were waiting for this lecturer to take his class, one dandy boy threw a coin at a Sikh girl student sitting on a bench in front. We had a couple of girls in our class, and they always sat in the front separately. When I saw the coin being thrown add the girl, I got up from my seat, in the centre of the desk at the back of the class, my usual position, and came to the front and challenged the students and asked that the one who had thrown the coin should come to the front too. When no one came and I started going up to my seat, the lecturer entered. He shouted and enquired from the class what was going on. Then he looked at me and asked me to get up and said he knew who was creating the disturbance. He said something to me but that I do not recollect now. Most probably he reprimanded me. I did not speak as I was too angry to say anything, but nobody else spoke either. It was only when I sat down that a youngish looking Sikh boy got up and said that I had done nothing but a good deed. The lecturer at this said it was all right. There was no apology from him, neither was there any appreciation and nor did he want to know what had happened. Whatever he did or did not do did not matter, but I am glad that I did what I had to do, as I cannot stand hooligans who denigrate or degrade women.

There is another incident in this connection, which rebounded badly on me. One day this lecturer gave us some home task and I did not do it, either because I did not know how to do it or I was too busy otherwise. Next morning he came to the class and asked five students to show him their notebooks. I was one of them. I knew he would humiliate me if I told him I had not done the hometask, so I asked another student, Jabar, sitting beside me to give me his notebook. He resisted, but I snatched his notebook, went and showed the lecturer that notebbook. He called Jabar and asked him to produce his notebook. Jabar pointed to the notebook lying before him. All the while I had been struggling get Jabar's notebook, the lecturer had been watching. Even otherwise he would have found out the real owner of the notebook just by looking at the first page of the notebook where Jabar's name was written. It was sheer madness on my part to produce Jabar's book as mine, but as I was in dread of his mocking tone, I thought I would be able to escape that by this ruse, but in the bargain I was called a cheat in the presence of the whole class and was awarded 14 days detention classes. I was never called a cheat again, but that humiliation still rankles me. I, however, could not complete my detention classes, for whenever one did not attend a class, one had to suffer the penalty of another additional class. Similary, if one was late even for a few minutes, that particular attendance did not count. And I, unfortunately, either missed a class or often came late. The net result was that a major portion of my punishment was still outstanding when I left that college.

During the summer vacation, I had met my cousin, Krishan Dass, who was doing B.T. (bachelor of teaching) in Islamia College, Peshawar. He told me that I should do Bachelor of Science in Agriculture, as there was going to be great scope for agriculture graduates in the future. During our converstion, he mentioned casually that there were some scholarships also for the undergraduates. The scholarships got me interested in an agriculture degree, so I asked him to send me the full particulars about scholarships after the vacation. Chaudhri Krishan Dass or Krishan Dass Verma, as he used to write his name, was the son of my father's sister. He had done M.A. from Aligarh University and, at the time of my talk with him, he was studying in Islamia College, Peshawar. He did not write for quite sometime. I got his letter after about a couple of months of the reopening of the college. As there were some scholarships from the state government of Rs. 25/- a month and a few of Rs. 15/- a month from the district boards, I knew there was good scope of getting a scholarship. He again took time in informing me, on my query, that the college could accept me even if I joined that late. By the time I completed my migration formalities and landed in Islamia College, Peshawar, it was the 1st week of December 1942. I was lucky that there was a complete strike in the month of November in the college, and so I was saved from at least a month of studies in order to catch up with the other students. The strike call was given by the students against the bad quality of the bread supplied in the hostels.

Students had carried out demonstration and shouted slogans against the English Principal, Hedow Haris. The college was closed for about a month to prevent the situation from deteriorating further. Actually the other hostellers arrived back the same day as I did. The Governor of the province at that time was Sir George Cunningham, the man who was very familiar with N.W.F.P. and was known to be the best expert the British had on N.W.F.P. He was the patron or such like authority of Islamia College, because he was somehow responsible for the administration of the college as the college was financially supported by the provincial government. Hedow Haris was no longer the principal when the college reopened in December. In his place I.D. Scot, I.C.S., was appointed as principal. Hedow Haris was retained as a professor in the English Department. Soon after, in a meeting, we heard from Mr. Scot that the Governor had brought him in, as according to him, the administration of the Islamia College was more important than that of a district. Mr. Scot was an M.A from Cambridge or Oxford.

I missed Rawalpindi. It was the first real city I had seen. I had visited it twice earlier; once, when I was a young boy, I had come with my uncle and brother to visit mother when she was lying ill in nursing home. The second time I had come with a friend, from Kohat, to see 'Dussehra' at Rawalpindi. Rawalpindi was the fashion centre of West Punjab and N.W.F.P., as Lahore was of the rest of Punjab. Mothers used to come here from far and wide to get the trousseau of their daughters prepared. Peshawar was a rustic town in comparison.

I, however, liked the atmosphere and the surroundings at Islamia College, Peshawar. College was five miles from Peshawar Cantt, and five miles from college was the famous Jamrod Fort on the road to Landi Kota, about 18 miles from the latter. The college was completely isolated from any centre of population. Opposite the college gate, across the road, was situated the college for the training of teachers of the senior vernacular and junior vernacular classes. This college was called the Normal College. The college was kept spotlessly clean. All the roads were lined with trees on both sides. All open spaces were lawns, playgrounds or turned into groves of trees. The college had a farm attached to it. The Government had established a small dairy farm also adjacent to it. The college must have been situated roughly in an area of 500 yards x 500 yards. The college looked like an oasis, in the surrounding wilderness, from a distance.

The college had, I think, seven hostels. The largest, newest and most imposing was Osmania, which was constructed with a donation from the Nizam of Hyderabad. One hostel was named Harding, after the British viceroy in India. All Hindu students were kept in Rahim Shah Ward. They called it ward, perhaps, because it was small. Only 30 or 35 students could be accommodated there, while the other hostels could accommodate more than double this number. In this hostel there were two single rooms, two double rooms, four seaters and three seaters. All hostels were in a near square shape. The rooms were arranged on the four sides of an open square in the middle. Just above the entrance gate were the superintendent's bachelor quarters. All superintendents had to live in the hostels and they had to live there without their families. The latrine and bathroom block was in a corner. There was no flush system; all the latrines were dry. Every hostel had a warden as well, who used to be a senior professor. For all practical purposes, the superintendent was the most important authority for us. The wardens came only once a week to inspect the hostels.

Every hostel had a monitor and a proctor. They were nominated from among senior students on the recommendation of the superintendent. The monitor was responsible for the general discipline in the hostel and all matters connected with victuals. There was a proctorial department in the college under a senior professor.

Another middle level professor looked after the day-to-day business. The proctors were responsible for maintaining the discipline inside and outside the college. They were also to see that students were always dressed properly during college and outside the college compound at all times and in public. The prescribed dress for the students was black or blue achkan or sherwani and white salwar.

The college had a debating hall, where debates were periodically held. The debating hall was in a separate building of its own. It was a newly built building put up a short time before my arrival there. The debates were run by an organization, the Khyber Union. The Khyber Union's office holders were elected by the college students. The elections were hotly contested. Demonstrations were held, processions were taken aound hostels and speeches were made. Though politics played a great part in these elections, they were supposed to be apolitical. The president of the Khyber Union was given a suite of rooms on the first floor above the gate of the Osmania Hostel. The elections were dominated mostly by the students from Peshawar, Charsadah tehsil (in district Peshawar) and Mardan district. Sometimes tribal loyalties in the above areas overshadowed political loyalties.

College hostels were situated in two rows facing the road. Between the two rows there was considerable distance. In the intervening space there were groves of trees and grassy patches. Between the adjacent hostels in the same row also there was sufficient space. There used to be inter-hostel tournaments in the winters.

The main college building was at a raised level, where the Principal's office, college secretariat arts faculty lecture rooms and the college hall were situated, in a 'L' shaped formation. Facing the longer arm of the 'L' was the right-angled 'U' shaped science block. On the middle arm of the 'U', in the center of which was the entrance gate and its portal, there was another floor in which were the offices of the Heads of Departments of the science faculty and their lecture rooms. The Head of the Department of Agriculture, Professor Mushtaq, used to take his classes there. The two blocks were not joined by any structure. Both looked like actually separate blocks, but they fit the general lay out, and there was an impression of a vast unbuilt area, enclosed on two sides by some low-slung structures. As the science block was at a lower level than the main block, it harmonized with the natural setting. All the open space was dotted with shrubs and hedges, which formed the passageway from the entrance to the main block. Colourful flowers, in the open space facing the main block, provided the soft touch to the austere appearance of the brick buildings.

Two lecturers in the Agriculture Department took their classes in the open or in a small building, especially put up for the Agriculture Department. It contained a shed for agricultural implements such as cultivators, ploughs and winowers. It was situated in the fields, in the northeastern corner of the college. It was situated at the farthest distance from the college, as compared to the other buildings, but it was nearer to the Rahim Shah Ward than the main college building, as Rahim Shah Ward was the eastern most hostel in the second row, and thus the hostel which was the furthest from the college. In this building, the dairy equipment of the college was also stored. In the Agriculture Department, there were very few students. B.Sc. Agriculture was a four year course, and in the four classes the number of students did not exceed 30. In our class, when I joined, there were seven students. One dropped out in a year's time. Another one dropped out in the third year, as he got selected into the Air Force. The number of students in other classes was much more than in the agriculture classes, but still, I feel, their number was less than what it was in the corresponding classes in Gordon College.

College had a coffee shop, where one could buy fruit and pound cake. I assume, if the name of the shop was coffee shop, then at some stage they must have been serving coffee and tea, but I do not remember any such service. In Gordon College, such a shop was called a tuck shop. To go to Peshawar Cantt, one hired a seat or the whole tonga from outside the main gate. A seat cost one four annas and the whole tonga one rupee. On return, one could pick up a tonga from a stand for college at the same price. Outside the college gate, one person was seen to be selling 'shami kabab' which he cooked from beef while sitting on the ground. I rarely saw a student eating his kababs. Mostly common folks going on the road or farmers or domestic servants patronized him. In hostels beef or pork was not served. Lamb was the only meat that was served there.

For food, Rs. 15/- per month was charged. Daily, meat was served at both the meals. In addition one vegetable was also served. At two meals in a week, 'Pulao" was served in addition. Similarly, a sweet dish was served twice in a week. Soft 'nans' were supplied by a bakery maintained for the purpose. The 'ghee' used in the preparation of meals was pure, being prepared from milk. This ghee was supplied by the Nawab of Swat. Vegetarians were served 'dal' (pulse) of different types but mostly of gram, in lieu of meat, and onion pulao instead of meat pulao. The flour for the nans was kneaded by the bakers with their feet.Their feet,however, were checked periodically by a doctor.

In college, the number of students enrolled was about 550. Out of them, 100 to 150 were day scholars, while the rest were residents. Among the Hindus, about 20 to 25 were residents, the rest, about 60 to 75, were day scholars. About a month before the University examination, which took place in the 12th and 14th classes for other subjects and was held every year for the Agricultural students, some day scholars used to get admitted into the hostels.I liked the location, the greenery, the quiet atmosphere and the feeling of openness of the college tremendously.

I preferred Islamia College to Gordon College in nearly every respect. Though in Gordon College two students were accommodated in each room, the rooms were dark, small and stuffy. While in Islamia College the rooms were well lit and airy and gave one the feeling of spaciousness even if one had to share a room with three others. In the case of food, in Gordon College the monthly expense for food came to about Rs.22/- while in the case of Islamia College the charges were fixed at Rs/ 15/- per month. They were not increased at all in my four years there, which I am sure would have been increased in Gordon College, as there the account of the mess was maintained by a student secretary and the charges would have increased with the increase of prices of food stuff, there being no fixity of charges. In Islamia College the ghee was pure, while the ghee used in Gordon College was made of vegetable oil. In Islamia College, however, one had to have his own milk and sugar if one wanted tea. Sugar remained with the respective students while the milk remained in the kitchen. The Hindu students took another advantage. It was regarding 'Paranthas'. For every student, two nans were provided, while students normally did not eat more than 1 1/2 nan, so some students had arranged with the hostel bearers to get a lesser number of nans, and in lieu of them to get some kneaded flour. They used to have a breakfast of paranthas as they kept a small tin of ghee in the hostel kitchen and with a small quantity of ghee from there, the cook used to cook paranthas for them. I did not eat paranthas in the morning. However, whenever I wanted a parantha, the bearers cooked for me using butter instead of ghee, which I kept on my table to use on toast for breakfast.

I had one distinct advantage in the hostel and that was my bearing. Servants always treated me with deference. I was a Hindu, and so could not be a Nawab, but they gave me the respect which they usually reserved for a person superior in status or rank. For some period we had Hindu bearers, and they also gave me greater respect than they gave to others, but the respect I got from Muslim bearers was qualitatively of a higher order. Bearers never refused me a service I asked for, though they refused to perform the same service for others. Even when I rebuked them for some lapse, they kept quiet, while they usually argued with many others. In the hostel, we had a cook named Sant Ram. He had been at that job for a considerable period. He was a good cook. He could cook all sorts of dishes. However, he was rather weak with age and disease. He would never refuse me whenever I asked him to cook for me.

The hostel had another advantage: whenever one fell ill, the superintendent called for the college doctor. Either the doctor treated you in the hostel itself or shifted you to a small hospital in the college or in case prolonged hospitalization was needed, the patient was shifted to a government hospital in Peshawar city. Such medical service is usually not available in other colleges.

In the hostels in Islamia College, the superintendents exercised an effective control and so criminal elements could not be housed in the hostels nor could the students indulge in any untoward practice. However, this system and the arrangement of rooms around an open square had one disadvantage, and that was the loss of privacy of the boarders, as the superintendent came to know the people who visited you or with whom you left the hostel, through servants, and the students came to know because your room was visible from other rooms. If they were open, which some of them always were, at least people coming in or going out could always be seen from the windows on one or two sides. Such a lack of privacy was altogether absent in Gordon and other colleges I have seen. The hostel rooms in Gordon College were in a row. All doors opened onto one side, in every floor, and that was the front side, and the windows opened onto the back. The doors were always closed, as they opened onto a verandah, which was a public passage. Rooms opened onto verandahs in Islamia College hostels also, but people at large did not use them. They were used by the boarders who had rooms on that side.

The classrooms in Gordon College looked small and dark, while they were spacious and well lit in Islamia College, Peshawar. The contrast, which struck me the most, was in the method of teaching and the personalities of the teachers of the two colleges. In Gordon College teachers seemed to be in a hurry. They presumed that students knew something of the fundementals of the subjects or at least they would learn them at home while doing homework, if they did not know them already. The situation was that the students from convent schools or from some outside areas had done something more in mathematics and chemistry than the students who had passed the examination of the Punjab Matriculation Board. My roommate, Rekhi, was a migrant from Rangoon (Burma), and he had already done what we were doing in the first year. Similarly, some students were regular in their studies, and used to mug up all essentials. However, there were others like me who could not mug up and so they took time to understand. The result was that while an overwhelming majority of the students were struggling to understand the fundementals, the lecturers were rushing ahead, for no rhyme or reason. Even in that rush, there was no consistency. While some of the lecturers were rushing ahead to finish their course early, the lecturer in physics practicals took two months to ingrain in us the wisdom to read a vernier, a job for which one period should have been enough. The lecturer, who taught us mathematics and was prejudiced against me, most of the time tried to show off his knowledge in trigonometry to the first year students, who were struggling to learn the essentials. The result was undue anxiety in the students, ultimately leading to their dropping the class. A little attention by teachers to late starters or even a bit of a sympathetic attitude to the class as a whole, would have prevented the lecturers from proceeding further until at least the majority of the class had understood what had already been taught.

In Islamia College, Peshawar, I was lucky to have only a few classmates, and so the attention of the lecturer was on every student. No one felt neglected. Lecturers taught at a slow and steady pace, in spite of having lost about six weeks of teaching in the strike and the college closure. Actually the courses were not long enough to rush through. For example, the course in trignometey was quite short. I think it is the outlook of a teacher that matters and not the level of intelligence that he has, which is the determining factor in the assessment of him as a teacher. I found the lecturers in Gordon College self-opinionated and non-accessible in general. Some like my lecturer in mathematics were sarcastic in their behaviour rather than sympathetic towards the students. In Islamia College, I found them all, without exception, sympathetic. Even in the worst cases, they employed humour and not sarcasm. I think, it had to do something with the stock they came from. Lecturers were Muslims from Punjab, except for a small minority, who came from N.W.F.P and the Principal and the professor of English, Hedow Haris, were from England. They were simple people and had good family backgrounds. None of them seemed to have a superiority complex or, perhaps, it was the culture of the college, which had affected every lecturer. They had inexhaustible patience. They never refused to explain a topic even if asked umpteen times. At worst, the lecturer concerned might have made a joke of it.

Another practice, which led to the improvement of teacher student relations in the college, was that once a year every class teacher invited his students to his place, in batches in case the class was large, for tea, in which a number of delicious eatables were served. Students eagerly awaited this treat.

My first night in college was spent with my cousin, Krishan Dass, who as a B.T. student had a cubicle. At the hostel he was staying in there were a large number of cubicles, as all B.T. students had cubicles. There were six or seven Hindus in the B.T. class. They all stayed with their Muslim class fellows in the same hostel, but came for their meals to the Rahim Shah Ward. A bearer used to deliver milk or tea to them in their rooms. Five of the Hindu B.T. students were from Kashmir. They all were Brahmins. My cousin enjoyed good food. At night, after dinner we went to the cofee shop, where we had three oranges each. On return to his room we had some dry fruit, a quantity of which he had purchased in the city on his last visit. In the morningt we both had a glass of milk each with buttered buns. In addition we had a delicacy, which he had brought from home in Kohat. The day I arrived at the college I accompanied my cousin and two or three of his class fellows on a walk of four miles. There were milestones on the road outside the village. We went out upto third milestone towards Jamrod and then turned back.

Their group daily went for this walk, and having nothing else to do and not knowing anybody else, I also used to accompany them on this walk. Even when they stopped going out in the evenings during their examination and after they had left college on completion of their course, I continued this practice. Whenever possible, I took a friend or two with me on the walk. Friends dropped out in between, but I kept on this practice. I imitated my cousin's other habits as well. I went for jogging as he did. After the evening walk, he used to go to the parallel bars in the ground. I did the same. Similarly, I had for breakfast a glass of milk and a buttered bun. I also ate three oranges at the coffee shop after dinner. I also started having French toast (three slices) with my evening tea. They prepared French toast by mixing sugar with two eggs and then dipping three slices of bread in this mass and frying them in a frying pan.

During these walks with my cousin and his friends, I got acquainted with a class fellow of his, Majid. As Majid was a follower of Jinnah and the Muslim League, our topic of conversation used to be mostly about the then political scene of the country, and especially the Muslim League. He had formed the Muslim Students Federation in the college, and he was its president. He was from Lahore (Punjab). So, one day I told him that he was from Punjab, but his machinations would not succeed here, as the Frontier was not Punjab. He asked whether I had not met any Muslim Leaguer here. I replied that though the intelligentsia was sympathetic to the Muslim League, the people at large were with the Congress. He asked whether I did not think that once the intelligentsia had come round, the common people would follow suit. I did not reply, but he knew what I was thinking about, as any intelligent man would know that whatever the time lag, ultimately the common people follow the intelligentsia. The only hope for the nationalist forces in the Frontier I could see was that the Congress's strength was in the villages and villages did not change soon, so if meanwhile nationalist forces could stop the creeping pernicious influence of communal forces, and then launched a vigorous campaign of their own, the situation could be saved. Majid left after a few months, after the completion of his course. But the situation instead of improving rapidly deteriorated in the next three years. The inexorable march of history could not be stopped, what to talk of reversed, by the nationalist forces headed by a rightist dominated Congress.

Coming to my college life, when I shited to Rahim Shah Ward from my cousin's hostel, I was put in a four seater room. Mine was the only bed in that room, and I put it in a corner near the door. I felt very lonely, away from home and the hostel of Gordon College with its congested room, thinking that I knew nobody there. However, in a couple of days I came to know that a classmate in the Government High School, Kohat, Ram Rakha, was there. So, it was a comfort to know that I knew somebody in the hostel. After some days, I had two roommates. Both had been day scholars earlier. They had joined the hostel, as they thought they would be able to prepare for the second year university examination better there. They put their beds in another corner across from mine, near the large and the only window. Even with three people in the room, it looked nearly empty. The room was so large, I thought that unless all the corners were occupied, the room would not look fully occupied.

I had nearly three months to prepare for my 1st year university examination. The subjects I had to appear in were Mathematics (Trignometry, Algebra and Land Survey) and Physics. In the second year, we had to appear in Chemistry, Organic Chemistry, Zoology, Botany and English. In the third year, we had to appear in Soil Chemistry, Dairying, Microbiology and English. In the fourth year, we had to appear for a university examination. Some subjects we read two or three years, but subjects like Mathematics, Physics, Soil Chemistry, Crop Botany, Dairying, Microbiology and Entomology were studied for only one year. In March 1943 we were given 15 days preparatory holidays for the examination. I went to Kohat for the duration of the holidays. My second cousin, Purshotam Lal, who had returned from Karachi after doing a three-year diploma course in Civil Engineering, was surprised that I had come home for preparation while everybody stayed in the hostel during the preparatory holidays. However, though I did not do very well in the first year examination, I did get 122 marks out of 175.

In the Christmas holidays in 1942, I had gone home to Kohat. There I found mother lying ill and in a bad shape. One night, I had to get a doctor out of his bed at 2 a.m. The doctor was a sub-assistant surgeon in the Civil Hospital and was living near our house, down the lane, in a Muslim locality. Actually our house was the first house in the lane and the second one was that of our landlord, and then the Muslim houses started. The doctor's house was situated in the row opposite ours, down the lane. A passage, open to the sky, led from the front door, for about eight yards, to an inner door and inside the inner gate were the doctor's sleeping quarters. Both the doors were locked, so my voice could not carry to the doctor. I threw stones in the passage so that at least the noise of the falling stones on the floor would wake the doctor up, and all the while I kept on shouting, though I was scared of the stray dogs who had started barking. I was planning on climbing the wall to get inside, but, luckily, the doctor woke up at the shouting of a neighbour of his. He came with me. Next morning, on his advice, mother was carried in a bus, the seats of which were removed, lying on a cot, to Peshawar Civil Hospital. My uncle, brother and sister-in-law accompanied her. She was admitted into the Womens' Hospital, and the same morning was operated upon by a lady doctor, who wore a black 'burqa' (a two piece garment worn over the normal dress, one covering the whole body from the shoulders downward, and the other covering the head with a flap like piece of cloth, loose on on three sides and stitched to the headpiece in the front, with small woven holes in the middle to see through when the flap is down; otherwise the user can lift it over the head to leave the face uncovered). The operation was successful. The doctor removed a good size tumor from the abdomen. My uncle came back to Kohat in the evening, but my brother and sister-in-law remained at Peshawar with my mother. My sister-in- law stayed with mother in the special room, while my brother stayed in a hotel. On my return from the vacation, I used to visit them in the hospital.

In the second year, my old classmate, Ram Rakha, and I stayed in a double room. Agriculture students, besides the advantage of having a good chance of getting a scholarship, also had the priority in the allotment of room over the other students in the same class. Otherwise, the inter se seniority for students in the same class was on the basis of marks.

My scholarship of Rs.15/-per month from the district board had come through within a few days, but I wanted a scholarship from the state government, as it was Rs. 25/- per month. The district board was easy as there was nobody else from the Kohat area, covered by the district board, except for me. The provincial scholarship also came through in about the middle of January 1943 on the basis of my first divison in the matriculation examination and the fact that I owned some agricultural land.

In college I also joined the University Official Training Corps (U.O.T.C). I believe it was established the same year in college as when I joined. One Captain Felstead, an Englishman, was the adjutant and a British sergeant was his sergeant to assist him in the work of training. We had a company of cadets, with three platoons and nine sections. Professor Mutlab, a senior lecturer in the Physics Department had been given an honorary commission as major, and he was nominally in command of the company. Adal Khan, the Director of Physical Training in the college had been given an honorary rank of a lieutenant, and so had his assistant Razaq.

Captain Feldsted was short and a bit plumpish. He was a very nice man. He was, perhaps, of 45 years of age, and more like a father figure for us than a captain. But inspite of his age and plumpness, he was more active than all the other commissioned officers on the field. Professor Mutlab was of Iranian desent. He was fair, reasonably tall, slim and had a well exercised body. He also looked about 45 years old.

Adal Khan was over six feet tall, dark, heavy in built, with a paunch but a powerful figure. Razaq was of medium height, dark, active but with a paunch and was putting on fat. Adal Khan and Razaq were both Punjabis. Adal Khan was our hostel superintendent as well. He was a nice man. He showed himself to be a disciplinarian, but as is usual with the physical fitness enthusiast, his toughness was a veneer for his could not careless attitude. He spoke in Punjabi with us. His tone usually was sarcastic when he spoke to us.

My studies in college went on satisfactorily, as the teachers in college were sympathetic and I had got the recognition of being an intelligent student. The Professor who taught us English once remarked that I was I.C.S. (Indian Civil Services) material. He always felt a regret that my subjects were not condusive to help me get into the I.C.S. as I had not studied any subject of a higher standard than F.Sc. (12th class) while for the I.C.S. a standard higher than B.Sc. or B.A. was required. I told him that I could study on my own. But he replied that a subject I had studied in college for four years could not be covered that thoroughly in a few months on my own. Professor Hedow Harris also used to take our class two or three times a week in English. He seemed to use his lips more than the teeth and the palate while speaking, and therefore, we could understand him only with great difficulty. I, however, could always engage him in arguments. He was not a bad sort. He was a scholar and different from the run of the mill English men we usually came across.

In October and November, the Khybar Union's election took place. The candidates for Presidency were Ali, son of Khan Abdul Ghaffar Khan the famous Red Shirts or Khuda Khidmatgar leader, and Nasim Anwarebeg. Ali was a tall, slightly plumpish, fair complexioned, handsome and gruff man. Nasim Anwar Beg was the son of Professor Anwar Beg, head of the Chemistry Departmnt of the college. He was about five feet six inches tall, slight in built, soft spoken and very good looking with rosy cheeks. He always looked neat and tidy. He was a very good debater, and had won many prizes in Lahore and other places. Ali, on the contrary, was a public speaker.

Nasim was identified with the Muslim League and so on purely arithmatical calculations he should have won, but he lost. What stood between him and success were the tribal feelings. Ali belonged to Utman Zai in Charsada Tehsil, and so had come from a pure Pathan stock while Nasim carried the surname Beg, which is a Turkish name but he was identified with Punjab, as his family came from there and they did not speak Pashto.

Saadulah Khan, the Muslim League leader in N.W.F.P. was an antagonist of Khan Abdul Ghafar Khan in politics, but both were neighbours, living in adjacent villages. All the younger members of the Saadullah clan supported Ali. Actually they were good friends of his. Students of Kohat and Bannu districts also called separate meetings to put up a united front to be counted in the elections. I attended the meeting of the students from Kohat. The main theme of the meeting was that students from Peshwar and Mardan always played an important part in the elections, and they did not entertain students from other distiricts, not even the Pathans, and so we should vote in block against Ali to teach the students from Peshawar and Mardan a lesson. I knew the underlying idea was to defeat Ali, the son of the Red Shirts leader, under the garb of narrow loyalties.

Demonstrations were taken out and speeches were made by the rival candidates in all the hostels, except in Rahim Shah Ward. When some of the Hindu boarders showed surprise at the indifference shown to them, I told them there was nothing to be surprised at. Both sides had taken us for granted. If the Hindus would not vote for the son of Khan Abdul Ghafar Khan, who else would they would vote for. Ali won the election that year and a year later also. Ali and Nasim, both were in the third year when they fought the election the first time. Ali was in the 5th year in 1945. He could have fought the election the third time, but I do not recollect it. In Ali's winning, the Hindu students also played a considerable part, as 70 to 100 students do matter when the total polling strength is 500 to 550. Ali's success was not due to the Congress's popularity in the college, as explained above, but the Congress's sympathiser papers hailed it as the Congress's victory. If the elections had been conducted on a party basis, Ali would have been definitely defeated by a Muslim League candidate.

I attended a U.O.T.C. camp in October and November of 1943 of 3 or 4 days duration. I attended three such camps. The one in 1944 is the one I remember. I cannot forget it even if I wanted to. I will write about it a little later. Now I may mention that after the U.O.T.C. camp, our second year Agriculture class went on a tour of

7 to 10 days to Lyalpur. Laylapur is situated in the canal colonies of the River Chenab. The farmers there, when we visited it, were very well off. Most of them seemed to be Sikhs. Majority were pensioners from the army. They had been given a 'muraba' or two. A muraba was equal to 25 acres. Canal imrrigation had made them rich.

A muraba at that time fetched a price of 1 1/2 to 2 Lakh of rupees in the canal colonies, if sold. Wheat's yield per acre at that time was a minimum of 16 mands (about 6 quintals) of approved varieties in Layalpur, while the average yield in the Frontier was half of that. The Laylapur Agricultural College was the premier institution of research and studies at the undergraduate level in Punjab, or even in India. In the Punjab University, besides Lyalpaur and Islamia College, Peshawar, degree level education in agriculture was provided in the Khalsa College, Amritsar. All these colleges were residential colleges. We spent a number of days at the college at Lyalpur and in visiting farm area near about. We visited a number of other places but I do not recollect the names. I remember having stopped at the Montgomery's station, as I met somebody named Ghulam Sarwar there who was known known to me from Tehri. He was a goodlooking man, a few years older to me. He was the son of a retired subedar, who was an important and wealthy person. He was in Montgomery to look after the few 'murabas' of land, which had been allotted to his father by the government. He was wearing a revolver on a belt slung over his right shoulder. He took conspicious care to show us his revolver by repeatedly thrusting his chest forward and throwing his jacket backwards. He was not a revolver carrying man at Tehri but in Punjab he was showing off.

In my third year in the college, we visited Lyalpur, Ferozpur, Rohtak, Hissar and Delhi. This was our most extensive tour. Hissar and Rohtak were very primitive places when we visited them. Hissar at least was an open place, but Rohtak was very disappointing. Brij Mohan, from Kashmir, and I were the only Hindus among the group, the rest four or rather five (counting the lecturer accompanying us) were Muslims. In small places, the servant accompanying us cooked for the Muslims, while Brij Mohan and I ate in a restaurant outside. At Rohtak, at lunchtime, Brij Mohan and I went out to eat. We did not find any eating palce. It was a sad specacle of misery and want. At Hissar, we went to see a desert control station (I do not remember the name). Actually, we visited the Central Dairy Institute also. They were doing some useful work. They had good facilities for research. They were cross breeding the Montgomery Sahiwal breed, which was the most productive in the country in milk, with the Holstein Frezian breed, the best milk yielder in the world, in order to have hybrids that would be producing more milk than the Sahiwal breed but would be more resistant to diseases than the Holstein Frezian. Similarly, they were cross breeding the Hissar breed with the Dhani breed of Western Punjab in order to have hybrid bullock for drought purposes, which would combine the strength of the Hissar breed and the doggedness of the Dhano breed.

At Delhi, we saw some poultry farms. However, our greatest pleasure was in having tea with pastries in Devico. While moving around in Connaught Place, we met an army captain, or rather he met us, for he came towards us when he saw us, as he was an ex-student of the Islamia College in Peshawar. He was not known to us, but most probably some of us were in sherwani, the uniform of the college, and he recognized us from that. The tea served to us was not sumptuous but our delight was in having tea in a restaurant where the elite like army officers, Englishmen and other dignitaries were also having tea and the band was playing.

In Delhi, we stayed in a Muslim hotel in Fatehpuri. Brij Mohan and I used to have our meals in restaurants together while the others had their meals in Muslim restaurants. Fatehpuri in those days had good Indian style (bare accommodation, nothing fancy, but cheap in price) hotels and restaurants, but they had all deteriorated when I visited them after the partition of the country. What we liked best in the hotel where we stayed was that it prepared green tea which we liked to drink after meals or when we were sitting at leisure in the winter.

In this tour I had an occasion to show off. We had to change trains at Bhatinda to go to Delhi. Because of the troop movement those days, it was quite difficult to get onto a train especially at a wayside station. Not that it is any easier now after forty years of independence. We were travelling in the third class while our lecturer was travelling in the inter-class. We missed one train, as we could not get in because of overcrowding. When after a couple of hours, I saw a train approaching our platfrom, I asked the servant accompanying us to lift the bedding and luggage and stand close behind while I stood near the edge of the platform to jump into a compartment opposite us when the train stopped or even when it appreciably slowed down. I advised my other colleagues also to follow suit. As soon as the train stopped, I jumped into the compartment, but I got stuck in the doorway as some passengers were getting down and many others were trying to get in. A Sikh soldier in uniform saw me struggling to get in. He rushed towards me shouting for me to get down as it was a compartment reserved for the military. He raised a stick in his hand to hit me, but I did not care. I caught the descending end of the stick in my one hand and shouted, in Pashto, to the servant to get in by pushing hard and not to be afraid. When the other Sikh soldiers in the compartment saw me grappling with the soldier's stick, some of them, about six, ran towards me to tackle me. I was determined to fight it out, even if the odds were heavily against me. When all of these soldiers were grappling with me, some Pathans soldiers rushed towards us and separated us, and restored peace. It was a compartment large enough to seat about 48 passengers, but the number of passengers was less.

On the side opposite to where we entered, a Sikh gentlemen and his wife had taken two long berths, and were lying there under quilts. The six or seven of us took the corner seats on the other side and we were more than comfortable, so much so that our lecturer, Ghulam Sarwar, at a subsequent halt of the train, came into our compartment as he found his inter-class compartment more crowded. He played cards with me for a couple of hours, but then he went back to his compartment, as he was afraid one of my colleagues, Malik, would involve him in a quarrel. The problem was that Malik had been continuously passing remarks at the two people lying flat under their quilts on the wooden benches. He addressed those remarks to me about those persons, in a loud voice, in Pashto, across a distance of about five feet. Inspite of my requests to the contrary, he did not stop. At this our lecturer left the compartment in order not to get involved in a quarrel, which Malik's remarks might generate. Malik's remarks were symptomatic of the envy of the individuals he felt within himself, who paid the same fare as himself but still could manage to sleep in peace, while he himself had to sit uncomfortably the whole night. This was quite common in wartime for a few military personnel to occupy the whole compartment and not allow any civilian in their compartment under the pretext that it was reserved for Military personnel, which actually it was not. Even civilians indulged in such practices, by occupying a whole berth, on which they had no legitimate claim, and depriving other ticket holders the seats to which they were entitled. This adage, of might is right, one can still see in practice in the unreserved compartments of Indian Railways.

Coming back to this particular journey, which I described above, when we had taken seats and were relaxed, some of the Pathan soldiers got in conversation with Malik and told him that I was a very brave man, as even knowing the tremendous odds against me, I was going to take on single handedly so many soldiers. They said I escaped being seriously mauled when I called the servant, in 'Pashto', to come on. From my 'Pashto' speaking, they had thought that I was a Pathan and, so, had come to intervene.

When we returned from this tour, we came to know that within a week we were having our home examination; the examination which was held three or four months before the university examination. We were taken aback as none of us was really ready. We went in a deputation to the principal, Mr.Scot. He remained adamant. He said that the dates had been fixed for various papers of not only our class but for all the classes in the college and, so, the examination could not be postponed. When our results came out, I stood first and all my classmates had failed. All our teachers were happy as they all were of the opinion that I was more intelligent, but in all the other previous examinations Abdul Malik had come first and I second. Our lecturer, Ghulam Sarvar, said in class that it had been the only examination to prove who was actually really intelligent. Professor Mushtaq, the Head of the Department of Agriculture, also said more or less the same thing. This was the first and only time that I was awarded a prize of books, worth Rs. 25/-, in an award function in college.

Professor Anwar Beg, the Head of the Department of Chemistry, used to take our chemistry class. When he used to teach, I used to be, usually, absorbed in my thoughts on a back bench. Sometimes he used to throw a chalk at me or shout, or do both, but I did not change. In the beginning he used to be curt while drawing my attention to the class, but as time passed, the tone of his voice become affectionate and humorous. He used to ask what he should do with me, and wondered whether I was dopey or had come to college after taking opium. He humorously used to say that his regret was that he could not punish me, as I was good in studies. Invariably, Malik came first and I second in the examinations. In individual papers, I used to come first in some papers like English, Economics and Zoology. I came first in those subjects in which I did not have to study much. Malik was a very neat and steady student. After taking notes in class, we took extra lengthy notes in subjects like soil chemistry, dairying, entomology, microbiology and agriculture, because of the non-availability of books. Malik used to make a fairy copy of these notes in another notebook, using red ink to write the headings and the important points and blue ink for narrations. In practicals also he was very tidy and methodical, while in contrast I was very clumsy. I used to dirty up the whole place. Malik was very studious and regular. He used to study two or three hours daily, but during examination days he never remained awake after 12 o'clock at night, while I was not regular at all. I used to concentrate on my reading only in the preparatory holidays and during examination days. During examination days I used to study sometimes upto 2 or 3 a.m.

In my second year, I tried to venture into the debating arena of the Khyber Union, but I got so clobbered that I did not dare to venture again into this thorny business. The debate was on Womens' Education, and I spoke in favour of it. I was speaking all right, but the audience was making noises. I thought that they were shouting to demoralize me. Actually they were shouting, as they could not hear me. I, however, stuck on and carried on till the end of the ten minutes, the maximum time allowed to each speaker. However, I understand that Ali, who was in the chair, pressed the bell one or two minutes before my allotted time to indicate my time was up. Actually, I had never spoken in such a large hall without a loudspeaker. So, while I was speaking, I had no conception that I could not be heard. The students were a noisy lot. They tried to disturb even the best speaker, though the latter usually prevailed over the hecklers after a short while.

I went for a debate in Urdu also, arranged by the Urdu Association in the College's main hall, not in the Khyber Union hall. The judges gave a student, named Tehmasap and myself cqual number of marks. Then thcy decided to ask us to speak extempore for three minutes. I was asked to speak first. Tehmasap won. Tehmasap shortly thereafter became the president of the Muslim Students Federation.

In the winter of 1941, I went to the U.O.T.C camp at Landikotal. It was the last garrison post of the British Indian army near the frontier with Afghanistan. The border post, Torkham, was seven miles from there. I was at that time a corporal in the U.O.T.C, and this rank got me in trouble. One morning when I came to my tent, which I shared with four or five other cadets, after bathing at the tap, I saw that three of my tent mates, Manohar, Lajpat and one other whose name I do not recollect, sitting downcast. After a minute or so, one of them asked whether I knew what was happening there. Then the second one said what could one do. All of them were senior to me in college by one year, but I was senior to them in the U.O.T.C. by virtue of my rank. I then made them tell me their story. What had transpired was that the previous night, when everyone was asleep, Adal Khan went to the tent where our two Hindu bearers were sleeping. The flaps of the tents were up. The bearers were two brothers from Garhwal. They were young in age. They were working in our hostel, and were brought to Landikotal to cook for the Hindu cadets. Adal Khan woke up the younger brother and made sexual advances towards him. The bearers kicked him and Adal Khan went away. In the morning, the bearers brought this to the notice of the Hindu students who they came across. After acertaining the facts from the bearers, I went and reported the matter to the adjudent, Captain Felstead. After a little while, Professor Mutlab, the company commander, called me. He just talked to me for a minute or two about the matter and let me go. This case remained dormant for a few months but then suddenly erupted into prominence and then fizzled out completely. At one stage it appeared to achieve province wise prominence and was expected to create dissension in the college, but I will write about it later.

One day we marched to Torkahn Border. It was an important day for me to stand at the entrance of the pass and contemplate the succession of invaders who had passed through this narrow pass and dominated and influenced the political and cultural life of India since time immemorial. The Aryans, the Huns, the Turks, the Afghans and the Mughals all came through this pass, and contributed towards the development and formation of India as it is today. Tyrants and plunderers like Alexander, Mahmood Ghaznavi, Chingaz Khan and Timur also came through this pass. They indulged in carnage and plunder, but left no durable effect, except of their bloodthirst and love of ill gotten treasures. Being interested in History, the visit to the Khyber Pass was a very important occasion for me. I still remember that while at Khyber Pass, it occurred to me that had there been no Khyber Pass, perhaps India would have been spared the misery, which was brought upon its people during the course of various invasions. The Khyber Pass, in my mind, at that time, stood responsible for all the misery, poverty, exploitation, bloodshed, strife and discord which the people of India had been exposed to during those past invasions and subsequently. But, today, after more than forty years, I realize, a pass like a gate is for entrance and exit. It enables people to move to and fro but it can bring in raiders as well. As a gate is essential to enable the people of the house to go for education, trade and recreation, so does the pass. As a household cannot live in isolation, so cannot a nation. For the development and progress of a country, it is essential that there should be free interaction between the people of different countries. Without it some countries would be perpetually backward and some advanced. It would be against the law of nature, as nature is moving towards synthesis and ultimate unity.

On the last day at Landikotal, a lieutenant from the cavalry regiment came to enquire if any of us would want to do horse riding. I was among those five who replied in the affirmative. He came in the evening, riding on a horse, with five horses in trail. He asked us who was a good rider. All the others kept quiet, but I replied that I was. So, we all got onto the horses and followed the lieutenant at a trot, which developed into a canter shortly afterwards. As we started, I knew I had trouble on my hand as the horse, I was riding on, was resisting my commands. He seemed to follow his own whims. He did not like to follow another horse. He wanted to be ahead of all the other horses. Anyhow the onward journey passed without any trouble, but I was perturbed in my mind. When we turned back, the trouble started. My horse overtook all the other horses including that of the lieutenant and galloped straight towards the camp. On the homeward journey the speed of all the horses had increased and so the lieutenant did not say anything, as he knew mine was a spirited horse. However, when the distance between my horse and his increased sufficiently, he started shouting 'not that fast'. I answered back that I could not stop him in spite of my best efforts. The lieutenant galloped his horse fast to catch up with me but he could not gain on me, as my horse, it looked, ran even faster when it knew that a race was on. I had pulled the reins tightly, and the horse was bleeding slightly at the corner of its mouth, but there was no stopping him. It had taken the bit in its teeth and ran towards its base at full speed, with foam coming over the injured corners of its mouth. The lieutenant had given up the chase. My only worry at that time was that to go to our base, we had to turn to the left pass and through the strong iron gate and mounted on its top were thick iron spikes of about 8 inches in length. I was liable to be badly lacerated by the spikes of the open left hand part of the gate, as we were approaching from that side, with the horse turning at speed. Luckily for my safety, but unlucky for my reputation as a horse rider, the horse slipped on the paved cemented surface of stones in the bed of a small rain water 'nallah' (stream) and fell down on its belly. The only injuries I suffered were a small cut on my left shoulder, as the momentum of the running horse had thrown my shoulders forward. The inner thighs became raw. The horse's belly also had become raw. It suffered no broken bones. This occurred very near our camp; so providential help came just in time.

That evening, our lecturer, Sarwar, also came to participate in the last night's fun at the invitation of Adal Khan, as he was a friend of his. At night when I met him, he already knew about the fall. He drawled in his inimitable style 'Were you an uncle of the horse that you had to ride it?' When I narrated the whole story to him, he turned to Adal Khan and told him that if the horse had fallen, how could I be blamed. Adal Khan stated that it was the best horse in the base; and that they had had to shoot him and that would entail a loss of Rs.10,000/- to the government. Sarwar remarked that if it cost the government Rs.10,000/- let it, but Sehgal was not responsible for it. I am narrating this incident with a view to firstly illustrate how down-to-earth and versatile the Punjabi idiom was and secondly to show how full of pun and humour Sarwar's day-to-day speech was in Punjabi. He enjoyed speaking in Punjabi, and spoke Punjabi where he could. Later on in college, I asked him one day whether Adal Khan had told him about the accusation against him when he visited the U.O.T.C camp. He replied in the negative and then asked how he could have told him about such a matter. When I said because he was his friend, he replied that even friends were too ashamed about such matters to talk about them to their friends. He, however, was not happy why I had got myself involved in such a matter. I replied that it was a matter of duty. But then promptly came his rejoinder, "Is duty your aunt or what? Sometimes things recoil on the person who performs duties such as these."

On our return journey from Landikotal to the college, the truck, in which the servants were riding skidded and turned athwart on the road. The tow rear wheels of the truck came to rest on the edge or on the slope itself. I was sitting on the front seat of the truck following the servant's truck. I saw from a distance of about fifteen feet, how suddenly and smoothly the truck turned and the men in the truck in ones and twos rolled over the slope. The whole incident, however, was over in less than a minute. Luckily, the slope was not very steep, nor rocky on the surface and nor deep. Most of the men got superficial injuries. Our Hindu servants could not get up on their own, so they had to be lifted up into the trucks. When we went to lift them up, I saw that the flesh of their forearms had been torn off. All the injured were removed to the main hospital of Peshawar City.

In April 1944 I had moved into a three-seater room in the hostel. Earlier my roommate in the two-seater, Mr Ram Rakha, had got admission, from the quota of seats allotted to the state, into the Medical College Amritsar, as the N.W.F.P had no medical college of its own. Such seats were not allotted on the basis of merit, but on political clout or on the system of sharing the spoils. The Member of Parliament from the Hindu constituency of Kohat district was a relation of his, and so he got him the admission. I do not think the quota of medical admissions for Hindus was more than two in a year, in case Muslim candidates were available for all the seats allotted to that community.

In the three-seater, I had moved in with only one student, Kundan Lal, a second year student from Kohat. Sometime later a third person, Raghubir Singh, was also put in with us. He had migrated from some other college in third year. In the hostel room allocation was based on some point system. Sixth year students had the maximum points followed by 4th, 2nd, 5th, 3rd and 1st year students in that order. Within the same class, agricultural students had the highest priority, followed by science and arts students. In third year I had lost the relative seniority to the 2nd year students and so could not get a two-seater room, which I had in third year. This preference of 2nd year over third year students was based on the fact that 2nd years students had to take the university examination while the third year students did not, as the University examinations were every second year. The preference of agriculture students over their contemporaries in the same class was most probably due to the fact that they had to take university examinations every year, or as they had to study more subjects.

Raghubir, before joining our college, had been an active member of the Student's Congress. This was a student organization having political affiliations with the Indian National Congress. It was a new organization. It was most probably formed by students sympathetic to the Indian National Congress, as most probably, the Students' Federation, which had been earlier representative of patriotic students, had become dominated by communists. As the Congress was the main political party and had ministries in most of the provinces, the Student Congress had at that time became quite an influencial organization. The Congress, after remaining in the wilderness in N.W.F.P for about two years, had formed the government at the end of 1944, when the arrested members of the province's Legislative Assembly had been released.

It was in February 1945, I believe, that Dinker Sakrekar, the Secretary General of the All India Students Congress, visited Islamia College. He stayed with Raghubir, but as Kundan and myself were also sharing Raghubir's room, we both had become co-hosts as well. Dinker Sakrekar's purpose was to establish a branch of the Indian National Congress in other institutions as well. At night we fell into talking of his project and I told him that in the Frontier he had no chance of success, as people in general had turned away from the Congress, in the case of students in particular, as their sympathy was with the Muslim League. I gave him the general background of the situation uptil then. I told him that in N.W.F.P the Khudai Khidmatgar movement (Red Shirts) had lost much of its influence to the Muslim League. The next morning he, along with Raghbir, went to see Ali. Ali catagorically informed him that he did not see any possibility for the establishment of the Students Congress in Islamia College. He however advised him to see me in the matter. On his return from Ali, when he told me about his talk with Ali, I told him that I did not want to take part in politics while studying, and even otherwise I did think it would do any good to establish a national students organization on the strength of students belonging to an infinitesimal minority. I knew when Ali referred Dinkar Sakrekar to me he meant that I would be able to form the N.W.F.P Students Congress mostly on the strength of Hindu students.

Dinker Sakrekar was to see Dr.Khan Saheb, the Premier of N.W.F.P. the same morning. He asked me to accompany him to the meeting. I refused on the plea that, as I did not want to join politics while studying, my seeing Dr.Khan would be of no avail.

I had realized that any effort to establish a student's organization in the Frontier would be futile. Firstly, because the student community in the Frontier was limited; there being only Islamia College, Inter Arts College, Edward College in Peshawar and, I believe, a degree college in Dehra Ismail Khan. Secondly, the Muslims in the Frontier in 1945 were much more inclined towards the Muslim League than towards the Congress, especially among the intelligentsia. Dr.Khan Saheb's (Congress's) ministry did not do anything during the time it was in power. A national government comes to power after centuries of oppression and deprivation. People expect things will change: consumer goods would become cheaper; there would be plenty of everything. Croppers would become owners of the land they tilled, water would be provided in villages for drinking as well as irrigation, industry would be established to offer employment to the unemployed, bureaucracy would become courteous and responsive to public need. Nothing of the sort happened. The Congress government ran the administration as it was being run before. One could not have expected all the above listed things to happen in the period they were in power, which was over five years, as they were in power from 1937 to 1943 in their first ministry, but actually nothing was done to improve the lot of the common man. The Congress came into power on the votes of the people in the rural area. It should at least have done something to alleviate the misery of the common people in the villages. The ministers were corrupt from the beginning. Favouritism and parochialism were the culture of the day. Dr.Khan Saheb was a very honest man himself, but what could one person do, and especially when he himself had to reward or satisfy the expectations of his long deprived colleagues and party workers. The wealthy could get things done from the ministers or bureaucracy through the power of money, but the common people suffered and became dissatisfied.

The League Ministry, which followed, was even worse. Their cronies, and hangers-on prospered and so one set of people prospered at the expense of the other. Though the Muslim League was worse than the Congress when in power, as far as corruption was concerned, yet the Congress suffered. The reason was that the people knew that the Muslim League was the party of Nawabs and big landlords and rich city merchants, but when the party of the masses, patriots, and the self-proclaimed reformers proved to be as good or even worse than the lackies of the empire, they switched their loyalties to the Muslim League, as it at least stood for the Prophet and the Quran.The religious appeal of the Muslim League had meant nothing to them earlier, as they knew that religion was a personal matter and it had nothing to do with getting independence and bettering their lot. After all Khan Abdul Ghafar Khan himself was a very religious person and the men opposing him in the Muslim League were not good Muslims. It was commonly stated at that time that the top brass of the Muslim League took hard drinks and did not observe the various practices enjoined by the religion. It was stated by the pious Muslims that Khan Abdul Ghafar's hands, when his arms were fully extended to the sides, reached his knees, like those of Hazrat Muhammad, the

Prophet of Islam. It was not an act of faith that turned the village folk towards the Muslim League, but the betrayal by the nationalist leaders that led to secularism losing its appeal for them, and on the rebound they went into the lap of the party of rich zamindars and Nawabs.

I had told Dinker Sakrekar that even in the 1942's Quit India agitation the masses showed much less enthusiasm than what they did in 1930-31 and 1932-32. In his History of Modern India 1885-1947, Sumit Sarkar has stated that in the Quit India Movement only 2500 persons went to jail in N.W.F.P.

Dinker Sakerakar and Raghubir, on return from their meeting with Dr.Khan Saheb, told me what had transpired at their meeting. When Dinker Sakeraker told him that he had heard that the Congress had lost much of its influence in the province, Dr. Khan Saheb became very angry and asked him the name of the person who had told such lies. Dinker Sakerakar was smiling when he narrated his conversation with Dr. Khan Saheb, as he had come to know by that time, from his conversation with Ali and me, and one or two others, that the Congress's popularity had suffered a severe setback. I laughed and said that it was a good moment when I decided not to go with him to see Dr. Khan Saheb, as he would have given me a good lashing of his tongue. Dr. Khan Saheb was a very simple man. There was no dissimulation in him. He said what he felt. Personally, he was honest to the core. He lambasted people even for a small lapse if he felt there was one, but which actually on verification could have been found not to be the case. I heard of one incident from a provincial Civil Service officer about Dr.Khan Saheb, which I describe here to illustrate his simple nature. Once a farmer approached him, when he was the premier of N.W.F.P, and asked him what was the use of having him as a premier when the police could commit atrocities on the people. On being asked to explain, the farmer said that his son had been put into prison without a charge. Dr.Khan was in charge of Law and Order also. He immediately issued orders for the suspension of the sub-inspector concerned and the release of the son of the farmer. It however transpired ultimately that the farmer's son was neither arrested and nor was the sub-inspector posted at the station where he was supposed to have arrested the farmer's son. The farmer had taken advantage of the simple nature and zeal of Dr.Khan Saheb for speedy justice to settle a personal score with the sub-inspector concerned.

Dr.Khan Saheb, having full trust in his belief, engendered by sycophants and favour seekers, in the overwhelming popularity of the Congress, would have lambasted me for circulating wrong information. He was assassinated, a few years after the partition of the country, in Lahore, by an unknown assassin.

In April 1945, one day in the morning when I was leaving for college, I saw Prem, who had appeared in the B.Sc examination the same year from our college, but was no longer a student of the college then, in the compound of our hostel. He was talking in a loud voice, about the affair of Adil Khan vis a vis the bearer of the hostel, to some students who were going to college. When he saw me, he said what justice was this that more than four months had passed and still no action had been taken against Adil Khan. He then gathered all of us and took us to my room, which was open. We never locked our rooms when we went to college, as the hostel sweeper swept the room and the room bearer made the bed and put the other things in order.

Prem got the boys from the other rooms, who were in the hostel, rounded up also. There were two more boys also with him. I understood they were students of the college before my time. All the other boys were also very unhappy about the college having hushed up the whole matter, but the initiative was taken by Prem. He said that we should write about the whole matter to the Premier, Dr.Khan Saheb and send copies to the Director of Education. Then the drafting exercise began. Ultimately, I took over the drafting exercise and drafted the letter. As someone in the hostel had a typewriter, we got the letter and the copies typed and all present signed, except Prem and his two friends as they were outsiders. We all took this letter to Captain Felsted. Captain Felsted was taken aback, as he had never expected to receive such a letter. He did not make any other comment except to state that we all should see the Principal. Prem, at that stage, departed taking with him the copies of the letter to be sent to the Premier and others. We went to the office of the Principal and there Captain Felsted presented the copy to the Principal. The Principal at that time was Sheikh Taimur. J.D. Scot had left to take up his new position as Deputy Secretary to the viceroy at New Delhi.

Sheikh Taimur, while he was reading our letter, showed considerable signs of apprehension. When I started talking of the authorities' partisan attitude and lack of justice, his hands started shaking. He did not know what to do, as most probably, he had hushed up the matter. But he got help soon in the shape of Mahmood Ahmed, lecturer in biology, but more relevant to the occasion was that he was the superintendent of our hostel. He came on his own. Nobody had called him. I think he saw the Hindu students going together from the hostel. He must have found out from the bearers what had happened. The bearers must have found out as to what was happening from our conversation. Later when he saw the Hindu students going into the principal's office, he came running to join the party. When Sheikh Taimur was sitting spellbound, Mahmood Ahmed started talking, "The whole exercise was engineered by Jagdish Dass (my name). He called the students who assembled in his room; he drafted the letter and he led the students to Captain Felsted and the Principal.'

I then knew that my goose was cooked. Mahmood Ahmed, like a clever manipulator, had put the whole responsibility on the ringleader. I immediately realized that Mahmood Ahmed had put the noose around my neck and suddenly the accuser had become not the accused but the culprit. Sheikh Taimur, immediately like a weak person, jumped up at the chance offered to catch the other man by the neck and take him down with him. However Mahmood Ahmed was a shrewd man. He knew hanging the arraigned man would not serve their purpose though his cooperation may. So when Sheikh Taimur said that he would take action against me, Mahmood Ahmed said that they would give me upto the evening to get the copies of the letter from the other authorities to the principal, otherwise I would be rusticated from the college. I had told Mahmood Ahmed earlier, on his query regarding the whereabouts of the other copies of the letter, that the copies had been taken by Prem to post and I did not where he lived, but he knew that to save myself I would get the copies.

I was so frightened that I could not think of anything else but of saving my career. I did not think whether they would or could rusticate me. A mouse, on seeing a snake, does not ask himself whether he could successfully fight it or not. The only thing he thinks of is saving his life and runs for it. I did the same. I thought of only somehow of getting hold of the copies of the letter before Prem posted them. The same was the reaction of Sheikh Taimur. As soon as he heard Mahmood Ahmed suggesting a way out for him without getting hurt, he readily agreed. I depended upon Opinder Bakhshi, a very good friend, for recovery of the copies. He knew Prem's house address, and he had a motorcycle which could take us there fast. Opinder was one of the three or four hostellers who had a motorcycle.

We missed our lunch and drove straight to Prem's house in the old city of Peshawar. From our hostel, Peshawar cantonment was more than five miles, and from there Prem's house was about 2 1/2 miles, though the famous Quissa Khani Bazaar was about two miles from the tonga stand for Islamia College, which was at a short distance from Odeon Cinema. Prem was a tough man. He was a wrestler, very combative and obstinate to boot. I was afraid he might refuse to hand over the copies. Opinder, who was from Peshawar like Prem, had the same feeling. He knew him well, being from Peshawar and from even the same locality in the city from which Prem came. Our one worry was that he might have posted the copies before going home or he might have gone to some other place instead of his house which would have made it impossible for us to make contact with him before the posting of the letters. However, our fears were unfounded. He was at home and the letters were with him, and on top of it all, he straight away handed over the letters to us saying, after he heard us, that under the circumstance there was no way out except to hand over the letters to the Principal. After taking the letters, we immediately drove to the Principal's house in the college. It was after 3 in the afternoon and he was having a siesta. We woke him up and handed over the letters to him. He received the letters without saying anything.

The news of this incident, however, spread over all the college. One day Tehmasap met me and he said that we Hindu students had conspired to frame a Muslim lecturer, Adil Khan. I told him that he knew that it was nothing of the sort and I would not do such a thing. He said that whatever I might say they were going to agitate in favour of Adil Khan. A few days later, Ali met me. He asked why we had to complain against Adil Khan and was I aware that others were going to make it a communal affair. I only said in reply that I could not help it. With these words the dialogue ended.

One say, during that time, Adil Khan by chance met me on a deserted road & spoke to me. He looked sad. He said, "Look what you have done to me. He knew I had done nothing to him. What had happened was his own doing. I had no enmity with him and nor had the servants. Why would they involve themselves in such a thing? They had rather everything to lose, in addition to their honour, by complaining. I was conveyed the news of Adil Khan's supposed heinous attempt by other students. I did not even hear it from the servants at first hand. The irony is that I did not even meet them after I came back to college. They remained in hospital for quite a long time, and some of our hostellers and the other Hindu camp mates of mine visited them in the hospital, but, for one reason or another, I could not visit them. It could be due to my laziness, but normally I am very prompt in visiting sick or distressed friends. Another aspect of the case was that these two servant brothers were very decent. They were always cheerful. They were not cantankerous or bad workers. They never complained nor gave any cause for complaint. I later on regretted my inability very much for not visiting them in hospital. Seeing the pathetic condition he was in, I really felt a surge of sympathy within me for Adil Khan. I could not imagine a powerful person like Adil Khan being affected that much by any misfortune. The only reply I could muster up at that time was to ask what could have I done.

About six weeks later I was called before an enquiry committee, composed of Professor Mutlab, Mahmood Ahmed Khan and Captain Felsted. Adil Khan was also there. He, however, did not ask me any question. He could not have because I was not a witness to the commission of offence. Mine was only hearsay evidence. However, Mahmood Ahmed asked Captain Felsted in my presence whether it was in line of my duty to report about the matter under question. Captain Felsted replied in the affirmative as I was the senior most Hindu cadet available on the spot.

I later on asked Opinder, my friend, whether Mahmood Ahmed was trying to get me fixed, but he was of the opinion that Mahmood Ahmed was cleverly putting it on record that my action was in line of duty and not because of any ulterior moive. My only worry was that under pressure, which I understood they were under, the servant brothers may retract their earlier oral statement, ascribing it to the pressure exerted over them by me. They however remained steadfast in their allegation.

For this they lost their jobs in the hostel. I lost my proctorship. I had been appointed proctor of our hostel in April 1945. Brij Lal Kaul, my classmate in B.Sc. 4th year, was appointed the hostel monitor. I took my proctorship in earnest. Within the first week of my appointment, I had sent up a list of about 50 students for dress infringement rule. As a proctor, I could report students for misbehavior also in or out of the college premises, but such cases were few. This must have been a record, as I understand Professor Qureshi, who was our incharge, told other proctors about my accomplishment. Other proctors used to overlook the infringements of their friends or of others in order not to be unpopular, but I executed my duties with great zeal. This was remarkable for a Hindu, as normally Hindus were careful not to annoy their Muslim brethren who were in a great majority and were more aggressive as well. I at least got more money for the kitchen fund, as all the amount collected for fines went into that account and helped the college not to incure any loss on account of hostel messing, or at least reduced the amount of the loss. After the summer vacation, I found my name was not included in the proctor's list, not were the servant brothers visible. Justice had been done. The accusers and their lawyer were punished and this was obvious to everyone, but nothing was known about what had happened to the accused; perhaps he was honourably acquitted.

I had learnt at the U.O.T.C office, from the sergeant that I was being promoted to sergeant. It was at least some relief, as it would enable me to miss the morning roll call's parade. I however abstained from attending the parade after the vacation. I had got used to taking easy in the morning, as I was excused from attendance at the morning roll call taken by the superintendent, being a proctor. So every morning, the superintendent fined me half a rupee for my absence. In the college, half a rupee was the usual punishment for such offences. For not being in the proper dress also the punishment was half a rupee, whether one was not properly attired at the morning parade or in the college or outside it. Meanwhile, I had ascertained from Captain Felsted that I had been promoted to sergeant, and the list of new promotions would be shortly out. However, when for about 15 days I did not attend the morning roll call parade, the superintendent called for me, thinking I was most probably challenging the authorities. When I told him I had been promoted to sergeant (I had one day earlier seen my name on the list of promotion on the notice board the U.O.C'S office), he first showed surprise, most probably thinking I could not have been promoted under the circumstances. He then asked me to get him a copy of the order form the U.O.T.C'S, which I got him the next day.

Mahmood Ahmed had come from Kohat. However he looked more like from South India than from Kohat. He was a short man of about 5 feet 6 inches, of a thin built and dark complexion. He had sharp and well-chiselled features. He always spoke with intensity.

He had become our hostel superintendent, I think, in the summer of 1945. He was quite different from Adil Khan. While Adil Khan was gross, Mahmood Ahmed was a neat, tidy and precise man. Mahmood Ahmed did everything precisely. He spoke deliberately while Adil Khan spoke whatever came to his mind. Mahmood Ahmed Khan had a sharp intellect while Adil Khan was mostly brawn.

I do not know how it happened, but he liked me from our first meeting. Maybe because I was from Kohat the place he also came from but, most probably, I think, it was because I had an honest face, a sense of honour and was well informed that made him like me a little more than the others. He taught us Entomology in the 3rd and 4th years. He was a lecturer far above the run of lecturers we had come across in college. Even in practicals he was very good. He went through every detail with us. You could not goof off and get away with it when he was present. One could not talk frivolously in his presence. He had a sense of humour, but he was not loud. His humour also displayed his breeding and the sense of proportion he always maintained. All his students, even in the class before us, considered him a lecturer par excellence. Even in class, he behaved towards me as if I were one of his very promising students, even though, as was my habit, in the class I tried to remain in the background.

But this same Mahmood Ahmed attacked me vehemently in the Principal's office and was nearly the cause of my being thrown out of this college. I never held it against him, as he was doing his duty as I was doing mine. He got mad because he thought I had collected students in his hostel to protest against the inaction of the Principal. He thought I had let him down, the same as I thought inversely. I knew, Mahmood Ahmed would not do me any harm if he knew I was not guilty, as he was too good a gentleman to do otherwise.

He called me to his quarters one day after I had handed over to the Principal the copies of the offensive (to them) letter. He said that he had called me on our return from the U.O.T.C. camp and had enquired what had happened at the camp as some rumours were going round. I remembered he had asked that and I had told him what had happened. He had then inquired whether anybody from the hostel was involved and I had replied in the negative. He had then finished the conversation by saying that was good. He now asked me why I had not told him earlier about my part in it. I replied that he had asked about the involvement of anybody from the hostel, and nobody was involved. I had only reported the matter to the higher authorities, but I was not involved.

I never went to him and asked the reason for my removal as a proctor. I was too proud to do that. Mahmood Ahmed had a good espionage system in the hostel. If anything happened out of the routine in the hostel, he came to know about it through the servants. After the incident at the camp, we never had any Hindu servants again. A tall Muslim servant reported everything to Mahmood Ahmed. This servant was not designated as head bearer, but he acted as one. He always exercised his authority and refused food for an unexpected guest. But that was to others; he was submissive towards me. In the beginning, he was difficult once or twice but later on his behavior towards me became quite respectful. But my innocent movements also he saw with suspicion and reported them to the superintendent. One day, for example, during the examination days, I became tired of studying at about 1.30 P.M and went to another room, which had three boarders. Among other things, which we talked about, the subject of 'paranthas', which some boarders ate for breakfast in the morning, also came up. These three boarders were unhappy because the superintendent had stopped the serving of 'paranthas' which were in any case not included in the hostel cuisine. I cannot remember the exact position now. I might have said something in sympathy with them, as I am against the imposition of autocratic orders without consultation with the affected party. I had immediately surmised that the so-called head bearer was behind this move. The Superintendent would not have bothered about such things unless the bearers had complained. The next day I was called up before the Superintendent. He mentioned my visit to another room at 11.30 P.M. I thought he had called me for the infringement of the hostel rule that no boarder could go to another room after 10 p.m. After seeing my reaction, he stated that I was planning to start an application about the non-serving of 'parathas' and for that I was going to the rooms to mobilize support. I laughed and said I did not take 'parathas' and I went only to one room and not to all the rooms and that also was not to mobilize opinion in favour of an agitation. I told him that he was being misled by a bearer, who deliberately magnified everything to curry favour with him. I asked him to call the bearer concerned, and I would prove to him how he magnified things. He felt embarrassed, as instead of me he had become the accused. He said it was good that I was not involved, because the problem was that things sometime looked minor, but when I got involved they became important.

Irrespective of what happened, I always instinctively felt that he liked me. Once when I came back from the summer vacation, he called me to his quarters for tea, knowing that as I was not then organized, I would miss my tea, which was very much needed after my journey, if he did not offer it to me.

I would quote here an instant to illustrate how bad the communal situation was in N.W.F.P, especially in the premier institution of the province. In the college, apart from the Khyber Union, every year, elections were held for literary and scientific societies. On the science side, elections were held for the scientific society. The Agricultural Department had its own society, the Agricultural Society. In the autumn of 1945, at the instance of Opinder, I stood for election as secretary. The Head of Department of Agriculture used to be the official president. Opinder, who was junior to me by one year, was the assistant secretary. As the previous secretary had left the college after passing the 4th year examination, the nominations were to be given to Opinder. At the time I gave in my nomination (actually my dear and good friend Opinder did everything himself) there was no other nomination. If I had known that somebody else was also contesting the election, I would not have volunteered to contest it, as I did not consider the secretaryship important enough to spoil my peace of mind even for a day. However, later on, I came to know that Abdul Malik, my classmate and the brightest student in the class, was also contesting. It really came as a shock to me. If Malik could call anybody a friend in class or in college, it was me. I always took an interest in what he said while others sometimes even laughed at him. He could not be a friend to any other except to a student called Maulvi, because he considered them persons of no substance. I had somewhat a common background with him; both of us having come from rural areas. I was quite popular amongst the students of Agriculture, but I saw that not a single Muslim vote in my class would be cast in my favour. The only vote in a secret ballot from a Muslim, which I could expect, was from Maulvi Saheb. He was the roommate of Malik but he did not like him. He liked me very much, but in an atmosphere charged with communalism, he, perhaps, would not have given me his vote openly. He however was very unhappy with Malik for standing for election against me. Maulvi was a meek and simple person with a beard. He was blind of one eye. His friend and nephew in relation had hit him in his eye with an arrow. It was a child's mistake. His nephew asked him to hold a machine woven woolen cap in front of him as a target for the arrow, which his nephew was to shoot from his small child's bow, none of them realizing the serious consequence of that action.

I was not scared of Malik standing against me. I knew, with my popularity and the general impression prevalent that I was a good speaker and better than Malik in extra curricular activities and otherwise capable, that I would win hands down. It was only in the classroom that Hamid, one of my classmates, told me that I should not depend upon his vote, as he would vote for Malik as he was a Muslim. Hamid should have been the last person to vote for Malik, as he always teased Malik in class. Hamid was a small boy. He was small in build, short in stature and his head was also small, but he was very witty and jovial in a down-to-earth manner. His wit deserted him when the teacher was in the class and in a big gathering, but in a small gathering, among his friends, he gave his humor full rein. He had one man Friday; Bashir. Whatever Hamid said, Bashir dittoed it. Bashir was from Kohat City. The peculiar thing was that Bashir was a muscular chap and still he danced to the tune of that midget of a man, Hamid. This shows how a nimble brain can command brawn. When Hamid teased Malik, Bashir supported him. This was very convenient for Hamid, as Hamid was very scared of physical violence and Bashir's muscles guaranteed against any rough handling. Malik considered them both to be without any brains. They were at the bottom of the class. Bashir had the privilege of being the last in the class and Hamid followed him. Jugal, a Hindu classmate in the high school of Hamid, had left college just after completing one year in our class, not being able to pull on.

When Hamid said that he would not give me his vote, I knew Bashir would also do the same thing, though when the Muslim students of Kohat were mobilizing opinion against Ali in the Khyber elections, he had taken me to their meeting to ask me to vote against Ali in the name of a collective fight of the students of Kohat against the hegemony of the students of Mardan and Peshawar.But that day when Hamid said that he would not give me his vote, I looked at Bashir and asked him about his position in the case. Bashir, instead of giving me an answer, looked down and avoided meeting my eyes. I then knew that the pull of religious bond was greater than that of friendship and common citizenship.

The Muslims in the 1st year, 2nd year and 3rd year Agriculture classes also looked away when they met me, avoiding meeting my eyes. I knew that the message of solidarity of Muslims had gone round, and that the bond was too strong for me to beat. Actually, I then felt so disgusted that I lost interest in this contest altogether. There were five Hindus and one Sikh among a total strength of about 30 students in Agriculture. I was sure of 6 votes of the Hindu and Sikh students, as all of them were good friends of mine, being my hostel mates. Some students would not attend the elections, and there was the possibility of some Muslim votes coming to me in a secret ballot (though they may not have materialized for fear of disclosure). So, there was a possibility of a good fight, but the desertion of my friends had made me lose heart. I told Opinder about my intention. After some discussion, Opinder said we must ensure Malik's defeat even if I withdrew my name from the contest. We then asked Hamid to stand for election stating that I would withdraw in his favour. He agreed and gave in his nomination paper. I withdrew my nomination. Immediately after that Hamid withdrew his nomination also. So it meant Malik's unopposed election. I asked Hamid the reason for his treachery. He replied in his usual inimitable style, humorously smiling and saying that I was indulging in the usual Hindu game of dividing the Muslims, but he was not going to play my game. At this Opinder flared up. He said that Hamid had played a clever game, so we would reply in the same coin. He told Hamid Mr.Sehgal had not withdrawn. Hamid said how could he do that. Opinder said he could do that because I had not withdrawn my nomination. However, I felt bad, because after all I had withdrawn my nomination. I was entrapped into withdrawing my name by Hamid but that was my fault. When I persisted in my withdrawal, Opinder said that in that case he was entering his name for election. It was with great difficulty that I could persuade Opinder to desist from the latter course. Hamid said that I was planning to make Muslims fight among themselves, though this thought was the farthest from my mind.

Opinder knew of my relationship with Malik. He thought it was a betrayal on the part of Malik to stand against me. He wanted Malik to be defeated, and I entirely agreed with him. I am not sure whether this idea of putting up Hamid against Malik was Opinder's or mine, but we both agreed that it was the best way of defeating Malik, as I myself stood the least chance of doing it. Even otherwise Hamid's allegation was frivolous, and he knew it, as in elections in college it was always Muslims fighting Muslims. My case was an exception. But my nomination ensured Malik's unopposed election, as otherwise some other Muslim, most probably, would have stood against him, and I would have canvassed and voted for him. I am sure Malik would have done the same thing if some Muslim other than himself had opposed me. It was only self-interest, which drove Malik into the lap of communalists; otherwise Malik was a nationalist, a rare thing in college. It was because of his father, who was a 'khudai khidmatgar' and a staunch follower of Khan Abdul Ghafar Khan. Surakhposh and khudai khidmatgar denote the same individual. Surakhposh means the one who wears a red uniform, and khudai khidmatgar means the servant of God.

Malik was very religious. Maulvi was also very religious, but while he liberally interpreted religious injuctions, Malik meticulously carried them out. Malik came from a rural area. His father was a farmer. He was rustic in appearance, dress and manners. He gradually picked up some essentials of modern life of the middle class educated Indians, but his rusticity so clung to him that it had become a part, rather the main part, of his personality. However, my liberalism touched him. He knew people like me always talked of brotherhood of men, and I in particular said that according to Hinduism, man is known for his deeds and not which religion he belonged to. But according to the Koran, during a conquest, learned people, and the followers of Judaism and Christianity must be spared, but others would be asked to pay the Jezia and if they did not do that, they would be killed. He knew that I had read the Koran and knew something of Islam. One day we went out for a walk together. On the way aprops of nothing he said, 'You know, Hazrat Mohommad was born in Arabia. He knew about the Christians and the Jews as he came into contact with them and knew that they were learned people, but he had not heard of the Hindus and so did not know that they were a learned people, and so this injunction of non-learned being 'Kafir' and thus being liable to put to death did not apply to the Hindus. Malik was a conservative, and this interpretation from him was a big advance towards humanism and communal amity. At first I thought Malik would have thought of this interpretation himself, but then it occurred to me that it might have come from Frontier Gandhi, Khan Abdul Ghafar Khan, whose appeal to 'pukhtoons' (Pathans) was based on religion.

In 1945 our class went on its once a year tour of Punjab. We visited Lahore, Amritsar, Lyallpur, Multan and one or two other places. The whole tour was of about fourteen days. From Lahore we went to visit Kala Shah Kaku, a rice research farm. It was about seven miles from Lahore. Here the rice was grown on alkaline soil. The manager took us round. During this round I remarked about a variety 'jhona', which was mostly grown there, and wondered who would eat it. He said that today at lunch he would serve that rice to us and we should judge for ourselves. I told him I would not be able to eat it as I was a vegetarian and he would serve only meat. He said that I would definitely eat it, and I did. He served me rice and 'dal' (lentil). I was surprised that a coarse grained rice was that delicious. The grain of that rice was coarse with a red tinge on the surface. On top of it, it had more minerals than the finest variety of rice known; basmati. Basmati was aromatic, slim and good to eat. It came to me as a pleasant surprise that a coarse grained variety was richer in nutrients than a fine-grained rice. On our way back to Lahore, we got down from the train at a wayside station to see the Mausoleum of the Mughal Emperor Jahangir and his Queen Noor Jahan.

At Amritsar, we visited Khalsa College and its farms. Khalsa College was larger than Islamia College but I found Islamia College more impressive. It was quieter, cleaner, had a better lay out and over all created a better impression than Khalsa College.

I have visited other institutions as well, like Shanti Naketan, but in India, I have not seen a more impressive institution. It was marked to become the seat of a university. We knew when we were there that it would become a university within a couple of years. The partition of the country delayed, I think, the establishment of Khyber University, but this happened shortly after the partition, as was envisaged.

We also visited Multan. I liked the visit for historical reasons. In olden days Multan was an important city as were Lahore and Peshawar. The invaders from the northwest and north invariably tried to take Multan before going towards Delhi. Muhammad Bin Qasim attacked and conquered Sindh. In 712 A.D. the Arabs took Multan. In 713 A.D. Mahmood Ghaznavi also attacked and took Multan in one of his earliest raids. Muhammad Ghori took Multan in 1175. He subsequently attacked Delhi in 1192 and again in 1103 and took it in the second attack. Actually for the invaders from the north, after they crossed the Indus, Multan was the most important city before Delhi. Multan was quite a large city and was the centre of trade. My expectation of Multan was that of a small town, but I found it a large flourishing centre of trade.

It was near about Multan, I believe, that I came to know the traditional wisdom and the reservoir of knowledge, which our village folk possess. In one village, I commented to a farmer that I saw in that area they used country plough only and I wondered whether the use of 'Raja' plough would not be more useful as it inverted the soil and thus for each year or for each crop provided fresh soil. He said that my contention would be useful in areas where plenty of water was available but not in their area, as theirs was a 'barani' area, and if they used 'Raja' plough it would dig out the soil from the depth and thus make this exposure of more soil lose much of precious water, while their effort was to save as much water as possible. My classmates and I had not gained this knowledge of treating soil differently in different conditions from four years of reading books, while the common folk knew it because of their experience. The farmer was correct, it immediately occurred to me, as a country plough dug up to a maximum of 9 inches of depth, while the Raja plough (which was then a new invention) dug up an inverted soil up to a depth of 11/2 feet.

In the farmer's colonies, round about Layallpur, I came to the same decision that our people may need more resources, but they were not dumb farmers. They are the inheritors of age-old wisdom and experience. Those Sikh farmers delighted to talk to us at our level. They discussed every farming practice with us. They educated us about many things we did not know. They did not show any sense of superiority when they told us about their farming practices or rotations of cops, which we did not know, because they knew people learn from each other's experience. They offered us 'lassi' or cane juice, wherever it was available. This was the last tour from college in connection with my studies.

I liked these tours very much. On the one hand, they helped us to know much about the agricultural development taking place in Punjab, which was known to be the leading state in the country in this respect. On the other hand, we all, who came from villages or otherwise backward areas, got exposure to the world at large. I liked the opportunity to rough it out on the railway stations. Sleeping on platforms, under the stars in winter with only a quilt to cover you, (while at home we shivered even behind a bolted door) and this too when everything around you was in turmoil: people running about you, and even over you screaming and trains shrieking by was a novel experience. I enjoyed it because there was company to enjoy it with, otherwise it could be a harrowing experience. Sleeping on platforms alone, with the fear that somebody can take away your suitcase while you are asleep or that your train may pass by while you are sleeping without your being aware of it is quite distressing. Similarly, eating lunch or dinner at a dirty stall on a platform or spending night hours in an overcrowded compartment is not a pleasant contemplation, but company made it a pleasant experience, so much so that even writing about it more than four decades later makes one yearn for it.

I may mention that from Amritsar, we had made a day return trip to Batala to see the latest agricultural implements there.

In college one day I invited Captain Felsted for breakfast. I had invited our lecturer in economics, Shetty, also. I served them paranthas, stuffed with potatoes and cake. I kept the paranthas on the plates as they were brought in from the kitchen, but Shetty being more inexperienced in such things cut them into many pieces. Captain Felsted ate only half a parantha while we ate two paranthas each and some cake also. Later in the morning, I went to see Captain Felsted for some work. There were one or two other students also. While talking Captain Felsted kept on moving his right hand over his stomach and telling the students that he had eaten too much at my place. They asked my what I had given him. I told them that he had eaten only half a parantha. We all laughed at it, because it was not much, but Britishers not used to such greasy things naturally felt uncomfortable. This was after all flour fried in 'ghee'.

Professor Shetty had joined the college the same year he started teaching us. He, with his golden colour rimmed glasses, looked very handsome. He was soft-spoken and unaffected. He talked to us like a friend and not a lecturer. After all there was only a few years difference between our ages and his. One day he invited us to his place in the evening for tea. He lived with his family in his ancestral house in Peshawar City. It was an old but large house. He took us for tea to a room on the first floor. He served us quite a number of dishes. We had told him in advance that we would come only on the condition that he would serve us good food. He daily commuted between his house and the college. I do not know what mode of transport he used. Many day scholars used cycles and a few even used motorcycles.

Captain Felsted one day called me to his office, some time in the last quarter of 1945. When I reported in his office he suggested that we go to the city. While driving his jeep, he told me that he wanted me to meet Colonel Richardson. When we reached the bungalow, where Colonel. Richardson was staying, Captain Feltsted introduced me to him. It was only when Colonel Richardson started asking me about my educational qualifications that I understood that Captain Felsted had talked to him about me and he was expecting us, because he immediately, after the introduction, started talking to me about my particulars. After knowing the facts, he said that I first must take my degree, as only a few months of studies were left for this. According to him the war was over and there was no necessity for them to recruit more officers. He, however, noted down my name and address and told me that I would get a call for appearance before the Services Selection Board. So by then I would have sufficient time to make a decision about the matter.

Colonel Richardson, it seemed, was the talent spotter. Whoever he recommenced did not have to appear before a local selection board. He went straight for the final selection before the board.

I do not know why Captain Felsted took that much interest in me to recommend me for special selection. My own feeling is that he felt that the college authorities treatment of me was shabby in Adil Khan's case and he wanted to do what he could for me personally. He may otherwise also have formed an opinion about me that I was courageous and had officer like qualities. Many times in discussion with him I criticized the British policy in India, while my Muslim colleagues praised the British.

He invariably took my side. I am sure he must have wondered himself how could one talk against the interest of one's own country as my friends did. Felsted knew my interest as I borrowed many of his books on fiction and war, and occasionally there was some discussion. I think what Felsted did for me was an example of a sense of fair play on the part of an Englishman. When I went to Kohat during the Christmas holidays, my mother was very unhappy about my prospect of joining the army. Unhappy is euphemism for what she felt. She was actually very distraught. She told my grand uncle, Dewan Bhagwan Dass, who was in Kohat then. He came and lambasted me, called me a coward for not being sure of getting a job in civil and therefore going for a job in the army. I argued with him, but he neither changed his tone nor the content of his talk.

I received a call for an interview on 25th January 1946, but I did not go. In the beginning of 1946, General Shah Nawaz of I.N.A visited Peshawar. The Congress organized his tour. In the afternoon when he was to deliver his lecture, we mobilized ourselves and asked all the Hindu students to attend. We gathered all the Hindu students from the hostel while the day scholars promised to come directly to the chowk, the venue of the meeting. Everyone came willingly, as the trials of three I.N.A officers: General Shah Nawaz, Col. Sehgal and Col. Dhillon (all I.N.A ranks) which had taken place in the Red Fort, Delhi, only a couple of months ago had engendered great enthusiam. Even otherwise Subhash Chandra Bose was a great favorite with us. His raising of the I.N.A had made him even more popular with us, as after ages an Indian army was fighting to liberate the motherland. The next day pro-Congress papers mentioned that in the meeting students of Islamia college were present in full strength while others who believed in factual reporting stated that 70 students of Islamia college were present, which meant Hindu students were present in full strength while no Muslim student attended.

A couple of days later, Tehmasap again met me and said that they had played a trick for while no Muslim student had attended the meeting, people got the impression that they had attended. I said he could not stop us from attending a meeting if we chose to attend it. He said, we could attend it but without the sherwani or achkan. I told him that nobody could stop us from wearing any dress we more, but in this case, when we went to the city in accordance with the college's reputation, one had to wear a sherwani or achkan. Tehmasap said, he would put protest to the college authorities and take out demonstrations against our action. He departed on this note.

Islamia College had a unique position in N.W.F.P. It was not only the premier institute, or rather the only institute of standing in N.W.F.P, but was also the home of future politicians and leaders in the intellectual field. So when we went out in our achkans we carried the prestige of Islamia College with us and were accorded due respect by the people in the know of things. And that was the reason the nationalist press gave our attendance at General Shah Nawaz's meeting much vaunted importance. In this connection I am reminded of one incident, which I quote here to illustrate my point. In 1945, one day, our scientific association had organized a day return trip to Takhbai Sugar Mill in Mardan district, at that time the biggest sugar mill in Asia, and the Malakand Hydro electric project. I had also volunteered to go on this trip. We boarded a third class compartment of the train for Takhtbai at the Peshawar City station. After seeing the mill and the hydroelectric project, we were to come back by train in the evening. In the evening when we were waiting for the train somebody informed us that the bogies of the train were in the yard and the engine would be attached to them in about half-an-hour and then the train would leave. As we had nothing to do, and we were bored by the futile waiting we went to the yard. We saw there were a number of 1st class and 2nd class compartments in that train. A second-class compartment for us during those days was something to dream about and the 1st class was something we could not even dream about. Two or three second-class compartments were not even locked. As many of us could get in, got in and we waited for the train to start. Anyway, it was good to wait in second-class comfort. We had just settled down, when somebody shouted 'guard is coming'. We bolted from the compartment and watched from a safe distance like a monkey who waits from a distance for the gardener to depart to pounce on the fruit. The guard came. He unlocked all the first and second-class compartments and then looked at us and told us to get in. At first we hesitated. He said it again and added 'only the best for the students of Islamia College'. We all rushed into the compartments. I made a beeline for our old compartment, but others who could not get in earlier, got into the first class compartment. Lucky chaps!

In connection with Shah Nawaz's visit I may mention some more information to show the general mood of the people. My brother during this time was posted at Tonk. Shah Nawaz's tour itinerary took him there as well. Haridwar, my brother, was present at the meeting at which Shah Nawaz delivered his speech. While Shah Nawaz was speaking, a procession organized by the Nawab of Tonk passed near the venue of the meeting. The Nawab's followers were firing in the air and quite a number of shots were fired over the meeting. The procession went round the meeting, firing with rifles. According to Haridwar, Shah Nawaz looked guite perturbed. He announced a number of times during his speech that his visit was not connected with elections, which were than taking place in the Frontier and other states for legislative assemblies. His nervousness was so much that he had to sip water frequently. It is correct, Shah Nawaz's visit was not connected with the election, but I think, the Congress definitely took advantage of it for its own purpose. The Congress's bosses knew that there was widespread sympathy for the I.N.A. among the people of India. The Congress so cleverly organized the tours of known I.N.A. personnel that each one of them was sent to that place where he or she could get the maximum advantage for the Congress in that most important election which was being held about nine years after the first election, under the Government of India Act 1935, in 1937.

From the Hindu seat at Kohat a distant relative of mine stood for election, but ultimately he sat down in favor of a Congress candidate, Dr. Gulati, whose only credentials were that he was a favorite of Pir Shahanshah, the Congress boss of Kohat, and resident of Jungle Khel. Pir Shahanshah could not win even his own seat, but he was all powerful and could get anyone he wanted elected from the Hindu seats, because Hindus always voted for the Congress. Pir Shahanshah used Dr.Gulati's clinic as a place of meeting friends when in town. Dr. Gulati was handy for him to get his needy constituents free medicines and medical advice. After the partition of the country, Dr. Gulati took no interest in politics.

During these days, I saw Pandit Jawahar Lal Nehru, who had come there in connection with the elections, on an evening at the most important and renowned bazaar, Quasi Khan, where on 23rd April, 1930, crowds faced armored cars and cotingents and where in three hours firing, according to official files, 30 lives were lost although the non-official estimate was 200 to 250 (Modern India 1885-1947, Sumit Sarkar). Here also, a Garhwal battalion, composed of Hindus, refused to fire at demonstrators, all Muslim supporters of the Khudai Khidmatgar movement, as they could not fire on Indians.

Nehru at that time was either getting into a car or getting out of a car to go to go inside a place. Muhammad Yunus, the Chairman of the Trade Fair Authority now, was with him. It seemed Yunus, was looking after Nehru's arrangements. I recognized Yunus, as his family had come into prominence since the marriage of his brother Yaha Khan with the daughter of Khan Abdul Ghafar Khan. Yaha Khan was the Headmaster of the Islamia High School, Peshawar. Because of this marriage, there was an uproar in the Muslim circles in Peshwar, so much so that Yaha Khan had to resign his job. His job must have been an important one as his successor at that job was made the Director of Education. This marriage most probably took place in 1937, because I saw his successor, Shah Alam Khan, as Director of Education at Tehri on tour before the middle of 1939, when I migrated to Kohat. Yunus had played an important part in the social activities of the Islamia College, Peshwar, but I did not meet him there, as he had left college when I joined. I saw Yunus once again with Jawahar Lal Nehru the same year, but I will describe that event later in its proper sequence. However, it seems to me now that once having attached himself to the Nehru family, Yunus did not leave their company.

Muhammad Ali Jinnah came to our college, a few days after Shah Nawaz's visit. His visit was organized officially by the Muslim Students Federation, but the college authorities did everything, as people who ran the college were supporters of the Muslim League. Jinnah spoke for an hour. The refrain of his speech was that he had made everything possible. It was not about the Muslim League but about himself that he talked. He said some years ago Jawahar Lal Nehru spoke loudly that in India there were only two parties, the British Government and the Congress. Jinnah said that he had also spoken meekly like a lamb and said that there was a third party also, the Muslim League, but no one had bothered to pay attention. Yet today everybody recognized that they were very much there. He said they were saying that there should be an agreement and all the communities should live together, but they could not live in peace with the Hindus. How could they? The Hindus worship the cow and we eat it!

This was the most absurd logic one could have ever heard. Just because the Hindus worshipped the cow and he ate it, he could not live with them. A sensible answer would have been then do not eat cow. But let us take this logic to its logical conclusion, As Christians eat pig and Muslim abhor it, Muslim cannot live with Christians. Similarly, as Muslims eat halal meat and Sikhs jhatka, they cannot live with Sikhs either. If we extend this logic further, it means that Muslims cannot live with vegetarians over the world. Inversely it would mean that Muslims could live with Hindus who eat cow and there are many such, but a Muslim will not remain a Muslim if he becomes a vegetarian. The latter position is possible, as I became a vegetarian after being a strict non-vegetarian. I personally believe, no person can be a nature lover, humanitarian or animal lover without being a vegetarian. Love is universal. If a person claims to love human beings and humanism, he cannot truly do so when he is cruel to animals. Jinnah had based his argument for Pakistan on only one factor, in the Islamia College Peshawar, on cow eating. I wonder what would happen if tomorrow Muslims stopped eating beef for any of the numerous reasons such as the dicate of conscience, prevailing ethics, economy, or scarcity of cows. Would then the reason for the formation of Pakistan vanish? The irony was that when Jinnah was declaring, as Qaid-e-Azam of a Muslim nation (as he claimed), that Muslims could not live with Hindus because the former ate cows and the latter worshipped them, he was planning to leave half of the population of Muslims in India behind to live with cow worshippers. If the Hindus on the pattern of Pakistan had declared India a Hindu state and banned cow slaughter, Muslim would have had to live with it too.

What pained me more was the applause Jinnah got repeatedly for such utterances. There has been a mention in the press a couple of times recently that had Jinnah lived a little longer, Pakistan would not have been declared a Muslim state. This is mentally painting in pleasant colour what is actually lurid in actuality. What I saw of Jinnah in Isalmia College and read about him does not make him a liberal leader. He remained all through his political career a communal minded though not a practisting Muslim leader. He was a first class politician who all along waited for an opportunity, and when it came along he took advantage of it. He had never thought of Pakistan earlier. His idea earlier was to get the best terms possible from the Hindus for an understanding. He was a constitutionalist lacking widespread support and effective field organization. When he failed to make any worthwhile impact on the political scene, he retired from it and settled down in London after the second round table conference. He came back in 1936 when he saw that a constitutional experiment, under the Government of India Act, was being launched. In the 1937 elections the Muslim League could manage to get only 2 out of 84 seats reserved for the Muslims in Punjab, 3 out of 33 in Sindh and none in the N.W.F.P. It was only after the 1937 election debacle that the Muslim League revival in U.P. started and it was the Muslim League of the United Provinces and leaders like Khaliq-Ur-Rehman who constituted the main force behind the movement for Pakistan and it was they alone who made Pakistan ultimately possible, otherwise, the Muslims of the provinces, which were to constitute Pakistan, nearly until the end did not support the call for Pakistan.

The fallacy of Jinnah's argument can be seen from the fact that East Bengal is now no longer a part of Pakistan. N.W.F.P. and Baluchistan are not happy. They can never fit into an association where Punjab is predominant. It even seems that the people of Sindh are smarting under the domination of Punjab. The armed fights between the Pathans and the Mahajars, refugees from the erstwhile United Provinces at Karachi, presently taking place in Karachi show that commonality religion or the practice of beef eating cannot replace common culture, social practices or a common sharing of life spread over centuries.

Abdul Qyum, an erstwhile leader of the Congress also spoke. He had changed over to the Muslim League sometime before the arrival of Muhammad Ali Jinnah. He was an orator of the highest order. He could rouse an apathetic crowd to great frenzy. He earlier used his vituperative speech against the British and the Muslim League, but I saw him that day use it against the Hindus and the Congress. It seemed that day during the speeches of Jinnah and Abdul Qyum that India was not under the domination of the British but that of the Hindus and they had done great damage to the Muslims.

Abdul Qyum was a Kashmiri but he looked and acted like a fearsome Pathan. He had a doubtful reputation. The Khan brothers Abdul Gafar Khan and Dr. Khan Saheb did not trust him. Therefore they sent him to the Central Legislative Assembly, rather than giving him an important berth in the provincial ministry, to keep him away from mischief. Perhaps that could be the reason for his resentment. After the meeting was over, the people remained there to chat with each other. Brij Lal Kaul, my class fellow and neighbour in the hostel, as we both had occupied the two adjacent cubicles in our fourth year in college, later on told me very agitatedly that he had asked Abdun Qyum in a conversation after the meeting what should Kashmiris do in the political situation prevailing then. Abdul Qyum replied that there was no way out for them but to assassinate the then Maharaja. Brij Lal, not expecting such advice, stated that he was a Hindu. On hearing that, Abdul Qyum kept quiet in embarrassment. He most probably thought that anyone wearing a blue sherwani would be a student of the college. He did not realize that a Hindu student of Islamia College would attend the Muslim League's meeting. But this incident shows what sort of politicians the League had at that time and what type of mental calibre they had to think that assassinations could achieve their political aspirations. Besides mental calibre, it shows the type of mentality and the perverse thinking of the Muslim League politicians of that day.

A few days later Tehmasap met me by chance. I asked him why he had not taken any action in the matter of our participation in the reception to General Shah Nawaz. He replied that they had thought that if they did anything in that matter we might retaliate by arranging hostile demonstrations against Jinnah when he came for the meeting. I asked him whether he really thought that. He said yes, they were afraid of that. It came as a surprise to me. The Hindus even otherwise are docile but we Hindus of the Frontier were meek like lambs. We were always afraid of the Muslims. No Hindu ever got involved in a quarrel with a Muslim. He avoided it at all cost, and ironically here, the Muslim students in Islamia College, who were the bastions of the most conservative elements of the Frontier, the Khans and the landlords, who were at the back of the Muslim League, were afraid of the reaction of a few unknown Hindu students. Here the tigers were afraid of lambs for the sake of the honour of their Qaide Azam.

Before I conclude this chapter, I must record here that when Malik stood against me for the post of the secretary of the Agricultural Society, our professors in Agriculture, Mustaq Sarwar and Tufail were very unhappy that students were going to vote for the candidates on communal lines. By the time Mushtaq came to know about it, I had already withdrawn my nomination. However when he showed his displeasure on communal line voting and said that students should vote only on the merits of the candidates, I told him that I had withdrawn from the contest. He was, as were all the Muslim students, happy that communal line voting was avoided, but from Mushtaq's countenance it appeared that he knew that I had withdrawn from the contest not as a good will gesture toward Malik but due to communal pressure.

As for my class fellows; Malik was selected as Assistant Conservator of Forests by the Punjab Public Service Commission in 1946 itself. Maulvi went for higher studies to the U.K. Hamid had left college before graduation to become a pilot in the Indian Air Force. According to Brij Lal Kaul, Hamid had become a Wing Commander in the Pakistan Air Force in the sixties when he met him at Delhi Airport. Brij Lal himself was Assistant Director, Gardens, in the Archaelogical Survey of India, when I met him in Srinagar in 1979. Opinder was one year junior to me, but I will mention him here as he was a friend. He was Secretary, Warehousing Corporation of India when I met him in 1979

Chapter Six

A PERIOD OF TRANSITION

I came back to Kohat after the completion of my studies. My uncle had gone on transfer to Murree about a couple of years earlier. My brother had been transferred from Tonk to Haripur in the Hazara district. My mother and sister-in-law lived in the same house, which mother and I had shared with my Uncle Shambhu Dass. Now, of course, there was a third person living with them, my nephew, and the son of my brother, who was born in 1945. He was named Avinash.

In June 1946, I went to Murree, a hill station, on the invitation of my uncle, for a few days. As luck would have it, during the few days I was there, Jawahar Lal Nehru passed it on his journey to Srinagar. Nehru's trip came about all of a sudden. Sheikh Abdullah, Sher-i-Kashmir, as he was called by the people of the Kashmir valley, had launched a movement for self-rule. As the movement gained strength and there were huge demonstrations of the people against the Maharaja's rule, the Maharaja appointed Ram Chand Kak, who believed in repressive measures to crush the movement, as the Prime Minister of the Jammu and Kashmir state. Sheikh Abdullah was arrested and repressive measure were instituted immediately on his appointment. When Nehru heard about the Sheikh's arrested, he left for Srinagar to show his solidarity with the Sheikh and the people of Kashmir. The whole country was agog with excitement and wondered what would happen; whether Nehru would be arrested and repressive measures would continue or would the Maharaja allow Nehru to do what he wanted unhindered. I read about Nehru's expected trip to Kashmir the same day he was passing Muree enroute. When I heard in the morning that he would be passing Muree at about 11 a.m. or so, I had just a chance to reach the road on which he was supposed to pass. I immediately started to go down the hill to reach the road. It was a downhill journey of about two miles. I went down in line with the slope of the hill; enroute I saw many others going and I followed them. Most probably if we had gone by road, the distance to the Rawalpindi – Srinagar Road would have been two miles. We went down more or less running as time was short and it seemed to be a matter of touch and go. It proved to be factually so, as no sooner had we reached the roadside than Nehru's car arrived. The car stopped on seeing us. As I was in the front, I could clearly see the occupants. I saw Nehru with Yunus in the back seat. There were two others also in their car but I could not recognize them. After about a couple of minutes the car started again. There were not many people there and nor was there any demand from them asking Nehru to speak and neither was there any garlanding. Perhaps the time was too short for people like those who do garlanding or anything else to make themselves visible.

In the beginning of winter I went to Peshawar to appear before the Punjab Public Service Commission for the post of Assistant Conservator of Forests in the Forest Department. There were only six or seven posts but only one was reserved for the Hindus. One year earlier also interviews were held for these posts and for the post reserved for the Hindus, Manohar Lal, brother of my brother-law, Seth Nand Ram, who was M.Sc. in Botony was selected, through an approach made to a member of the Punjab Public Service Commission, who was a Sikh gentleman from Rawalpindi and was known to a Sikh leader of Kohat. However, Manohar Lal had not been called for training until this time.

When I was going for my interview for the post, his family thought that as he had once been selected he would be called. So, my brother-in-law and one of his brothers said that I was unnecessarily going, as their brother had been selected and he was bound to be called against the quota reserved for the Hindus. However, I went for the interview. I knew during the interview itself that I had done badly. The Sikh gentlemen in the commission asked me what wood hockey sticks were made of. I did not know it nor had I bothered to gain knowledge about it, not even before the interview. I guessed and replied to the question, stating that hockey sticks were made of teak wood, as one very often heard that name. The Sikh gentleman guffawed and the other members also responded by smiling. I was dismissed in a couple of minutes. Though I knew that I had done badly, still I had hope, as I felt that while the Sikh gentleman may be running down other Hindu candidates, the others may decide on merit. Though I should have known that when every member wanted his candidate to go through, they all would help each other to succeed in their aim.

In the evening I want to Islamia College to refresh my memory of my Alma Mater. I spent the night with Opinder. In the evening I met Malik by chance while roaming about. He had also come for the interview. We spent quite some time together. He was in good spirits. He kept on smiling throughout. He normally did that when the tension of preparing for the examinations was not there. However, that day, from his jovial talk I knew he had been selected in the interview. So, I told him what I felt. He admitted that he had been selected. I knew if he said so it would be true due to the nearness of his father to Dr. Khan Saheb, the Chief Minister of N.W.F.P. He asked me about my future plans. I told him that I would first wait for the result of the interview for the post of Assistant Conservator of Forests and decide after it was out. He asked me not to waste time and try for something else. When, inspite of my assertion repeatedly that I would wait for sometime for the result of my interview, he went on saying that I should look for other avenues, I suddenly asked him, before taking leave of him on the road where he had come with me from the hostel he was staying in, whether he knew the result of our interview. After some hedging, he came out openly and stated that he knew the whole result, and that I had not been selected. He told me that against the Hindu quota, one Chuni Lal had been selected. I remembered that when I had gone for the interview, I had met one gentleman with the same name there from Dera Ismail Khan.

The next day, when I went to Kohat and passed my brother-in-law's chemist shop, which he was running with one of his younger brothers in the cantonment, my brother-in-law saw me and called me in. As I expected, he was anxious to know about my interview. He and his brothers were worried that I may supplant their brother from his rightful position. The brother concerned was the youngest. The one working with my brother-in-law was elder to the youngest brother but younger than my brother-in-law. My brother-in-law and his brother wanted to know about my performance, as they could not have guessed that I had come to know even the name of the person who had been selected. When I told them about that, at first they both were dumbstruck, then the younger brother, who was of a volatile temperament, burst out into invectives. He told his elder brother that all polticians and members of the Public Service Commission were alike. According to him, a bribe must have been paid, as that was the only criterion these people understood and that was their sole motivating force.

In the same connection, I would like to mention another incident to show how little faith even then people had in fair play, justice and equity. I attended three U.O.T.C. camps. The second was at Landikotal. At that camp, one day we were taken for firing practice. After some practice, we were given a demonstration in the battle of innoculation. It was the creation of a battle situation for the training of the troops. In the first exercise, Captain Felsted, Adil Khan, Abdul Razaq and two others were taken. These five marched in a line on a flat ground, while we all watched from a rock above. These five marched, rather walked loosely, in a single line abreast straight ahead. On the ground they were to trespass there were white lines, parallel to the line of their formation, at some selected locations, at varying distance to each other but at an average distance of about eight yards. While these five walked in their full battle dress with rifles, from a projecting shoulder of the rock, where we were standing, some soldiers were firing all around them with machine guns and rifles. They were firing very close to those five advancing to their destination. From the flying of the sand or earth, where the bullets hit, we could see how close the bullets were to them. However, the five kept up their uninterrupted advance at the same speed. The most awe-inspiring spectacle was when the shooters shifted their line of firing and started firing at the line (white), which the advancing party was to reach. The accurate firing on the line was continued right unto the time the party was to cross over the line, but by the time the men's feet came down on the line and crossed the line, the firing had shifted ahead of them. The white lines appeared to us as death traps. As the party neared the white line, we all, who were watching, held our breaths, though we knew that none in the party would be hit. Every time the men reached one step from a line, everyone stopped breathing, because no body was sure whether in the next moment all or anyone of the advancing party would be alive. We all thought that the soldiers firing the machine guns could set their machine guns accurately, but who could be sure of a rifleman. Even the best marksman cannot be always 100 per cent right, especially under strain. The army must have been employing their best marksmen for that job. And, of course, the persons who formed the advancing party must have been scared all the time.

After the above party came back, volunteers were asked from the cadets for the battle in innoculation. I was among the ten or twelve of those who volunteered for it. But they selected five persons seniority wise. I was not among them. One cadet, Zafar, who had been nominated, refused to go in for the exercise. I do not know how he was selected in the first instance. Maybe he had volunteered in the first instance, but later on backed out when nominated. Another cadet went in his place. I wondered to the people about me why he had refused such a good chance of this unique experience of walking under the shadow of bullets. Abdul Razaq, Assistant Director of Physical Training of the college, who was sitting nearby remarked that Zafar's father was a member of the Punjab Public Service Commission. He would be easily able to get him selected in the Province's Civil Service, so why should he run the risk of being shot. All others who were sitting near about concurred with him. I am sure Zafar also heard him, but he did not speak. It came to me as a surprise, to hear that only those participated in such exercises who were seekers of a career in the military, while I always thought people did those things for adventure. I had never thought of adopting the military as a career. The first time I thought of it was when Captain Felsted, on a later date, took me to Lt. Col. Richardson, and that too because I wanted a job soon in order not to be a burden on my brother any longer. To a slightly lesser extent, one motive was adventure. A job, which I was not seeking, was being offered to me and so by accepting it, on the one hand, I would be showing my appreciation of the efforts put on my behalf by Captain Felsted, and on the other, I could have adventure in the army for a short period. I narrated this incident here only to support my belief that in British times one could not get anything done from the government, except through approach or bribe, barring the intervention of many indiviual upright and enlightened British officers.

One day, after getting fed up with not doing anything useful or more correctly not doing anything remunerative as otherwise I was quite usefully employed reading quite a number of useful books, in January 1947 I went to Peshwar from Kohat to meet the Minister of Agriculture, Mehr Chand Khanna, in order to request him to send me for further studies to the Indian Agricultural Research Institute at Delhi at the government expense. During those days it was difficult to meet any bureaucrat, forget about meeting a minister. However, I went to his office. His private secretary, who knew me through my brother, sent my name chit in and I was called in after about ten minutes. Mehr Chand Khanna had a very forbidding appearance. He had a weatherbeaten face with wide eyes and a very bold stare. His voice when he spoke was full and had a loud Punjabi resonance. After I had told him of my errand, he asked what right did I have of coming to him with such a request. At first I was taken aback at this grating response, but then I said that I had come to see him as a citizen. He then said that everybody was a citizen. I replied that everybody had not come to see him for what I had come. I told him that I had come to him with a request; if he could do it on merit that would be fine, otherwise it was all right. He then asked why I had not come with an M.L.A. (Member Legislative Assembly). I asked him whether he would have done my job if I had brought an M.L.A. with me. He said it was not like that. He was just asking. I said that I did not feel it necessary to bring an M.L.A. I was already on my feet when I uttered my last sentence. After completing the sentence, I started walking off. At that very instant Khanna got a phone call. He picked up the phone and gestured for me to sit down. While sitting, I realized he was talking to the Director of Agriculture. After talking to him for a minute or so, he asked him what was the policy of the Department in the matter of sending students to the Agricultural Research Institute. After hearing the Director, he said that he did not consider it a good policy to send only the officials for such training. He said that he felt that they should advertise the vacancies in the papers, and after receiving the applications, select the best candidates. I heard the Director's reply while he was talking to the Minister on the telephone.

The Minister, after talking to the Director, put down the receiver and said to me, " Son, look you heard what the Director said. I was very much in favour of sending the best man for the postgraduate training, but the director does not agree. He says that even from outside we would send graduates in Agricultural and departmental candidates would also be B.Sc. Agriculture, and so if we send outsiders, there would be great resentment in the department. It would be best if you joined as Assistant in the department, of which there would be no problem, as are were a number of vacancies there because of post war development schemes. Once you joined there, we would see what could be done for you."

I thanked him and left his office. The next day I went to the Islamia College, Peshawar. I met my Professor of Botany. I told him of my decision to join the Department of Agriculture. He felt let down. He said that I used to make fun of the Department of Agriculture and its research, and now was joining the same department. I told him that it was a temporary arrangement just to make a living and that I would get out of it as soon I got an opportunity as I would be trying for better jobs outside while working at that job. But he was not convinced, as according to him, 'once you get into a job, you had it for your entire career, because jobs suck you in so hard, it becomes impossible to leave them.' Muhammad Sarwar, whom I met a little later, said the same thing, but in his inimitable style. He said I used to talk big, where was that talk now. When I told him of my financial limitations, he said that I was not starvng, was I? He then asked me to remember my big talk. In the evening, I met Mahmood Ahmed. He took me to tea. He also felt let down. He said that what I said about trying for better jobs, while working at the Agriculture Department, looked good in concept, but it would not work in practice. He said, once I got a job my family would get me married, and once I got married, I would get trapped, and would not be able to leave a secure job for greener pastures elsewhere. That night I talked to my friends, so I had no time to contemplate on what my professors had said earlier on during the day, but the next morning, I felt my chest congested with despair. On the return journet on a tonga to the cantonment, I had a great sense of helplessness. I knew I was in a trap. My ambitions were alive within me, but the necessity of earning a livelihood was stronger than the reality of ambitions. At that time, more than for myself, I was sorry for letting down my professors. I really had not known that they believed in me more than I did myself. They must have found in me a refreshing contrast from an ordinary intelligent and studious student. They most probably saw in me a could not care less student who did not study hard but managed to get good marks; who had high ambitions and did seem to give an impression of achieving them. They were normally used to thc ordinary run of the mill student who did everything according to expectations. They found me rather fascinating from my talk of improving everything I found bad in society; the educational system, the agricultural society, foreign rule or the lack of character in the Indians of our day. At that time I did not care for anything else except to get their trust restored in me.

The next morning, I went to Tarnab Farm, the premier research institute of the Department of Agriculture, N.W.F.P. as well as its headquarter, and met the Director of Agriculture, Mr. Shah. He said that he had a number of vacancies and I could join any day I liked. I joined the same day. He gave me the charge of looking after the draught bullocks and the growing of fodder. The person who was looking after them earlier had been given a research job. The Director told me that as bullocks were fed in the evening and given concentrates, I should stay at the farm to supervise the feeding, as otherwise the headman was very likely to steal the concentrates. This looked to me a difficult situation, as I had no utensils to cook food in, nor did I have any bedding or any servant to cook for me. I knew from the very beginning I had been put in a difficult situation. The situation was further complicated as I was mentally not prepared to live in a place away from a population center. I did not have even a single book, while one needed a good stock of them for living in such a place. Worst of all, I did not feel inclined to procure all the stuff. On the first day, I requested the person I had relieved, Jameel, to supervise the feeding on my behalf. He smiled and said that he was sick of that job, but he agreed to do it for me for a few days. He told me that meanwhile I should prepare to shift to the farm.

At Pehawar I was living with my aunt, whose family I had visited at Mansehra and Abbotabad. My uncle had been transferred there as an S.D.O. (sub divisional officer) in P.W.D. He had a house on rent in a nice locality in Peshawar cantonment. His next door neighbor was a Judicial Commissioner, one of the two top most legal officers in the province, there being no high court in the province. The high court at Lahore, Punjab, was the appellant authority against the decision of the Judicial Commissioner. Every morning my cousin, Gangadhar, used to take me to the spot in the city, from where the Tarnab farm bus used to start. I think, only about a dozen persons went there every morning from Peshawar. From that spot, Tanab farm was seven miles on the main Peshwar-Rawalpindi Road. My uncle's house was about two miles from the starting point of the bus. I had a good time there. Every evening after my return from the farm, Gangadhar and I used to go for a walk in the cantonment area. Sometime, we used to go to the movies.

I did not have much of western clothing. In my school days, I had decided not to use western clothes at all until India became independent. So I used to wear a shirt and salwar to school and to college, with a jacket or achkan, which was my college uniform, and shoes or peshawri chappals, as necessary. My headdress in college, whenever I used one, was a 'qaraqul' cap in light and dark gray shades. It was of a very good quality and highly priced. Even in those days when the price structure was not that much blown up as it is today, it was stated to be about Rs. 300/-. I discarded this cap somewhere around 1950 mostly because I stopped wearing caps, and to a lesser extent because that cap was a product of cruelty. This nagging guilt complex remained with me all the time I had been wearing it. Once, I did not wear it for a few days. I could not pick it up to wear as that cap had cost a new born calf, or possibly an unborn calf and its mother, their lives. These are the strange quirks of conscience that I knew the origin of my cap, I condemned this practice of obtaining 'Qaraqul' skins, but still I wore that cap, assuaging my conscience that I was not responsible for that deed; the deed was already done when I came into the picture and so there was harm in making a cap of that skin, but still the guilt complex remained in me. I still do not know how much a part did my guilt complex play when I actually discarded that cap. It shows how hypocritical I was, within myself, to subvert my conscience. So, when I see the super abundance of hypocrisy of my countrymen, I realize how much a part hypocrisy has become of each one of us, even though sometimes others may fail to realize it.

In the summer of 1946, Haridwar, my brother, got stitched for me two pairs of trousers for the summer, saying it was time for me to possess some. I broke the faith, which I had made to myself that I would not wear trousers until India was independent. Though I knew that I had failed in my resolve, I was later on happy, as these two pairs of trousers came very handy. To be truthful, a salwar is not a good dress for a workingman and nor is it smart. Though, I had started wearing trousers, I did not have many trousers or suits. Gangadhar, my cousin, had a good number of suits, and he gave me full freedom to use them. Actually, every evening, he and his sister, Kunta, forcibly dressed me in a different suit and tie before I went out. So, because of the generosity and the dress sense of these two cousins, I was one of the best dressed men in Peshawar at that time.

I did not carry any lunch with me to Tarnab farm, but during lunchtime, I used to go to the house of a senior Agricultural Assistant, Manan. He was a bachelor from Hangu, District Kohat. He had accomodation of two or three rooms with a large courtyard. We used to sit around in the sun in the courtyard and gossip. Old people called the sunlight in winter in N.W.F.P., the fruit of winter. Even otherwise, sometimes I used to go to his house when Manan was at home. There were always one or two other agricultural assistants like me there. Manan was a very good person and that made him quite popular. He liked me; rather he took me under his wing. He himself volunteered, a couple of days after I joined the farm, that in my absence he would supervise the feeding of the bullocks. In the farm, all Hindu officers were called 'Lala Saheb'. Lala has a connotation of 'bania' (trader). The word trader is a respectable word but bania in the vernacular is not. It smacks of moneylending and the cheating of peasants while weighing goods. One day, one Agricultural Assistant, senior to me in college and who also used to come daily from Peshawar, addressed me as 'Lala Saheb'. I objected to it. He said brashly that I was a Lala and so he would call me Lala. Manan just remarked in general in his insouciant manner that I was right, as I was not a Lala because I did not belong to a shopkeeper's family, and so if somebody wanted to call me anything other than my name, it would be appropriate to call me Dewan Saheb, as my family members were Dewans. This hushed up that uncouth fellow, but did not please me greatly, as I had tremendous aversion to being called 'Lala Saheb'. I am glad that nobody called me Lala Saheb ever, except for this incident. In N.W.F.P. it was a common practice for Muslim subordinates to call their Hindu superiors Lala. Sometimes one's colleagues also did that.

In Tarnab Farm, besides the Director, there were two officers. One was Thareja and the other was Ranjan. Thareja was a sugarcane specialist. Ranjan became a class two officer during my short tenure there. He had become a fruit fly scheme officer. The grades of these officers were not very high. Even the Director did not have a very good grade. My office space was in a laboratory, where I, along with Jameel and a senior assistant, used to sit. One day, while I was working on my stock register with my back to the entrance door, the Minister of Agriculture, along with the Director of Agriculture, entered the room. At first I did not realize who had entered the room, but later on I realized, from the voices and the fact that my other two colleagues had stood up, that the Minister and the Director had entered, but I did not get up as my back was towards them and I was not supposed to know who had entered the room and so I continued to work at my figures. Later on, at lunch break, Jameel asked me why I had not got up. Before I could answer Manan, repying on my behalf, asked why I should have got up. I had been working and I had continued to do so. If the Minister had asked me something I would have got up. However, I think, my reputation had spread that I was not one of the run-of-the-mill officers.

While I was working in Taranb farm, I saw an advertisement in a newspaper, about a one-year course in Horticulture for graduates in science, by the Fruit Development Advisor to the Government of India. I saw the Director about it as some candidates were to be sponsored by the provincial government. He stated that I could not hope for any such course for a few years, being the junior most. Later on Manan told me that an Agricultural Assistant, Sayeed, had been nominated for that course. I however, applied for the course directly. A month or so after I has sent my application, I took three days leave; two days were without pay. I went to Delhi to plead personally before the Fruit Development Advisor for the course. My childhood friend, Dayanand, who was at that time working as an insurance agent in Peshawar, came to see me off at the railway station. When I was sitting in a third class compartment and talking to Dayannad through the open window, he jokingly remarked that I was sitting in the 'gadandai'. Gadandai is a pushto word meaning fast. It also means fighter. How appropriate that word was, neither he nor I myself knew at that time, but since then I have been fighting all along outside forces that I cannot bear, or perhaps which are against my natural impulses, or both.

On arrival in Delhi the next evening, I stayed in a hotel in Fatehpuri, as I was familiar with that area, having stayed in a hotel there when I visited Delhi in my third year, with my classmates, on a training tour. The next morning, I went to the office of the Fruit Development Advisor, G.S.Cheema, which was situated in a barrack, near the Central Secretariat. He was on tour to the Andamans. So, I enquired about his Deputy, Sham Singh, but he was also on tour. So, I met the Assistant Director. His name, as I recollect, was Lal Singh. He was a fat Sikh with blunt manners. When I met him, he asked me why he should select me. I replied that as far as he was concerned, according to him, he had to select about a dozen prospective trainees from the open market, so why should he not select me as I had come from Peshawar rather than somebody else who was indifferent and had not even tried to get into the course. He did not give me any encouragement, but I always have faith in the judgemnt of blunt persons.

When I came out of the office of the Fruit Development Officer, I realized I had apparently seemed to have spent the little money I had to no purpose. While coming back to my hotel in a bus, I saw a poster about a convention of the Indian Science Congress from the window of the bus. The poster mentioned the visit of Pandit Nehru and General Aung Sang of Burma at the convention. In the evening, I left for the convention, without knowing the route to the University where the convention was being held or the date and time of the visit of the above mentioned celebrities. But all worked out well. After I reached the convention, Nehru and General Aung Sang arrived. Nehru himself was chaperoning the youthful general. Nehru immediately, on arrival, brought the general onto the stage. Pandit Nehru looked smart and exuberant, but it was General Aung Sang with his youthful figure, handsome smiling face, sprightly gait, resplendent in his well-cut uniform and its golden adornments, who was the cynosure of all eyes. General Aung Sang was a legendary figure, who first colloborated with the Japanese to drive away the British, but when because of the vicissitudes of fortune, the Japanese position in Burma had become untenable, he turned against the Japanese and added to the British efforts in driving them out of Burma. In this way, due to his sagacity, he was able to maintain his military presence in Burma after the departure of the Japanese. The British, unable to subdue him, left Burma altogether and thus at the end of World War II, Burma emerged as an independent nation like Indionesia.

After about a month of my return from Delhi, I met the Director, as it had occured to me that though I did not have much chance of being selected, still I should be ready, if it came, to ensure that he would put no obstacles in my way in the matter of my relief. He stated that I could not apply for any training or job without his approval, and in case I applied through him, he would not forward my application, as he himself was very much short of staff. I then said a bit vehemently that he could not expect me to spend my whole career in that hole. He said that was for me to think over. I asked him that if he came to know that I had applied directly for training or for a job, then what would be his reaction. He stated that I would get a black mark in my character roll. I then told him about my application for the post graduation horticulture training class. He said that he knew about that, as he had come to know that the leave I had taken was for going to Delhi and not for another work. I had not mentioned in my application that I was going to Delhi and he had guessed the purpose of my visit. I am sure Manan must have told him about the purpose of the leave, as Manan also had come from the same village, Hangu, as the Director. I asked the Director what should I do about the job or training I had already applied for directly. He said that I should resign before I got a letter for training or for a job, and once I had gone no would bother. However, I was not to tell anyone that he had told me that.

The Director of Agriculture, M.I.Shah, was known to be strict and ascerbic in temperament, but he had been nice to me. Once or twice, when he met me, he reminded me that I had to shift to the farm, but he did not issue an order that I had to shift to the farm by a given date. He had, I think, come to realize that I would not shift to the farm, for when I was talking to him, in the meeting mentioned above, he said that he did not know what I saw in the Horticulture course as the place where the course was being held, Mirpur Khas Sindh, was not known as a fruit growing centre. Secondly, there did not seem to be to a good horticulturist with the Fruit Development Advisor to make the course worthwhile. Thirdly, I would not get any benefit for that course in the province, as the agriculture department went by seniority and it sent its own officers whenever a specialized opening occurred in the department. He further said that the scheme for the control of pests on the fruit trees had come into being and Rajan had been appointed as officer in charge of the scheme, and I was being posted as fruit fly inspector of Kohat. I would get Rs. 100 per month as salary as usual and Rs. 40 per month for the office permises. I could take a house and use it as an office cum residence. He advised me to take up that job as I would be able to manage in my salary comfortably well. He said that he was posting me at my home town to give me an opportunity to settle down, and for the same reason, inspite of the pressure on him to post somebody else there, he was posting me. He said, he was sure I would get opportunities for a better course in the future than the one I wanted to go for. Manan had earlier told me that one agriculture assistant, Ved, who was from Kohat and whom I knew well, had written to the Director for the post at Kohat and the new fruit fly scheme officer had also recommended his name, and he was accordingly being posted at Kohat. It meant that Manan had not heen correctly informed about the last piece of information. At that age and time, however, I was not looking forward to settling down at a cushy job. I, therefore, told the Director that I wanted to resign, as I did not want to take a risk of the Director not forwarding my applications in the future. The Director wanted to bind me to my post, while I wanted freedom of action in case of an opportunity arising in the future. I, therefore, told the Director that I wanted to resign. He asked me to give it in writing, which I did there and then.

When I came out of the Director's room and handed over my accepted resignation letter to the Office Superintendent, as directed by the Director, the Superintendent gave me back that letter as well as my appointment letter to Kohat and asked me to choose whether I wanted to pick up my appointment letter or hand over my resignation letter. For a few seconds I was in suspense wondering what to do, for even though I had decided to resign and had actually resigned, but when a choice was given to me again in the shape of the letters, to choose between two alternatives of accepting a comfortable job in my home town or having freedom of action and hope for a better job sometime in the future, I hesitated because giving up something tangible was painful when there was no sign of reward in the immediate future and I would be without a job then. But I handed over both the letters, without the minimum of delay, to the Superintendent, and thus I had become a man without a job again on 21st January, 1947, after a service of less than three months, as I had joined the Department of Agriculture on 2nd November, 1946.

Manan also thought that even if my admission to the course in Horticulture came through it would not amount to much, as Mirpur Khas Sindh was not a place to hold a course. He thought that if a course in Horticulture was to be held, it should be held in N.W.F.P.which abounded in fruit. According to even my own limited knowledge then, I had not heard of any fruit which Sindh exported to any other province, while N.W.F.P., because of its varied climate and terrain, produced a variety of fruit, which no other province, or even regions put together in India produced. Peshawar was known for its Washington Navel oranges and grapes, Hazara for apricots and walnuts, Kohat for peaches, guava, loquat, melons, watermelons and mulberry. Bannu exported melons, dates (palm) and plums. Dehra Ismael Khan produced melons. Varieties of berries were produced all over N.W.F.P. A few mango trees in the company bagh of Kohat produced delicious mangoes. As their quality was limited, the fruit of those trees was reserved for V.I.P's. In the Kaghan valley, the growing of 'chilghoza' (pinus gerardiana) had started. The like of peaches (shalils) of Parachinar and juicy apricots of Haripur (Hazara) I have yet to see anywhere. I am sure, since the partition of the country, the fruit plantations and the variety of fruit grown there would have greatly increased. I knew about Manan's implication and entirely agreed with him that the choice of Mirpur Khas as the location of the training center of Horticulture for postgraduate students was determined by the interest of somebody higher up in the Department of Agriculture in the centre than on the intrinsic value of the place.

On being relieved, I went to Kohat. My mother, sister-in-law, and my young nephew were living in the house there while my brother was at his place of posting, Haripur (Hazar), as Excise Sub-Inspector. I did not get any letter from the office of the Fruit Development Advisor for quite sometime, not did I hear from the Central Board of Revenue to whom I had applied, in response to their advertisement, for the post of Income Tax Officer Class II.

When I went to Delhi in connection with the admission to the postgraduate Horticulture Training Course, it occurred to me to call on my ex-principal of Islamia College, Peshawar, I.D. Scot, who been transferred to Delhi as Deputy Principal Private Secretary to the Viceroy, in order to ask him whether he could help me get the post of an Income Tax Officer. I had no hope but I thought there was no harm, as beggars cannot be choosers. One day, in the morning, I reached his bungalow. It was on Duplex Road. I reached his bungalow after inquiring about its whereabouts, though one hardly met anybody on the road in that area. I reached later than I had planned, but it worked out fine. As I entered the bungalow and approached the residence, Mr. and Mrs. Scot came out. As soon as Mr and Mrs Scot saw me, she went in and Mr. Scot shook hands with me and asked me the purpose of my visit. On hearing about it from me, he stated that he would not be able to do anything in the matter, as it did not concern him. He said that the authority concerned was the Central Board of Revenue and it was upto them whom they selected. After saying that, he called his wife and both went away in a car before I had even reached the gate.

In the dreary days that followed my arrival at Kohat, I waited for news of an opening everyday, but none came. Worse than my own disappointment was the political and the communal strife situation, which seemed to get worse. Being a member of a minuscule minority in N.W.F.P., and with the escalating communal tensions and irreconcilable differences between the Congress and Muslim League, the danger to the personal safety of my relatives and myself and all other Hindus, was increasing with the passage of each day.

On 20th February 1947, Atlee, the British Prime Minister made a statement in the House of Commons that the British desired to leave India by 30th June, 1948. This was the news that nearly every Indian of my generation had been dying to hear since he was old enough to understand things, but even this news did not bring much joy, as in a situation in which the country was divided into two hostile and warring camps, no deliverance seemed possible, for how and to whom would the British hand over power. However, this news brought a flicker of hope that the mighty and unbeatable British Empire had been forced by events to decide to give up India which was the foundation of its power and the main source of its wealth.

However, the problem of self preservation had become the main concern of the minorities, Hindus and Sikhs on one side and Muslims on the other, since 16th August, 1946, was the date the Muslim League, under its leader, Qaide Azam Muhammad Ali Jinnah, had declared as direct action day. The Muslim League had not launched any agitation earlier in pursuit of its objective. Its role had been only to oppose the Congress and raise cries of Hindu perfidy and aggrandizement, but on 27th July 1947 the Muslim League working committee drew up a plan of direct action and fixed 16th August as the day of its enforcement. Jinnah perceived that hitherto they had been sticking to constitutional means but they were discarding it that day. According to Jinnah, that day they had forged a pistol and they were in a position to use it, and they did use it on 26th August, 1946. They reverberations of that pistol shot did not stop even with the division of the country. Its reverberations started from Calcutta and were carried on in a chain reaction to other places and provinces. In Calcutta, the trouble was engineered by the Muslim League Ministry of Bengal. Its Prime Minister, Hassan Shaheed Suhravardy personally supervised over the interests of his community, but when the reaction to his handwork started, even he could not control the riots. It took many days and a visit from Pandit Nehru, then the member of the Viceroy's Executive Council responsible for External Affairs, before the riots subsided. Sunravardy must have come to know for the first time in his life that it is easy to set fire to a thing, but it is much more difficult to control it.

Once it caught hold, communal riots in Calcutta were followed by riots in East Bengal, Bihar, Sindh, Ahmedabad and in other places and provinces. Mutual hatred between the members of the two major communities and the all pervasive sense of fear which the above riots had engendered had made the atmosphere so volatile that a rumour, a personal quarrel or a speech by a fanatic was enough to send the people of one community at the necks of the people of the other community. In this atmosphere, when on the 3rd of March, 1947, the coalition ministry of Punjab, formed jointly by the Unionist, Hindu and the Sikhs members of the Punjab legislative assembly, resigned under the overwhelming pressure of the Muslim communists of Punjab, the flood gates of restraint burst open against the flood of passions, hatred and fear. There was a spate of riots in different areas of the Punjab. It had an immediate effect in N.W.F.P. Hindus were openly insulted and stabbing incidents took place in different towns. Many well-to-do Hindu families temporarily left for places like Haridwar, with the intention of returning when the atmosphere cleared up. In Kohat's bazaar, a Hindu Manohar was stabbed to death. The atmosphere had become surcharged and the Hindus knew a simple incident could lead to conflagaration. The Hindus remained alert and careful not to give any chance to the Muslims to get annoyed and start on a destructive path. Rumours of impending attacks on Hindus were galore.

Our family, however, continued to live as usual a secluded life in a Muslim locality, just outside the Hindu Mohollah. One day, my sister-in-law's brother-in-law (her sister's husband), who was working in a transport company, came hurriedly and told my sister-in-law to come with him to the cantonment, as an attack was imminent. I did not believe it but when somebody comes and states that your life is in danger and that he would save you, you cannot insult him by saying he was wrong. You accept his proffered help, because it is safe as well as prudent and we did the same. Om, my sister-in-law's brother-in-law, did not give us any time. He asked us to come along as we were. The bus, which he had brought, was parked at Sangadi, at a raised level about 100 yards from our house. Sangad was outside the residential area but on the road, which led to the main bazaar. My mother and sister-in-law carried whatever came in their hands by way of luggage. I ran and made two trips to the bus, carrying whatever I could carry in my two hands. By the time, I came out of the house the second time, my mother and my sister-in-law were with me. They locked the door, and we went towards the bus and safety. Within five minutes of Om's arrival, we were off. We did not carry much with us. It was not that we were scared. It was just because Om was hurrying us. Most probably, he believed that an attack was imminent. Om himself was staying with a friend of his who had a quarter in the cantonment. I thought he was taking us there and my sister-in-law, most probably, thought the same, but mother like a real head of the family was applying her mind.

As soon as we reched the cantonment, mother asked Om to take us to her sister's bungalow. My uncle, Dewan Harichand, was at that time posted at Kohat as a Sub-Divisional Officer in the Public Works Department. He had come on transfer from Peshawar and had a bungalow, with a very large compound, in Kohat cantonment, and so we went there. My uncle already had his sister's family, his parents and his brother's family staying with him. It was quite a large gathering. All were eating from one kitchen. Mother insisted that we would have a separate kitchen but my aunt did not agree. She stated that when so many were eating from kitchen, two more additional mouths would not make much difference, as it was accepted that my mother would not be prepared to eat at her sister's place. So, mother had a separate kitchen for herself while we ate from the common kitchen.

During the days, we played cards or chatted about everything on earth. In addition to myself, the other male members, who were my constant companions were my uncle's brother-in- law, Dewan Mathura Dass, a retired provincial Civil Service officer of Baluchistan, one of the brothers of my uncle, Duni Chand, Dewan Mathura Dass's son, Hari Dass, my cousin, Gangadhar, and one other relative of my uncle. There were others like uncle's father and Dewan Mathura Dass's other sons but they were not my companions. In addition to the above, there were ladies and children. It was an occasion just like that of an Indian marriage, when so many relatives gather under one roof. You cannot have privacy at all in such circumstances. And a marriage did take place. My cousin, Gangadhar, got married. The marriage procession went from my uncle's place to another place in the cantonment itself.

One day, we got the news that the previous night an attempt had been make to burn our house. Miscreants has made a clumsy attempt to burn the outer gate by burning some papers but the fire was extinguished by our Muslim neighbours and some pandits (Hindus) from the Hindu Mohollah. Mother asked me to get a few suitcases out if I could. I went to the city. I was fortunate to find and hire a wooden luggage carrier, with two wheels, which shopkeepers normally used for transportation of sacks from one place in the city to another. This carrier was pulled by two labourers. From the house, we pulled out 5 or 6 trunks and suitcases and a bundle of carpets which Haridwar, my brother, had acquired in Thal, when he was posted there as custom officer, from the pavindas, the sheep herders from Afghanistan and had brought them to my uncle's place in the cantonment. All along I was scared that the Afghan labourers might do some mischief. They were very strong and if they were so inclined, they could have murdered me in our house and carried off everything themselves, without any harm coming to them in these troubled days. But I was glad also that I had Afghan labourers with me as they were very simple people. Local people were not reliable at all. They were fanatics, and most of the city folk (not from Jungle Khel) were liable to do mischief if a chance presented itself to them. They, at the least, would have taken advantage of the chance and charged much more than the agreed sum.

After about a week or so, another incident of setting the house on fire occurred. The fire was extinguished as before. And just like before I went and brought 5 or 6 suitcases. It was apparent somebody wanted to do mischief just because the house belonged to a Hindu.

During those days an advertisement appeared in the newspapers about the competitive examination for the Indian Civil Services (I.C.S.) and I got the forms from the office of the Federal Service Commission, New Delhi. The form was to be sent after a recommendation from the Deputy Commissioner and the Chief Secretary of the province on the form. Bureacracy in India still strikes a terror in the minds of the ordinary Indian people, but during the British days it was really unapproachable without any influence. However, I approached the Deputy Commissioner through his office and gave them all the necessary papers, about my domicile at Tehri, as the people in the office demanded. My job was done in two or three days, much earlier than my expectations. One day, I left in the morning for Peshawar to get the signature of the Chief Secretary on the form. I told mother, before leaving, that I would be back home in the evening, but in my mind there was a doubt whether I would be back because the Chief Secretary could be on tour or might not see me the same day. I did not carry any change of clothes with me, as I had the optimism of youth those days. My optimism proved justified. From the bus stand at Peshawar, I went straight to the Chief Secretary's office. I was there about 2.30 p.m. I was admitted to his room straight away. I put the form before him. He looked up at me and signed the form and stamped it with his office's stamp and handed over the form to me. I thanked him and walked away with the form. I have always talked against the British because they had occupied my country and as such they were the enemy of my country, and by the same token they were my enemies as well, but in all my encounters with them I met with kindness. If an Indian had been in the Chief Secretary's place, he would not have met me at all. The form would have gone through the proper channel and come back through the same channel.

We Indians are masters of copying. We did not only learn time consuming procedures from the British but improved upon them. It is the bane of Indian administration that Indians copied what the British did to keep the British officers aloof from the masses in a deliberate policy to enhance the prestige of the foreign ruling class and present the members of that class as unapproachable but kind God like personages when encountered at rare moments. This policy made the India subordinates look like the villains responsible for all the omissions and commissions of the government, resulting in injustice to the supplicants and ill and indifferent treatment of the people at large on one hand. On the other hand it made the British bosses appear as just, kind, considerate and benevolent masters. Indians copied this policy, but in doing so added some of their own innovations, as all imitators do, in making the policy through proper channel more comprehensive. The British had ensured that the policies laid down by them for the administration of the country ran smoothly, but the Indian administration is now so comprehensive and democratic that even in the smallest matter many people have to be consulted before a decision is arrived at. The result has been that even the highest functionary is incapable of taking an independent decision. What normally should take minutes now takes days. Responsibility is divided, so nobody can be held responsible for a bad decision and delay. Corruption is rampant. At every stage, one has to pay to get a file moved. The days when a British officer could take an on the spot decision are over. I will write about certain aspects of it later.

The communal and law and order situation in the province continued to deteriorate. Every succeeding day was worse than the previous day. It was stated that the Muslim mobs daily demonstrated outside Dr. Khan Saheb's house and kept him continuously under siege, so much so that he could not move out of his house. Naturally it had led people to believe that the Congree Government had been rendered ineffective. Omens had been there even earlier. There was a time when the Khan brothers writ ran everywhere whether in office of otherwise, but in the winter in 1946 when Pandit Nehru had come to the Frontier and visited the Malkand agency area in the company of Dr. Khan Saheb, the Premier, they had been subjected to a fierce attack of stone throwing by the people there. I had written to Pandit Jawahar Lal Nehru, then the member of the Viceroy's Executive Council for External Affairs, that the situation in N.W.F.P. was very bad and he should not be misled by the statements of Dr. Khan Saheb that the situation in N.W.F.P. was normal. I further wrote that the safety of the Hindus could only be ensured if he could manage to deploy two divisions of Hindu troops. I received a letter of acknowledgement from his private secretary, Tarlok Singh in May. In May itself I got a letter from the office of the Fruit Development Advisor that I had been selected for admission to the Post Graduate Horticultural course, and that I should report for that course at Anand Parbat, Delhi on 4th June 1947. I informed my brother at Haripur about it. He stated in his reply that I should take my sister-in-law also with me and leave her with her parents at Dehra Dun before I went to Delhi. He had also written that I should take some of the boxes with me as well.

In my childhood, I used to go sometimes with my father to the Krishan Dwara of my father's guru, 'Maharaj ji' and with friends very occasionally to the tomb of the parent guru of Tehr, but really I had no faith in either of kind of worship. All kinds of worship are based on certain rituals and I abhor rituals and inane recitations. Many Hindu youth of my generation felt the same as I did and even now quite a larger number of Hindus do not care for ritualistic prayers, but as I normally show quite an indifference to rituals and hypocrites, I quite often became the butt of attack by those older people who showed themselves as religious people. I never took notice of such attacks, knowing that was the way to pull me down from my high horse of indifference and detachment. One day at Kohat, while I was staying with my aunt and uncle in their bungalow in the cantonment, my uncle remarked in the company of his brother-in-law, Dewan Mathura Dass, and others,"Look at Jagdish, he gets up in the morning and sits down to breakfast without saying Ram or Rahim and the whole day does not say a prayer or remember God". I kept quiet at this onslaught, as doing otherwise, I would have exposed myself to more ridicule, but help came from an unexpected quarter. Dewan Mathura Dass said that he found me a person of very high ideas. My uncle said that was all right but one should remember God sometime also. Dewan Mathura Dass hotly asked what he was talking about. He said my uncle should not run me down, as I was much beyond his mumbo-jumbo. At this my uncle became quiet as his brother-in-law was older than him, and more aggressive and known to be more knowledgeable. Dewan Mathura Dass took my side, for because of the enforced inactivity we had to spend long hours together and there I had had the opportunity to show off some of my bookish knowledge. His son, Hari Dass, who was my friend might have built me up too.

At the end of May, one day I left Kohat with my sister-in-law, Padma Vati, and my young nephew, of about two years, for Rawalpandi by the night train. We reached Rawalpindi in the morning. At the platform waiting for us was my brother, Haridwar. He had come from Haripur to Peshawar and from there had taken a night train to Rawalpindi. He had arived only a few minutes before us. We were not aware of his coming. According to him he had suddenly decided to meet us to ensure we did not run into any difficulty. We spent the day in the waiting room. The train for Dehra Dun left in the early evening. There was a large crowd waiting for the train when it came to the platrorm. It appeared that the Hindus had started leaving Rawalpindi and the surrounding area in appreciable numbers, most probably temporarily, to pass the period of danger in tranquility and await the coming of good days in safety. As soon the train came to the platform, people rushed for the compartments to get seats and luggage racks. We were able to do so with the help of porters without difficulty. When we were comfortably seated and the train was going to start, a Sikh gentleman, who was an important personality among the Sikhs of Kohat, came hurriedly towards our compartment with a large number of packages. He wanted to throw his packages in through the windows we were sitting by as the passage from the door was blocked by luggage and people. We objected. He remonstrated a little bit but we did not yield. He then gave up. I felt so bad in not allowing him to come through the windows that even today I feel remorse. I did not know him personally, but I knew that he was from my town. I should not have said no to him, but unfortunately, he himself was a heavy set man and he had a large number of boxes. I know we would had some packages on our laps and been miserable all through the journey, but still I feel we should have helped him.

It is in time of trouble that one needs help, but because of one's own safety and comfort we are reluctant to extend it. This much I know, that if he had pressed us further, we would have agreed. To continue the narrative, we reached Dehra Dun the next morning on 1st June 1947. On 3rd June 1947, I took the night train for Delhi. The next morning, I reached Delhi. It was at the Delhi Railway Station that I heard being broadcast over the loudspeaker when I alighted on the platform from the train, that Lord Mountbatten had declared on 3rd June, 1947, that the British had resolved to vacate India on 15th August, 1947. Earlier, Atlee, the Prime Minister of Great British had made a statement on 20th February, 1947 in the House of Commons, that the British Government had desired to hand over their responsibility in India to the authorities established by a constitution approved by all the parties in India in accordance with the Cabinet Mission Plan, but as there were no prospects of such a constitution and such authorities emerging, the British Government intended to take necessary steps to effect the transfer of power to responsible Indian hands by a date not later than June 1948.

So Mountbatten had brought that deadline of June 1948 down to 15th August 1947 and thus the prospect of India becoming independent ten months earlier seemed real.

When Atlee's statement was announced, we the people at large, did not believe that the British were sincere, as it was unimaginable in those days of imperialism that an imperial power would give up its power on its own volition. We, at that time, did not have the benefit of hindsight to know the reason behind the British decision, but when Mountbatten's announcement came, I immediately believed it because it was so worded that the urgency of the move seemed very real. One could feel it. I always thought of sacrificing my life for the freedom of the country, but when it was palpably near, my heart was heavy and fulled of foreboding. I did not know that Mountrabetten had prepared a plan for handing over power. It seemed from the announcement that the British would leave India whether parties came to an agreement or not. I saw prospects of bloodshed between the Hindus and the Muslims for gaining advantageous positions. The destination was close but the future looked full of despair. At that time I was not aware that Mountbatten had a partition plan, which he had got approved by all the political parties. When I heard of it or rather read about it later, I was very happy about it. Actually everybody seemed to be happy about it.

The Hindus of West Punjab and the Frontier knew that they were in great danger there, and such was the situation, at a lesser scale, in Bengal, and, therefore, they were agreeable to give up some territory in lieu of safety. A paradoxical situation had arisen. The Congress, which had along stood for the integrity of India, and the Hindus, for whom the integrity of India was a question of faith, historical reality and geographical necessity, had to suddenly sue for peace and agree to the partition of their country. All the resolves and the vision held sacred for years by all patriots had been swept away by communal frenzy. As Jinnah was bent upon refusing any constitutional plan for a free India, short of partition of the country, and, without it, on creation of communal trouble in Punjab and the Frontier, Pandit Nehru told Lord Mountbatten that the Congress would be agreeable to the partition if Punjab and Bengal were also partitioned on communal lines. Jinnah won by the threat of the use of the weapon, coined by him, of mutual discord and slaughter on a mass scale and the Congress succumbed to this pressure, but people still died in millions as the poison of communalism and neutral hatred, preached incessantly from political and religious platforms over the years, had so infested the minds of the people that when the agreement about the partition came through, even this antidote was not enough to cleanse the minds of the people of it entirely. A substantial part of it remained.

The reason was that the country had been divided on communal basis. The basis of communalism was religion. A people of the same cultural and genetical stock had been divided on religious basis. Religion, instead of uniting people, as it should do, had divided it. There is a saying in 'Pushto' that a cousin turned hostile is the worst enemy and that happened in India. Pakistan and India, the successor states to the India that was, are now perpetually aligned against each other because of what happened years ago in the name of religion. Pakistan does not have any Hindu population, except a small one in Sindh, but India has a very large population of Muslims, and therefore the communal problem was very much there, as Jinnah had his Pakistan but left his communalism, which he had nursed so assiduously, here.

Chapter Seven

A Period of Turbulence

On Anand Parbat, we were accommodated in a hostel, which was a sort of temporary structure originally built for officers of the American Forces during the war. We each had a room to ourselves. A large bathroom was attached to each room, but there was no provision of running water in them. For a bath, we had to go to a common bathroom, where water taps had been provided in different enclosures. Anand Parbat was situated on a flat-topped low hillock. The whole surface was rugged with boulders everywhere. Boulders had been cleared off only from the sites of a few structures there, the main passage, and a few subsidiary passages connecting the structures with the main passage. The main passage joined the Original Road stretching from a point on Faiz Road, running in a south-north direction on the eastern extremity of Karol Bagh to a point on the upward slope of Anand Parbat, a little below the plateau on the top.

Except for a couple of houses on the Original Road slope there was no habitation on Anand Parbat when we came there. The place was absolutely desolate, windswept and without any vegetation. When we first came, it was the month of June. Hot winds blew day and night. The winds were so hot and searing, with sand particles, that in the scorching heat of the afternoon, we remained indoors keeping our doors and windows shut, to escape the burning and suffocating 'loo'. This loo, as this hot wind was called in local parlance, pestered us day and night. At night its intensity was less but we could not sleep. We slept outside for fresh air but we got the same hot air slightly cooled down. The water in the taps, even in the morning, was hot. It used to be very hot in the afternoon and evening. For bathing, we put our body under the tap part by part, for a couple of seconds. The water pipes bringing water to Anand Parbat were exposed, so the water in the pipes got very hot in the summer heat. The water in the pipes, which were exposed in the bathroom, cooled down at night. One got cool water and that too to a small extent if one was the first one to use the bathroom in the morning.

The surface of the ground was so congested with boulders that the builders instead of clearing the passages between the different structures and main building and outhouses of boulders had cemented the path, as it was cheaper. Our hostel was a large one, with rooms arranged in a quadrangle around a large courtyard. This courtyard had been made for growing vegetation and flowers by packing its surface with dirt, but when we came, this place was devoid of any vegetation expect that it was mostly full of tall dry grass.

There were twenty students in our class; ten were deputies from the open market, one was from N.W.F.P., two were from Sindh, two from Assam, two from Bihar, two from the Central Provinces and one from Coorg. As for those taken from the modern market, one was from N.W.F.P., Daljit Singh; Nirmaljit Songh, Surijit Singh, Surinder Singh, Kuldip Sady Dugal and Sant Lal were from Punjab. Khosla was from Patiala State and one was from the United Provinces. From the composition of the class, it appeared that the course was not given much importance. Punjab and the United Provinces, the two most important provinces from the point of view of agriculture and horticulture, had not nominated even a single person for this course, and nor had Madras and Bombay, the two other important provinces. The course had first started at Mirpur Khas Sindh, with the deputies from the provinces, but as no proper facilities were provided there, the course was shifted to Delhi as a last resort to save it from going into oblivion. Otherwise Delhi was not the place for such a course as firstly, Delhi was not a fruit-growing centre and secondly, there was no fruit orchard available for the class to see things in practice or to do their practicals in. As for the accommodation, it was not near any cultivated area.

There were no catering arrangements for us when we arrived. Later on a servant was employed for cooking meals, but he was hopeless. We kept up this arrangement for sometime, but later on, when we had the chance, we shifted to another arrangement. All of us had kept electric stoves for making tea. There was no library either. We used to go to the library of the Indian Institute of Agricultural Research for consulting books, but that was not situated at a convenient distance. It took a long time to go there. Firstly, we had to walk down to the bus stand on the slope of Anand Parbat or down below to the one on the Original Road, depending on the time, as Anand Parbat was touched only by two routes and that too at infrequent intervals. We had to change the bus once to reach the bus stand outside the Institute's premises and then had to walk quite a distance within the perimeter of the institute to reach the library. We normally preferred to walk the whole distance, as it was faster though we had to first traverse a rough ground full of very inconvenient dark and craggy boulders for about half a mile on Anand Prabat, about a quarter of a mile of the slope and a further distance of about ¾ mile on the level ground. The buses took a much longer route. The buses took an easterly route to Faiz Road on the Original Road and then went at right angles to the south to Pusa Road, which led from Faiz Road to the west to the outer gate of the Agricultural Research Institute (or the Pusa Institute) in the southwest corner of a large square. On foot we went in a northwesterly direction from our hostel. Actually at first it came as a great surprise to us when we went on foot in a northwesterly direction and found ourselves in the vicinity of the Agricultural Institute as soon as we came down to level ground after coming down the slope of Anand Parabt.

The Indian Agricultural Institute was originally situated in Pusa in the Bihar province, but after a devastating earthquake in Bihar in 1934, the Institute was shifted to its site in Delhi. It would be a point of interest to note that the Institute's library did not contain any book on Indian horticulture. A book on horticulture had come out just about the time we joined the course, so we all were made to buy it. I think we had to pay Rs 25/ each for this book. It was far from exhaustive. It did not contain much worthwhile information about the cultural practices in the various parts of the country and nor had it much researched information about the fruit growing provinces and their soils, climate and geographical positions nor of the fruit growing areas. But as it was the only book available in the market we were happy to acquire it.

As for our faculty members, we had one lecturer and one demonstrator. The name of the lecturer was Ranjit Singh. He was not a horticulturist but a M.Sc. in Botany. The demonstrator's name was Mohan Singh. He was B.Sc. (Agriculture.). Ranjit Singh did not know much about horticulture but otherwise was intelligent. Some of the provinces' representatives like Skukula and Bari from Bihar, Chaudhry from Assam and Vankhede and his colleague from the Central provinces were much more knowledgeable than Ranjit Singh, but Ranjit Singh aptly and intelligently handled them and always gave the impression that he was in control. I think, along with us, he also educated himself in horticulture. As for Mohan Singh, he was completely overshadowed by our colleagues from the provinces. Actually we learnt more from our colleagues than from Mohan Singh. I do not think he took us out for more than one or two days and that also for actual demonstration of not more than half an hour each. The book on fruit growing, which we had purchased, was our textbook and our lecturer used to teach us from there. However, we learnt a great deal from our tours on which we were taken. We, and especially our Muslim colleagues, used to often humorously comment on the fact that all the official posts in the Horticulture Department, from the Fruit Development Advisor to the demonstrator, were held by Sikhs.

About a month or so of our joining the class, we had to shift from our hostel, as accommodation was required for the research officers of the Agriculture Ministry, who were being transferred from Punjab, the Frontier, Baluchistan and Bengal consequent upon the June 3rd partition plan. One of the requirements of this plan was that all the Government of India officials would be asked their options whether they would like to serve in India or Pakistan, and as per their option they were to be transferred to the territory of their choice. We were shifted to the first floor of a hostel, which, most probably, belonged to Ramjas College as there was a school building there which later on was occupied by the Central Agricultural College but, earlier on, it was stated, it had belonged to Ramjas College. We were on the first floor of a two-storied building, which was quadrangular in shape with a narrow court between the walls, the width of the court being much smaller than the length. It was situated in line and adjacent to another hostel of a similar type. In front of these hostels was the building, which was shortly to become the Central Agricultural College. Within about a month of our arrival in the new building, the college started functioning and the ground floor of our hostel was occupied by the first year students of the Central Agricultural College. Our rooms in the new hostel were much smaller than the rooms in the other hostel, but for one person they were satisfactory. There was a running verandah along the rooms; so, it was convenient for us to pull our cots outside in the verandah at night in the summer. Our rooms were situated on the front side facing the college. On the front side there were about ten to twelve rooms with bathrooms at each corner and the superintendent's large room in the middle of our row of rooms.

The Hostel Superintendent had been appointed by the college authorities. He had nothing to do with us, but still the maintenance of the discipline of the hostel, in which we were living, was his responsibility. He was a junior lecturer in college. He had a tiff with one or two of our classmates in the beginning as a consequence of his exertion of his authority over us, but he left us alone either realizing himself or perhaps on somebody else's advice that he would himself lose by getting entangled with senior trainees.

In our new hostel, pipes all lay underground. I had mentioned earlier that we shifted over to another arrangement being dissatisfied with our cook. The other arrangement was that of the Central Agricultural College for their hostel. The Central Agricultural College entrusted the catering to a contractor, which was perhaps the reason why their catering was also bad. But as we were seniors in every way, the contractor cared for us more than for the first year students, being afraid we could harm him by complaining to the higher authorities. We ate under tents or in the open, as there was no dining room at the time we were there. The contractor supplied us a bucket of warm water, in the winter at half a rupee a bucket, for bathing or washing.

A few words about Karol Bagh at this stage would be appropriate. Karol Bagh is situtated three miles from Connaught Place, the main and the most fashionable shopping centre of New Delhi, just west of the ridge, which extends from Dhaula Kuan in the south to the University in the north. Near Karol Bagh is the centre part of the ridge. Just below the ridge, to the west is Faiz Road running from the north to the south. Parallel to Faiz Road to the west is Gurdwara Road a couple of blocks away. Similarly situated is Ajmal Khan Road, the main and only shopping place in the locality to the further west. A little distance away, in the same direction towards the south is Regarpura. A little further away is Deopura. The Original Road, as I mentioned earlier, cut Ajmal Khan Road in the middle, running from Faiz Road to Anand Parbat. Parallel to Original Road, to the south, is Pusa Road, on the southern extremity of Ajmal Khan Road. To the north runs Rohtak Road, parallel to Original Road.

On Faiz Road, facing the east, was a row of town houses. These were 3 or 4 room nicely built houses. Muslim families were living there. Gurdwara Road presented a deserted look. There was neither any market nor any residential place. The only thing I remember was a taxi stand there. On Ajmal Khan Road, there was a small restaurant of a reasonable standard. We occasionally came there to eat. Opposite the restaurant was a lowly tinsmith. There a very few nondescript shops, besides, in the central sector of Ajmal Khan Road on which was the main shopping area. This area was just south of Original Road. Near the junction of Original Road and Ajmal Khan Road, a few yards to the west, was the police station. At some distance to the north, from the junction, was Ajmal Khan Unani Hospital, on the left side of the road. Near about it and on two sides of a large park, which was situated just to the north of Original Road and the southern and the western boundaries of which were formed by Original and Ajmal Khan Road respectively, there were quite a number of houses. These houses were also mainly occupied by Muslims, though Hindus also had some houses. On Rohtak Road there were a number of two storied buildings, each one of which was in about 400 sq yards of area. Each storey constituted a decent flat. These flats were occupied by Hindus in September. That was the time I started going to that area to visit my cousin sister, who was residing there in a first floor flat with her husband and daughter.

Regarpura was from its very inception a slum area. Two small rooms were put together in such a way that one had to pass through one room to reach the other room. The whole house was put up in about twenty square yards. All houses were similar in construction and dingy in appearance. It seemed as if that locality was some sort of an area in isolation. It stood apart from Karol Bagh in the east and Deopura in the west. One only saw some truck drivers, Sikhs and Hindus, sitting in the open ground on stringed cots, gossiping together in the evening. Deopura was to the west of Regarpura but it was a relatively large area and the houses were larger and better built and meant for the middle class. Beyond Deopura to the west, except for the Indian Agricultural Research Institute, there was no urban habitation, but within a few years, one of the largest expansions of an urban area in that period of time had taken place in the west of Delhi. This was a record in India. Delhi, it is said, was built eight times after repeated destruction and each time, with every new construction, it moved towards the north with some aberration.The seventh Delhi was built by Shah Jahan, the fifth Mughal King, and was called Shahjahanabad. Its northern limit, at that time, was Kashmiri Gate. The British built their capital to the south, so it was called South Delhi. The British had reversed the general trend but they did build buildings to the northwest and west of Kashmiri Gate, like the Old Secretariat and the university area. During the Second World War the northern limits of Delhi were extended to Kingsway Camp and thereabouts. Actually the northern expansion of Delhi was limited to the flow of the River Jamuna which flows from the west to the east in the north of Delhi but forms an arc near the Old Secretariat and then flows in a nearly southern direction from about Red Fort. Delhi has now expanded to the east as well, as a result of a couple of bridges, constructed across the Jamuna, one at Vikas Minar and the other at Nizamuddin in recent times, but it expanded a great deal towards the south and west. Its expansion towards the south has combined all the eight Delhis of historical times from Tughlakabad near the Rai Pithora area to the right bank of the River Jamuna in the south, but Delhi's greatest expansion has been to the west.

In the summer, I went to Simla to appear in the I.C.S. Examination. I appeared in it wihout any preparation. There I stayed with Opinder, my college friend, who along with his parents, was himself staying with his brother's family. His brother was working in the Central Secretariat. The house had limited accommodation, but that is the tradition of the Hindu joint family all over India that when a guest comes, a house, which normally can accommodate only four members of a family with difficulty, stretches its accommodation to accommodate many times that number. I did not qualify in that examination, but I scored reasonably well considering that I had appeared in papers like Indian History, British History and Economics, which were not my subjects in college. Besides, there were compulsory subjecs like English Essay and General Knowledge. I think my highest marks were in Indian History and in that I got about 50% marks. The lowest marks I got were in the lower thirties. I had earlier given my centre as Peshawar, but later on when communal trouble in Punjab increasingly acquired serious proportions, the Federel Service Commission offered applicants, through newspaper advertisements, the choice for change of the examination centre, as migration of the people from the areas earmarked for Pakistan to truncated India and vice versa had started from March, 19th and had increased gradually to a considerable extent by July.

I was really worried about the safety of my mother and Haridwar, and especially Haridwar as he was at Haripur and Haripur and other parts of Hazara were areas which were with the Muslim League even in the heyday of the Khudai Khidamatgar Movement in the N.W.F.P., and not only that, the people there were viciously fanatic. Mother, at least, was in the cantonment of Kohat. But every Hindu in the Indian part of India was worried about the safety of his loved and dear ones in Pakistan. The Hindus were entering Delhi in great numbers, but the Muslims had moved out in trickles in the summer months as Delhi had not experienced any communal violence during the pre-independence days and the Muslims constituted a good proportion of the population of Delhi, which gave them the confidence that whatever happened they would be able to face it. Otherwise also the Hindus of Delhi were meek and docile while the Muslims were aggressive and confident of retaliating in case thay were attacked. No one was aware of the holocaust in which Punjab and the Frontier were going to be plunged into in the coming days. The Hindus were coming to the Indian part with the avowed object of returning to their respective areas after things settled down in the areas forming Pakistan. But this migration was confined to well-to-do persons. People with limited means, of course, had no wherewithals to stay in areas hundreds of miles away from their hometowns in an enforced exile for months.

By the beginning of August the Hindus were coming in such large numbers to Delhi that finding accomodation for them had become a big problem. My chilhood friend, Dayanand, had occupied a vacant Muslim house. It had two or three rooms on the ground floor and he was forced to admit another immigrant family from West Pakistan into the house. That family occupied the first floor. A few days later he had to perforce vacate one or two rooms on the ground floor. So ultimately, he had to remain contented with one room, which he shared with his wife, mother and a brother. Immigrants from the north were quarrelling among themselves for occupation of the houses. The farsighted and worldly-wise managed to occupy houses with their own or hired muscle power. At that time most of the immigrants were searching for a roof to put over their heads, oblivious of what the future had in store for them. I believe a few Muslim families in isolated places were forced to vacate their houses for their immigrant tormentors.

I feel that if the Government had been prepared and built up accomodation for the immigrants, there would have been no riots in Delhi.The Hindus flooding Delhi had no accommodation or shelter where the ever increasing number of Hindus could live, as neither had the government built any for them and nor had the Muslims vacated theirs. The trouble in Delhi was inevitable as the Muslim League was determined to get the Hindus out from the Muslim majority areas in order to form an Islamic state in Pakistan without fear of having to face a powerful minority of Hindus and Sikhs in West Punjab, the state which was destined to dominate Pakistan politically, militarily and economically because of its agricultural wealth, mineral wealth, extent and geographical nature of its area, its large population as compared to the other states in the west and the war like nature of its people. Even in March in Kohat, when we had to leave our house in the city and move to the cantonment, it was because of the inspired rumours. A stabbing case in the market and attempts to set our house on fire were all manouveres in this direction. In West Punjab these attempts were accompanied by much bloodshed. Larry Collins and Dominique Lapierre in their book "Freedom at Midnight" have stated that letters were sent to the Hindu and Sikh households in Lahore warning them of impending Muslim attacks in order to make them flee. The Government of India should have anticipated the movement of the people from the areas designed for Pakistan. One did not need any secret agency to provide them the intelligence of things to come. The League's aim and propoganda had provided enough clues of their intention. If mixed military units, composed of Hindu and Muslim personnel with British officers, had been deployed in West Punjab and the Frontier, Hindus would have faced no danger to their lives and hence there would have been no reciprocal migration from India and no bloodshed. But perhaps, this exercise would not have succeeded, considering the attitude of the Muslims in West Punjab and the Frontier at that time. Most probably as soon as the military were withdrawn, the slaughter would have begun. The Congress leaders of that time, unfortunately, were so preoccupied dealing with the aftermath of the acceptance of the partition plan into which they were forced by the blackmail of bloodshed by Jinnah that they did not realize that even in agreeing to partition the country to save it from bloodshed, they could not save it because of lack of foresight, experience and knowledge of the actual situation.

The movement of the Hindus and the Sikhs which had started in March from the areas of West Punjab and the Frontier into East Punjab and other areas of India, singly and in groups, remained unabated by 15th August, but the leaders of the Congress party and the people of Delhi, since June had been awaiting Independence Day on 15th August. I felt we should celebrate the day befittingly. I got together Shukla from Bihar, Wankhede from the Central Provinces and Sant Lal Jindal, a direct entry to the course from Punjab, and formed a committee, with myself as convener. In this connection I met Mr. Luthra, the Principal of the Central Agricultural College. He was very nice about it. He said that he and his college would fully co-operate and I should tell him whatever help I wanted from him. Our committee members went to meet some of the Viceroy's executive members and would be ministers. None of them even received us. We were informed through their personal assistants that the leaders concerned would not be available for our flag hoisting ceremony. In the case of Maulana Azad, we were not allowed even allowed to enter his bungalow. When we visited Maulana Azad's residence at about 11 o'clock in the morning, we were stopped at the gate and told that he was asleep. We waited outside the gate for him to get up from his morning siesta. An hour or so later we came to know, through the kindness of a peon or some such functionary, that the Maulana was up but was having tea. Quite sometime later we found out he was talking to Aruna Asif Ali. We decided to wait, but when even after a wait of an hour or so we were not called in to the Maulana's presence, we beat a retreat in the afternoon heat.

The futile wait at the gate of Maulana Azad's residence, indifference of the other ministers and a weary journey back to our hostel had induced a feeling of dejection and despondency in the minds of my colleagues. They went straight to their rooms on reaching the hostel without asking me about the future programme or telling me that we would meet again. I talked to Jindal later in the evening about it. He persuaded me to abandon the whole idea of a celebration on the 15th of August as none of my colleagues seemed to be enthusiastic any longer. I suddenly felt very dejected. My dejection was basically triggered off by the loss of interest of my colleagues, but it got accentuated when in this state of mind it suddenly occurred to me that mother and Haridwar might not survive the communal violence that had engulfed the North Western part of the country. Actually, we in our zeal, had become presumptious to think that any minister would come to our function. It was a folly to even think of it.

In the frame of mind I was in, after abandoning the idea of the celebration of the Independence Day on Anand Parbat, I felt homesick and so the next day I left for Dehradun by night train to see my sister-in-law and nephew, Avinash. The next morning I was in Dehradun. I stayed with the parents-in-law of my brother, where my sister-in-law and nephew were also staying. I had reached Dehradun on the morning of 14th August. On 15th morning, just before dawn, I suddenly woke up in my bed. I was sleeping under a mosquito net in the courtyard, just like the other members of the family. When I woke up, I heard two persons talking in whispers. For a few seconds I tried to fathom who was whispering, and then on a sudden impulse I lifted a corner of the mosquito net and saw my brother talking to his young son in whispers in the verandah behind my cot. I had barely got up and talked to him for a couple of minutes when the others also got up. His story of his journey put me in a sombre mood.

He, knowing the situation at Haripur, had applied for 15 days leave from the middle of August thinking that if there ensued violence after Pakistan came into being on the 15th of August, it would have ended by the end of August when he was to report back, little realizing the temper of those days. He came to Peshawar from Haripur on the afternoon of 14th. He left Peshawar the same evening by the Frontier Mail. At Gujranwala, about 40 miles from Lahore, the train was terminated, as there were serious riots in Lahore and even the Lahore station was involved. He became very frightened as he was stranded alone on the Gujranwala station with no hope of getting out of that place, and Gujranwala was burning. He could see from the station the flames from the burning city rising into the sky. Within a few minutes of the arrival of the Frontier Mail, a Military special train, which was carrying Hindu and Sikh soldiers to India, had also arrived. A few Hindus who had escaped from Gujranwala begged the military personnel to save the Hindus of Gujranwals, but their British officers refused to intervene inspite of repeated requests and knowing that barring their intervention the Hindus of Gujranwala had no hope, as according to them they were not supposed to do so. Hari-dwar, my brother, went to every compartment of the military train, begging the soldiers to help him, but they said they were not permitted to carry any non-military person with them. However, on his repeated requests, the soldiers in one compartment asked him to talk to the British officers. He approached them but they refused him pointblank, as he was a non-military person, but he continued begging the soldiers, going from one compartment to another, but in vain. However, as the train was going to start, soldiers in one compartment seeing his distress took, him in. At Lahore, he saw the cruel work of insane fanatical killers. The Lahore station was littered with corpses. The killer mobs had mercilessly killed the Hindus fleeing from their home in the city, in the building of which they had contributed a lot.

Lahore, the city of colleges, was the premier centre of fashion in pre-independence India, but on the first day of the existence of Pakistan it lay in ruins and the smoke from the burning buildings could be seen from the station. The handsome young men and beautiful women who formed a part of the city's splendour that day were either in flight or boarded up in their houses, stricken with grief and fear or lying dead on the streets or in their houses or at the railway station. They died while waiting for a train, which never came for them. People, in authority in Delhi, who should have known that people would die like that, did not know. They believed in the Muslim League whom they should not have from their experience. The dead at the Lahore Railway station included children, old men and women. Lahore, legend says, was founded in prehistoric days. It remained an mportant city during historical days. Though since 1008, when Mahmood Ghaznvi took it after defeating Anandapala, Lahore had remained under the domination of Muslims till 1802, when Maharaja Ranjit Singh took it over from Zaman Shah. Hindus remained in Lahore and constituted a good proportion of its population. In 1947 Hindus and Sikhs constituted about half its population. Lahore was lost to the Hindus altogether in 1947, as the Hindus had to vacate it then enbloc.

At Lahore, the Military special's driver ran away as he was a Muslim and was apprehensive, seeing the conditions at Lahore station, that he would be killed at Amritsar by Hindus and Sikhs when the train arrived there. However the military officers were able to catch hold of some other Muslim driver for the train. Naturally, no Hindu driver could be found there. The train started with an officer holding a revolver at the head of the driver. As there was danger of rails having been having been removed, some military personnel walked in front of the train at some places to prevent a mishap while in Pakistan territory.

After that his journey had been uneventful. We all, who heard this account of terror and gruesome killings of Hindus in areas of Pakistan, did not exhibit any anger or show any feeling of revenge, but thought of the future, wondering what would happen now. We knew in our hearts that the events Haridwar described were the harbinger of worse things to come, as such events in such a scale do not happen in isolation. We hoped for peaceful days ahead as Haridwar, his family and myself ultimately had to return to Pakistan, that being our country by residence and we did not want to return to destruction. When I returned to Delhi in this sombre mood, I came to know that communal violence had spread to East Punjab. Sikhs and Hindus in revenge or spite had started hitting Muslims everywhere in Punjab.This meant large scale slaughter and plunder on both sides of Punjab. Hindus had been fleeing from West Punjab and the Frontier at random to safety for quite some time, but when the trains were hit, the Hindus free-at-will migration came to a stop and they got marooned in pockets all over West Pakistan. The emergence of Pakistan had turned nearly the whole of Pakistan and East Punjab into a wide field of carnage. When refugees started leaving by special trains from both sides, the trains were hit and passengers were slaughtered indiscriminately. I do not remember the sequence of events, but every moment there was a fresh rumour or news. For example, I heard that the Hindus coming from Pind Dadan Khan and Bhira were slaughtered in trains bound for Pakistan. Similarly one heard about Muslims being slaughtered in trains bound for Pakistan.The more the violence, the more insatiable became the people's thirst for blood. Even people who could not harm an ant became killers in emulating others. It is a maxim that violence breeds violence, but inefficiency and lack of response of the law enforcement authorities encourage people to take the law into their own hands. Bad characters incite people and lead them, but when people see it is so easy to kill and rob, without danger, they became bold and indulge in killing and robbing on their own.

Hindus, being peace-loving, get scared easily. Even in Delhi one frequently heard rumours that Muslims were going to attack the Hindu areas. One reason was that Muslims were aggressive and somehow well armed. It was more so during those days, as in recent years a change is taking place in the Hindus attitude. If the conditions in India remain the same as they are now, this change may be more pronounced in the coming years.

One day I came to the hostel from outside just before sunset and saw that a lot of activity was taking place on the rooftop above the first floor of the hostel. I went above and saw that the 1st year students of the Central Agricultural College were gathering stones near the outer boundary wall, which was projecting about three feet from the roof level. My three Muslim classmates, Sayeed from N.W.F.P., Abbasi from Sindh and a third from Bihar were urging them on. I laughed at the efforts of the 1st year students and asked them jokingly which enemies were they preparing against. They said seven thousands Meos (Muslim residents of Mewat) were coming this side to attack. I had not heard anything more ridiculous. I thought they were afraid of an attack from the local Muslims. That itself was absurd, but to think of an attack by Meos who were known to be ferocious fighters was impossible. I asked them whether they seriously believed that Meos would come more than twelve miles to attack Delhi and in between no policemen or military men would stop them. They said that between the Meos and our hostel there was no habitation. It was correct that our hostel seemed to be situated on the western extremity of Delhi and one did not see any habitation to the west if one looked from the rooftop, but still an attack on Delhi by ill equipped Meo rabble was too far fetched to believe. But before I could say something to dissudade them from their futile exercise, Sayeed spoke up. He said that they were right, as there was definitely a danger of attack. I looked at Sayeed and realized he was supporting this foolhardy attempt at defence to guard against an attack by the Hindus. Shrewd as he was, he was supporting himself against a possible attack by Hindus. There had been no chance of that either. I did not say anything about that but only said that they may guard the place, however, I was going to my room. But before I left I had been imparted an impression by my Muslim friends that they were carrying a revolver with them. I knew they did not have a revolver, but to deter us Hindu from a possible attack on them they had concocted a story about having a revolver. In my mind I did not blame them because it is always better to take steps in advance to safeguard oneself, but I thought my Muslim friends should have realized that not a single soul in the hostel would have thought of harming them. I am sure that had a threat materialized to their safety every inmate of the hostel would have risen to their defence. We were all of a different temperament than robbers and killers. After all how could we have attacked our own colleagues or allowed them to be attacked by others.

One day in the morning of 1st September, I came to our class a few minutes late. All my colleagues were sitting in their chairs except for my three Muslim friends who were standing near the chair of our lecturer. I found out from one of my class fellows, who was sitting nearby, that communal trouble in Delhi had started. Karol Bagh was also in the grip of communal violence. Our three Muslim friends had approached our lecturer and asked to be evacuated. Our lecturer had taken them to Mr.Luthra, the principal of the Central Agricultural College. Luthra had rung up the commandant of a Gorkha battalion, which was stationed just below Anand Parbat to the southeast. The commandant had promised to send a truck with a couple of soldiers to escort our three Muslim friends to the Pakistan Embassy. While we were talking, the truck arrived with two armed soldiers. Our friends left within minutes with their baggage.

After that we went to the slope of Anand Parbat facing Original Road. Everything seemed to be quiet, except that an individual, the same or a different person each time, made three or four trips to the Original Road from the Rohtak Road side, and each time he dropped what looked like a corpse on the Original Road nearly opposite to the police station. Otherwise there had been absolutely no movement, neither of vehicles or that of the mobs that one would expect during disturbances. In the subsequent days, we heard rumours that in Pahar

Ganj and Darya Ganj, refugees had attacked Muslim houses, but Muslims with firearms had fired on them. Ultimately the Muslims, from the threatened areas, were evacuated by the police to camps set up for the same purpose. We were quite safe on Anand Parbat. There was no sign of trouble there and we could see the whole of the Original Road from our perch on the slope.

Karol Bagh area was absolutely quiet for days and there did not seem to appear to be any movement there except for a casual jeep coming to or going from the police station. On a night or two we saw a glow of fire towards the Sabzi Mandi (Vegetable Market) side. Perhaps some place or places had been set on fire. It seems strange that in Karol Bagh, the trouble started because a popular doctor, Joshi, had been killed by Muslims. We heard this on Anand Parbat, but later on when we were able to move about I heard it from different sources.

While sitting in idleness on Anand Parbat, from where the trouble seemed to be hundreds of miles away, I was worried about the safety of my friend Ajmal. Ajmal was one year senior to me in school. He was tall, slim in body and fair in complexion. He had very long legs. I never saw him walking slowly. He always seemed to be running while actually that was his normal gait. He was from Jungle Khel, as all my Muslim friends in Kohat were, and was a very nice man. He met me in the main bazaar of Darya Ganj by chance two days before the riots started. He took me to the first floor of a building to the east but very near the main bazaar. The place he led me to was a large hall. On both sides of the hall cots had been spread with their heads towards the wall along the length of the hall, with the bedding lying on them folded. It really was a barrack like place, but much larger. On each side there were about twenty cots, and between the rows of cots there was a passage of about eight feet wide. From there, instead of asking me to rest, he took me to Chandni Chowk on foot without telling me where he was taking me. At Chandi Chowk he took me to a Muslim sweetmeat shop. There he ordered habshi halwa. Habshi is the Urdu word for a Negro and halwa is any sweet made from flour, sugar and 'ghee' in which ghee, purified butter, is added in a great quantity. We both ate that halwa with great relish and in a very satisfying quantity. I had eaten that type of halwa earlier also and have eaten it often since then, but at no time was it as delicious as at that shop. This type of halwa was a specialiy of Dehra Ismail Khan, a district of N.W.F.P., and it was called and is still called 'son halwa'. This halwa is normally brown in colour but the halwa I ate that time was near black in colour and it was because of this that the halwa, most probably, was called "habshi". This halwa is not available in Delhi as that particular shop, which sold it, is no longer there. Most probably the owner has migrated to Pakistan. I did not meet Ajmal after that. I went to his place where he lived as soon as I could, but he was not there. Some person there told me that he had been evacuated to Pakistan. I still hope that he reached his home safe and sound.

A couple of days before the riots started, I had given a Muslim tailor cloth for two trousers and two cambric (cotton) shirts. It was very difficult those days to acquire pure cotton cloth. Actually everything was in short supply. Shirting material, I had acquired on my ration card and the velveteen for my trousers also I had got hold of from a similar source. After the riots had subsided, I went to the tailor's shop to find out whether he had stitched the clothes. On going there I found that the tailor had left the shop. My friend Dayanand, who lived nearby and knew that I had given the clothing material to that tailor to get stitched, told me that when the riots started he saw some people robbing that particular tailoring shop. He went there to retrieve my clothing material, but there was such a rush of people at the shop that he really could not reach the material. He saw two books lying in a corner near the door, and he picked them up. These books were of no practical value to him, as there was nothing worthwhile to read in them. He just picked them up, as they were there to be picked up. On hearing this I laughed and said that I had been robbed in the Frontier and then I had been robbed again in Delhi. I said that it looked like I was a born loser. I was happy that there had been no bloodshed there and the tailor and his family, the shop was the front room of the house, had got away without any physical harm.

During those days, I used to wear a shirt and a salwar with a qaraqul cap on the head and a pair of Peshawari chappals on the feet. A couple of Sikh boys, who were living in the houses facing Original Road on the slope of Anand Parbat, had fixed a volleyball net and marked the court with slaked lime. Some of us, Syeed Abasi, our Muslim friend from Bihar, Lal Jindal Khosla and I used to play with them the days we did not go out. Sayeed's way of encouraging me used to be to shout during play, "Well done, Khan.Come on, Khan." I used to think he called me Khan by way of complimenting me, as 'Khan' denoted a ruler or a member of the ruling class among the Turks and the Pathans. Even otherwise, he used to say occasionally during conversation, that I was a Khan. I thought that he did that because of my dress and bearing. However, one day after our Muslim colleagues had left, Sant Lal Jindal, who seemed to be much closer to our three Muslim colleagues than any other trainee, told me the reason he thought that Sayeed called me Khan. According to him, it was a deliberate ploy of Sayeed to set me up as a Muslim before those Sikh boys. He said those boys had fallen for that ploy and were planning to kill me. According to him those Sikh boys knew that there were two or three Muslim trainees but they did not know their identities. So, when I was addressed as Khan and with my Pathan attire, they were convinced I was a Muslim. So, when they mentioned their design to Jindal, they came to know my true identity. According to Jindal, Sayeed was a very tricky person and he knew about it all along while befriending him. He advised me to change my attire. He said that even those Sikh boys had told him to ask me to change my attire. I, however, did not do it. The peculiar thing was that he had this opinion about a Pathan but not about Abbasi from Sindh. Abbasi, was a simple fellow and Sayeed, tall and lean, looked a deep one. Bari from Bihar had sympathy with the Muslim League and talked with communal undertones. But inspite of that, and with his gruff speech and bulky body, he did not seem to be a bad chap. He was a big bluff. Luckily, none of our Hindu and Sikh students had communal leanings or spoke in that vein except Khosla from Patiala State who, sometimes, very rarely, spoke about what was happening in West Punjab.

Within about ten days of the happening in Delhi, my uncle, Dewan Ram Swarup, my father's cousin, along with Seth Parma Nand came to see me in a jeep. They both were sub-judges, fourth class, in the Frontier.They had left their wives and children at Anandpur, near Shivpuri, which was established by Swami Sarupa Nand of Tehri, and later developed by his successor guru, Swami Viraga Nand, and come to Delhi for a job. Their arrival in Delhi coincided with the commencement of riots.

Delhi's administration at that time was in disarray. Delhi's population at that time was even less than five hundred thousand. It was a centrally administered city and its population was more or less orderly, the central secretariat's employees and their dependents constituting a substantial proportion of the population. Delhi's administration was not prepared to deal with the influx of refugees and the large-scale riots, which followed. Delhi's commissioner at that time was Khurshid Ahmed Khan and the Deputy Commisioner was Randhawa. Law and order until a few years hence and the general administration had been the responsibility of the Deputy Commissioner; the commissioner being responsible for policy matters, dealing with the central government and other matters such as transport, excise and finance. Law and order a few years ago was put under the charge of a Police Commissioner, but of the time I am writing about, it was under the charge of the Deputy Commissioner. He, of course, was under the control of the Chief Commissioner, but in a situation like riots when the officer in-charge has to take on the spot or immediate decisions, all the authority starts shifting towards him, and finally gets consolidated in him. Even otherwise, Khurshid Ahmed Khan, being a Muslim, had a great disadvantage in dealing with refugees at that period of time, and so Randhawa had more or less had complete control as far as law and order was concerned. My uncle, Ram Swarup and Parma Nand contacted Randhawa at Delhi, and he immediately appointed them first class magistrates, being short of parties going out to control mobs or to administer different localities for peace keeping purposes. Randhawa, most probably, had been given powers to recruit officers on the spot for his immediate need.

My uncle gave me a curfew pass, though Parma Nand opposed it saying that my uncle should not give me the pass because I would be going out frequently during curfew hours and that would be dangerous for me. However my uncle warned me not to make too much use of the pass. They were going on a round. They asked me to go with them because they knew that I had been restricted to Anand Parbat and had not been out of that place for quite some time and would, therefore, like to go out and see for myself what had been happening. We passed through Karol Bagh, and it was absolutely quiet. On Faiz Road all the houses vacated by Muslims had been occupied by Sikhs. It had made Uncle Ram Swarup very angry. Some Skihs had occupied those two houses also which Uncle and Parma Nand had earmarked and locked for their own occupation. Their argument was that the right to the houses was determined by prior physical possession and not by who had locked the houses earlier. Uncle abused them, and at one stage he even snatched the rifle of one of the two policemen accompanying him in the jeep to threaten those Sikhs, but Parma Nand, myself and some other dignitary, who was also with Uncle and Parma Nand in the jeep, snatched it away from him. The Sikhs remained adamant in their possession. They said they could arrest them but not abuse them. Ultimately, Uncle and Parma Nand had to beat a retreat, leaving those adamant Sikhs in the possession of those two houses, which the magistrates of the area had earlier taken possession of and locked. At that time only pysical might counted to occupy a vacant house and to hold it in Delhi.

After the incident at Faiz Road, in the evening, Uncle and I went to the airport to see the arrival of aeroplanes, carrying refugees from the various cities of Pakistan. It was done at my request, as I expected mother and my Uncle Shambhu Dass to arrive on one of those planes. These planes used to leave in the morning for various destinations in West Pakistan and returned laden with refugees in the evening. Many a time, more than one plane came nearly empty or with very few refugees, as at many places in West Pakistan intended refugees could not reach the airports because the passage between their houses or camps and the airports was unsafe for them. In order to facilitate evacuation, All India Radio used to announce at night the names of those refugees who were to be evacuated the next day from various stations in Pakistan. The names were furnished to the All India Radio by friends and relations of those people a number of days in advance. Many Hindus in the cities of Pakistan used to take a chance of boarding a plane for India, even if their names were not announced over the radio, and they usually found seats, as people whose names were announced mostly did not turn up either because they did not hear the All India Radio's broadcasts announcing their names for the flight concerned or they could not get out of their localities for fear of attacks by Muslims gangs enroute to the airports. So it was mostly the daring or the influential persons, who were provided protection by the local authorities, who made use of these flights.

When we were at the airport, the flight from Peshawar arrived. In this flight the only person I knew by sight was Dr. Gupta, the Medical Superintendent of Lady Reading, the main hospital, in Peshawar. Uncle Ram Swarup knew him. He asked him about the persons waiting at Peshawar to be evacuated. But he did not know much about it. After a number of days I went to see my uncle. He was staying in a hotel near the main city railway station. He asked me to spend the night with him and I readily agreed, as during those days I always carried in my mind a sense of insecurity because of the uncertainty about the safety of my relatives in Pakistan and the uncertain future I faced. To talk and spend some time with an understanding close relative is very welcome when one is disturbed in mind.

I was perturbed about the safety of my mother and my uncle, Shamhu Dass, and his family because my brother's family and he himself, as well as my sister and her family were already in India. I was more worried about my uncle and his family than my mother, as mother was with my aunt and her family in Kohat Cantt, which was safe and my uncle, Hari Chand, was an influential official. I felt that he would somehow manage to get everyone living with him evacuated by air. Murree, where Uncle Shambhu Dass was posted, on the other hand, was a hill station, which had no railhead or air connection, and on top of it their line of escape was through Rawalpindi, which had seen a lot of communal trouble. Kahutta, near Murree, had witnessed the killing of nearly the whole population of Hindus and Sikhs in mob violence.

My brother, Haridwar, was to leave for Haripur on 24th August by train to report for duty there on expiry of his 15 day leave. I received a letter from him that I should book a seat for him on a plane from Delhi to Peshawar. I guessed he would go from Peshawar to Haripur by road. I knew he was worried about his job. He was an employee of the N.W.F.P government and he wanted to report there on expiry of his leave, but going there was very risky when all over West Punjab and N.W.F.P, according to rumours, Hindus and Sikhs were being killed. I did not know whether to try booking a seat for him or not. On the one hand, booking was against my judgement but on the other, not to do it would be against his wishes. I thought I would try to purchase a ticket. If I could not get a ticket so much the better, but if I could get it, I would try to persuade him not to proceed further and cancel the ticket. I thought he would have discussed the matter with his father-in-law and others. I did not know how they could have agreed with his move. I personally was even scared to go to the airline's office, having been there during one of my various wanderings, because of the huge crowds of prospective travelers, both Hindus and Muslims, to Pakistan.

Khosla, my classmate, had an uncle who was a senior official in Delhi. I asked him whether he could ask his uncle to use his influence to get a seat for my brother for Peshawar. I gave him the money for the ticket also, as he was going the same afternoon. I asked him to see his uncle. He told me in the evening that his uncle had stated that it was not difficult for him to get a booking but had asked whether Khosla's friend was a wellwisher of his brother or an enemy. Khosla always talked loudly, but that day he gave full vent to his feelings. He asked what type of a brother I was to send my brother to butchers. He went on talking in this vein. I knew he was right, but in the morning he had not said any such thing. He, of course, offered an explanation for that himself stating that in the morning he did not dissuade me from trying to arrange a booking because I would have thought that under that pretext he was trying to get away from the effort of making a booking.

It is true many mistakes are committed just because a person does not want to say no in order not to be misunderstood. I told Khosla that I agreed with him and his uncle. The advice of Khosla's uncle was what I needed to make up my mind. I sent Haridwar a telegram the day, 28th August, that I had not made the booking, as it was too risky to go to Pakistan during those days. The next day he telegraphed himself that I should not make the booking.

From Haridwar's change of his intentions one visualizes the rapidly deteriorating situation. He came to Dehra Dun on 15th August with the firm attention of reporting back to Haripur, a town in Pakistan, on expiry of his leave, inspite of the fact that he saw massacre or arson at various railway stations and cities during his outward railway journey. Still he did not think of remaining in India. I came back from Dehradun on the 17th, but we at that time did not talk of the possibility of his staying on in India. Things had deteriorated since then, but still he did not change his mind about going back to Haripur until the 25th of August, when he wrote to me to book his air seat, but on the 28th he sent a telegram that I should not book his seat. It was good that he changed his mind in time at the last moment, because I read in the papers, about the middle of September, that all the Hindus in Haripur, about 150 in number, had been killed. Haripur's Hindu population was much more than that, but that news item indicated that luckily many Hindus had left the place earlier.

At end of September, Haridwar wrote to Shahbaz at Tehri that he should go to Haripur and take his double barrel gun, which he had left behind, from his house and keep that gun as his own. Shahbaz was a friend and supporter of my father. He was a leader of his community and was respected for his courage and gentlemanliness. He always carried a 'Kulhari (an axe like implement but used as a weapon, with a long wooden handle and an iron piece attached at one end, to cut with its nearly arc shaped sharp edge, 4" to 6" in spread) on his shoulder and at least a sharp knife with a 6" to 8" blade, held under his long shirt by the drawstring of his 'salwar' in front. Many others did the same to show their prowess as fighters, or most likely as killers. They were mostly cowards, who carried these weapons to bolster their image to frighten Hindus and ordinary Muslims who were meek and gentle persons, except Shahbaz who was a gentleman but had to carry these weapons as a protection against attack, as people like him, who are fearless and come to help members of his community, are liable to attract a challenge or a sneak attack. Because of his attachment to our family, he had become friendly towards Hindus in general.

Shabaz wrote to him after some time that he had gone to Haripur, but the gun was not there at his house as his house had been looted. This house he had shared with Seth Parma Nand, who was posted there as sub-judge 4th class. He had also not taken his wife there.

Until the disturbances started in Delhi, most of those who had come from areas in West Pakistan because of the threat of communal disturbances had come as a temporary measure. They all had intended to go back after the situation became normal or near normal. But after the start of trouble in Delhi, or just before that, they knew that chances of going back had vanished altogether. The next two months had been a period of turmoil, gruesome killings, pillage and rape in nearly the whole of Punjab and the Frontier, but the situation in Delhi was brought under control within a few days.

We nearly faced the horror of bloodshedding at Anand Parbat itself. Adjacent to our hostel was another unoccupied hostel. After the 15th of August, we saw families coming to that hostel. Gradually, within a few days, a number of families were living there. We learnt that they were the employees, and their families, of the Post and Telegraph Department, who had opted for service in India. They had been evacuated from areas in the new Pakistan by the Central Government at Delhi. One night at about 10.30 P.M when four or five of us trainees were lying in our cots, but had not gone to sleep in the verandah of our hostel, the door of the room of the superintendent of the hostel towards our side of the wing opened. Two people, both from Punjab, emerged. The superintendent stayed at the door but the two Punjabis, in salwar and shirt, advanced and stood at a place where they could see and talk to all of us. The younger one said that they all had been evacutated from West Punjab and all families, except one, were Hindus. The exception was a Muslim family. According to him, they wanted to kill the members of the Muslim family; which comprised of a husband, wife and a young child. They did not succeed in their design, as that morning the lady of that family tied a rakhi (a silk thread, simple or adorned with tinsel) that Hindu women tie around the right wrist of their brothers on a particular day of the year, around the wrist of a Hindu neighbour, and that Hindu gentleman told these conspirators, who were planning the murder of that Muslim family, not to touch that family, as it was his sister's family. Having met with a setback they came to seek our help in their venture. They thought being young, we would be eager to join them in their nefarious design. That is the reason that their introduction of the project to us was not in the simple words as I mentioned above but in 'Come along, there is game'. As nobody else among us spoke, I said that the Muslim gentleman was a colleague of theirs and rather than killing him and his family, they should protect them. They both were annoyed at my words. They said that I did not know what Muslims had done to them: they had come from Bahawalpur state and there, Muslims had killed all the members of their families. They said that we could not realize the anguish they were going through. According to them they could not rest in peace until they had had their revenge. I told them revenge never provided peace of mind. They were already speaking heatedly, but on hearing my words they got aflamed and said that if we were true Hindus, we would join them in their venture, as it was the duty of every true Hindu to kill Muslims wherever they might be. I kept quiet; nobody else spoke. One of them asked after a while whether we were coming with them. We again kept quiet. At this the older of the two visitors told his companion that they should leave, as none of us had courage.

After they went away the way they had come, all my colleagues started to speak, though none had not uttered a word when the visitors were there. The superintendent, after seeing them off, came to his position at the door of his room where he had stood throughout the period the visitors were with us. I asked him why he had brought the visitors to us and why he had not turned them back from his room itself. He said that they had entered his room with a long knife, and he got scared, but instead of taking them to the 1st year Agriculture students, who were immature, he brought them to us, as we were mature. We appreciated his action. I knew that my colleagues were also afraid as they had somewhat admitted. I was actually no less scared, otherwise I would have admonished those two refugees and warned them of the consequences of their actions.

This incident demonstrated to me how, because of one's lack of courage, one allows others to indulge in dastardly actions without physically intervening to prevent them. My companions, who were lying on their cots beside me that night, such as Daljit Singh, Amarjit Singh, Surinder Singh and Sant Lal Jindal, were Punjabis and concerned about what was happening in Punjab, but none was a rabid communalist to countenance communal killings, but they did not speak that night because of the fear of fanatical killers. The superintendent was so afraid that he admitted possible killers in his hostel to meet the boarders although his duty was to prevent his wards from meeting such people. Of my own part, which I played that night, I am not proud. The reason for the lack of courage of very steadfast and liberal minded persons at a crucial moment is that fanatical killers are so imbued with the righteousness of their murderous intent that they are liable to kill their own if they are opposed by them at the time of putting into execution that intent.

The second time, however, I gave a better performance. One evening, when dusk had nearly turned into night, I saw a tonga at the foot of Anand Parbat facing north on the road cutting Original Road at the base of Anand Parbat and running from south to north. The tonga was standing just to the north of the crossing and two young men on bicycles on either side of the tonga were talking to the tonga driver, and two people, a young army captain and a girl, were sitting on the rear bench of the tonga. It seemed to me from the way the girl was bedecked with jewellery and dressed in fine clothes that the couple was newly married. The young men were saying to the driver that he was a Muslim and so they would kill him. The driver was so frightened that he could not even talk. He managed with difficulty to give monosyllabic answers. When he said that he was a Hindu, the young men asked him to show his 'janev', the sacred thread which all Hindus are supposed to have round their necks, but in modern times many do not have. When he could not show the janev, he was asked to show his 'choti, which all Hindus are supposed to have but few actually do. He picked up a few strands on the top of his head to indicate that he had a choti, but it was obvious that he did not have a choti. The distant resemblance to a choti could be a queue worn by the Chiness. But while the Chiness queue is a thick, long and broad sheet of strands of hair pulled back from the top of the head, the Hindu choti is normally a few strands of hair a few inches long and usually tied together, so that it lies on the head.

When the tonga driver could not produce a choti, he was asked which place he came from originally. This was done to give him another chance to produce proof of his being a Hindu. The tonga driver stated that he came from Rawalpindi (West Pakistan). Then he was asked about the locality he came from in Rawalpindi. He replied haltingly that he came from the Saidpuri locality. At this the captain jumped from the tonga and said," Kill him! No Hindu lived in Saidpuri Moholah. I know it because I came from that side." At this, his wife said in English, 'Madan, do not get involved. You are an army officer.' Her husband replied that as he was an army officer, it was his duty to do so. As if it was an army officer's duty to get Muslims killed by fanatics. At this juncture I intervened, as I saw that the questioning had finished and the next step would be to kill the driver. I asked the army officer very vehemently what he was talking about. I said I knew about Rawalpindi, and could definitely say that Hindus lived in Saidpuri Mohollah. At this the army officer was taken unawares. He could just ask, 'Oh, do they live there?' I am glad he gave in, otherwise an emphatic statement of an army officer would have been definitely accepted especially in those days of turbulance as during war or civil strife, army personnel enjoy exceptional prestige. The youth, at my intervention, became unsure of themselves. They asked the driver whether he knew anybody in Karol Bagh to identify him. On the driver's saying that he knew a 'halwai' who was supplied milk by him, they took him to the halwai's shop in Karol Bagh with the captain and his wife in the tonga and the two youth on cycles on either side of the tonga. I am sure that, whether the driver was proved to be a Muslim or not, he had escaped death because during those days when things had rather quietened down, it was not possible to kill a person even though he might belong to, supposedly, an undesirably community in the main bazaar when unarmed. However I wondered at the army officer, who instead of going to the place he was going to, involved himself in a dangerous game due to his injudicious and malicious intervention. However it occurred to me that I was lucky that those two youth did not mistake me for a Muslim, as I was dressed in my Pathan attire: salwar, shirt, Peshwari chapli and Qaraqul cap.

One day, I went to Fatehpuri and Old Delhi's railway station. I went to see how things were on that side. This was my normal practice those days to go to various areas to see the things for myself. Even before this communal strife, I visited outlying and other unknown areas, as it was a sort of hobby with me to discover new areas and familiarize myself with them. While I was at the station, at about 4 P.M, the curfew hooter sounded. I got stuck there. To spend the night there was not a pleasant prospect for me. Indian railway stations are as it is dirty, but the refugee influx and people camping on the platforms made them most unwelcome. I knew there was night curfew in Old Delhi, and I had never expected it to be otherwise but I was not prepared for curfew from 4 p.m. Most probably some trouble or possibility of trouble had made the authorities declare curfew earlier. I had a curfew pass, but to walk back about seven miles was not a happy prospect and that too in curfew hours when on the empty streets any mischief-maker could have stabbed me or taken a shot at me. Luckily while I was wondering what to do, I found myself face to face with Hari Dass, my friend of Kohat days. On hearing my dilemma, he advised me to go Mohiuddin Pur where he was going and so I went along with him by train. The train left within minutes of Hari Dass meeting me. He most probably knew about the train timing and so had just arrived in time at the station. Mohiuddin Pur was about 53 kilometers from Delhi. His stepbrother there was working in a sugar mill. He had sent for his father's family from Kohat, and Hari Dass, his father, mother and brother had been there since their arrival and had been staying in a separate house, which Hari Dass's stepbrother had been able to manage through the General Manager of the mill, who was from Kohat and who knew Hari Dass's father well. I spent the night with Hari Dass's family, and early in the morning left for Delhi by bus, as I knew my lecturer would be angry if I missed classes that day because even otherwise I had stayed the night without permission, though under circumstances beyond my control.

In November I went to the Services Selection Board at Meerut to appear before it in connection with an advertisement, in the newspapers, released by the Army Headquarters, in connection with the recruitment of commissioned officers in the various branches: Mechanical Engineering, Military Farms Supply and others. As only graduates were expected to reply and for Military Farms B.Sc. Agriculture was an acceptable qualification, I had applied for it. I was selected after about three days of tests. One of the charms of the selection process was the Army's mess life, which consisted of among other nice things, a furnished room to sleep in, very good food and a well-provided ward room.

Nearly all who came to the Service Selection Boards for recruitment in the officer cadre were from the middle class. For them, to be waited upon by bearers, to be served bedtime tea with a banana or a couple of biscuits and most of all to be served a full breakfast of fruit, cornflakes or porridge with milk, toast with butter and jam, eggs done according to one's choice and tea or coffee as desired, was something out of this world. Boys, who had been to the Selection Boards, used to talk to their relatives and friends about the good things they had when with the selection boards. Boys, who were called, as during the World War everyone who was a matriculate and had applied for a commission was called, looked forward to their stay with the Board. Some, who were not even interested in joining the services, went when called just to sample the hospitality of the services.

I was not informed by the Board about my selection, but as I was asked to stay back for a day for the medical examination, it meant that I had been selected. The rejected, naturally, were not medically examined. I was sure of my selection, as it was obvious to others and me that where there were group tests like discussions and field tests, I had done very well. However, I got a call from the Selection Board much later, maybe after about two months, stating that my name had been recommended to the Army Headquarters for a commission. During World War II, in connection with emergency commissions, such letters were not issued. Everybody who was medically examined got a letter of posting from the Army Headquarters a short time thereafter. I, however, did not hear from the Army Headquarters for quite sometime. I got anxious about it though everyone of my acquaintance said that once someone was selected by the Selection Board, the selection was irrevocable, the Army Headquarter's approval being just a routine. They were going by the war time precedent, but in my mind there was a doubt, as I had read a news item in a newspaper to the effect that in view of the post independence requirement of the Army, it had been decided to considerably increase the intake of mechanical engineers in the graduate course, and to that extent decrease the number of graduates in the other branches. When the communication from the Army Headquarter was delayed beyond what I thought was a reasonable period, I one day walked to the South Block of the Secretariat where the Army Headquarter was based, without the sentry stopping me at the gate on seeing my determined look. I straightaway entered the room of Lt. Col.Sarin who was dealing with selections. He asked a Major Gupta to attend to me. Major Gupta showed me a chart and explained that as they were taking only one graduate for the military farms my name had not come in the final selection due to somebody else being above me in merit. Later on in March 1948 I got a letter dated 1st March from the Army Headquarters confirming what I had already learnt.

My mother came from the Frontier about the middle of October. She came with her sister and her family. They came from Kohat to Rawalpindi by train, my uncle having arranged the police protection from the house to the station. From Rawalpindi, they were taken to Chaklala Cantonment, which had become a big transit camp for refugee evacuation. After a wait of many days, they could get rail passage to Sahranpur and then to Dehra Dun from there. My uncle, Dewan Hari Chand, himself later on came to Delhi by air on his way to Dehra Dun. My uncle, Dewan Shambhu Dass, was stuck in Murree. He was in the Military Engineering Service (M.E.S). He and all others who were in the All India or the Central Services were asked their choice at the time of the partition whether they would like to serve in India or Pakistan. He and others, who came from areas forming Pakistan, had opted for Pakistan, little realizing that in a short while Pakistan would become too hot for them. When just after the partition, reports about large-scale carnage, rape and arson and forcible conversions started coming, they realized the folly they had committed. Many perished, many escaped with some damage and others escaped without any damage.

My uncle belonged to the last category. He escaped through a stratagem. Murree was a hill station, forty miles from Rawalpindi. Its only link with Rawalpindi, from where he had a chance of escape, was a road, which connected Rawalpindi with Srinagar via Murree, Muzaffarpur and Baramula. But the local Muslim population, as well as that of the villages' enroute, was more than hostile to Hindus. One day he heard from some acquaintance that according to an announcement in All India Radio seats had been reserved for him and his family on a plane coming from Delhi to pick the refugees from Rawalpindi, but he could not avail of that opportunity because of the near impossibility of getting through to Rawalpindi airport. He came to know later, when he met me, that these seats had been reserved by me. At that time the only possible stratagem he could think of was to make a break for Rawalpindi by posing as Muslims. For this, he obtained three 'burqas' (cloaks worn by Muslim ladies) through a colleague of his whom he knew well. One day he quietly boarded a bus with his wife, two daughters and two sons with his wife and 13 year old and 11 year old daughters in burqas. His sons were quite young being 9 and 7 years of age. From Rawalpindi they managed to reach Chaklala cantonment. There uncle had another escape. He went with a senior officer of his to bring their luggage from the cantonment to the railway station. There they hired a truck for the luggage and started back for Chaklala. On the way back they noticed that the truck was not on the road to Chaklala but on some other road. As the driver was a Muslim they became suspicious. The senior officer had a double barrel gun. He handed the gun to Uncle who was sitting in the back of the truck (the senior officer was in the front seat with the driver) and asked him to shoot the driver without any question through the aperture, normally of 6 to 8 inch square in the broad board separating the front protion, where the driver sits, from the back of the truck, where normally the luggage is kept, in case he saw something wrong. They reached Chaklala safe but rather late. Mother, who was there when Uncle and his family had arrived at Chaklala, and others had been anxiously awaiting their arrival. When they got the accommodation in a train for India, Mother came to Dehra Dun and Uncle went to Agra where M.E.S. employees coming from Pakistan were being berthed. The intensity of carnage in West Pakistan had made the Indian government ignore the options exercised by the employees for service in India or Pakistan, as the Government of India knew that nearly the whole of the Hindu population of Pakistan was on the move towards India.

Uncle came to see me at Anand Parbat. I was washing my undergarments in the bathroom one day when he came upon me, guided by Daljit Singh, my neighbour. He told me his story and said that he was in a bad shape. Aunt and their two daughters did not have even a change of clothes. I had at that time managed to get cloth (cambric) for two shirts. I gave that to him. My earlier attempt to make two shirts had been foiled by the rioters and now once again I had lost two shirts. The problem at that time was that there was a tremendous scarcity of cloth. One could occasionally get some cloth on the ration card but that was rough cloth. Once in a while cambric cloth for shirts was made available at some places on the ration card, but the cloth was inadequate and not available everywhere and so only the fortunate ones who either had influence or money had access to sources of fine cloth. In the evening, I took uncle to Uncle Ram Swarup who, as a magistrate, had been allotted a good sized bungalow with plenty of open and grassy land attached to it. Uncle Ram Swarup also gave him cloth suitable for ladies garments, but it was not of a very good quality. The next day, he went to his transit camp at Agra.

My uncle, Dewan Hari Chand, was able to get out of Kohat nearly all his good quality household goods. He had formed friends with a number of Army officers. When those Army officers moved out to India in special trains with all their movable belongings, they carried some items of my uncle's housholds goods also. When my aunt moved out to India with her family and my mother, she also took with her a considerable amount of luggage. Mother, however, brought with her a small handy case of gramophone records, which she could carry herself easily. All the records in the case were those of songs of Sehgal, the immortal singer of India, of whom my father was very fond. The only worthwhile goods, which the Pakistan Muslim successor of my uncle in that house would have found, would have been ours, as uncle had managed to remove all his. He lost, however, one good sized Afghan carpet to a Hindu Army officer in India. That officer had carried that carpet for uncle to India. When uncle went to see him to retrieve the carpet in Ambala, where he was posted, he stated that it had been lost enroute, though at that time that particular time that carpet was adding to the splendour of the officer's drawing room. This carpet was recognized by the other members of his family as well in subsequent visits.

My future wife, Shakti, on the 15th of August was in Bhaun (district Chakwal) in West Pakistan with her parents. The eldest son of the family was with the Indian Army somewhere in India as a civilian officer in ordnance. The next in line, in order of age, was a son, Mohan, an assistant in the Central Secretariat. He was at Delhi. The next in line, Kamla, was married to a Captain in the Indian Army on an emergency commission. He was posted at Red Fort, Delhi. Kamla and he had got married at Bhaun in 1945. The next in line was my wife, Shakti. The last of the children was a daughter, Kunta. She was five years younger than my wife. Kamla's husband, Om Vohra, reached Bhaun somehow about the 20th of August to take his wife with him to Delhi. When he reached Rawalpindi he knew that to go alone to Bhaun, which was about 60 miles between Rawalpindi and Lahore, was to take a great risk. He therefore approached some Pakistan Army formation. There a Major agreed to go with him with a vehicle. From Bhaun he brought back with him the three Talwar sisters, Shakti's newly married brother's wife and two other relatives. He left behind his own parents and parents-in-law. At Chaklala railway station, the Pakistani major helped them to board a 2nd class compartement, which in those days used to be very well fitted and very confortable. They did not get down from the train, nor did they open their windows until they reached Indian territory. His parents and parents-in-law came to Chaklala. From there, they took a train, when they could manage it, and came to Delhi.

All trains between India and Pakistan after 15th August were running on account of the refugees, but where the transfer of millions of people was involved, a few trains running on refugee relief were grossly inadquate. Therefore refugees in columns miles long, were moving in both parts of Punjab to leave behind their homes, land and what they called 'watan' in Urdu and motherland in English. Wherever people could board trains, the fittest got the chance to leave their country earlier, as they were always the first to push their way through a crowd of people, all of whom were pushing and struggling, in order not to let go the available chance of escape.

Karol Bagh, which was like a sleepy village in June when I had first come there, had become an overcrowded town by the end of

September. One saw crowds of people wherever on went. The most crowded places were areas around the entire length of the Ajmal Khan Road. One had to push through the crowds to reach one's destination in this area. This was the condition in many other places also in Delhi: such as Darya Ganj and Pahar Ganj. At Kingsway Camp, a large camp was set up for refugees. Another camp near Delhi was at Faridabad, 20 miles away from Delhi in East Punjab. Such camps were established nearly in every city or town of East Punjab. In some places of Utter Pradesh also camps were established. One such camp was in Prem Nagar at Dehra Dun where many of my relatives went. My aunt, Baso, my mother's sister, with her four young children was also in this camp. I think this was the best camp among all the camps run by the Ministry of Rehabilitation and Resettlement, Government of India, that had come into being to rehabilitate refugees and settle their claims for immovable property left in Pakistan.

Against authenticated claims, compensation was offered from the land, houses or business enterprises left behind by Muslims evacuees to Pakistan. As properties left behind by Muslim evacuees were much less in value than those left behind by the Hindu and Sikh refugees, compensation claims were also adjusted against the urban land and houses in the housing colonies established by the Government. I do not know what was the rate of compensation, but it was much less in case of rural properties. Compensation against rural properties left in Pakistan was allowed only in case of agricultural land and not of housing properties.

We had left behind two houses in Tehri, 'kacha' and one 'pucca' but we were not allowed any compensation for them. For four acres of well-irrigated land and a few scattered pieces of land, we were offered two acres of land at Rajpura, near Dehra Dun, but we refused that. I wrote to the Assistant Settlement Commissioner concerned that we both, my brother and myself, were government servants and therefore it was not possible for us to us to manage agricultural land at a distant place and even otherwise it was the government's policy to consolidate land, but giving us, who were not engaged in agriculture, a small piece of land would only result in fragmentation of a larger holding.

No reply came to my letter. Ultimately, I got my share of approved claim as well as a portion of Haridwar's adjusted against the price of a plot in the new housing area called Defence Colony, called as such as it was sponsored by the Defence Ministry,Government of India, for the Armed Forces personnel. The area of the plot allotted to me was 325 sq.yds. and its price was about Rs.6800/-. This plot was allotted to me in 1953 and I got it registered in my name in 1954. I got our claim adjusted against the price in 1959. Until then, I had been paying Rs.350/- a year towards the ground rent and the yearly lease money (the plot had had been allotted on a 99 year lease); Rs. 102/- and Rs.248/- respectively against those two items. I was allotted the plot in 1953 when I was in the Indian Navy. I paid the full amount of the lease money in 1959, through the adjustment of our claims, when I was no longer in the Navy, and got the house constructed in 1962-63, though the plot was allotted to me on the undertaking that I would build the house within a year of registration of the plot and this constituted a clause of the lease deed. The costruction cost was about Rs.60,000/. I had got a loan of Rs.35,000/- from the Government for house construction, Rs.9,000/- came from my savings after working in the Naval Services and the rest came from relatives and friends as a personal loan.

To get one's claim registered and assessed was a long, torturous and tiresome process. To illustrate the difficulties refugees faced from the mismanagemnt of the Government, I narrate here my own experience. To get citizenship and the benefits sanctioned by the Government for them, the refugees had to get themselves registered in the offices set up by the Government for the purpose. On registration, every refugee was given a card for him and his dependants. This card contained the names of the refugee concerned and his dependants. To get a card for myself, one day I went to the refugees' registration office in Karol Bagh. I saw a long queue of about four abreast, and this queue was anything but orderly. At the registration window in front some people were pushing each other. Some people were lying flat on the heads of the people in the queue and trying to wriggle forward. The four abreast queue had provided the broad platform for their endeavour to beat the queue. Unfortunately Punjabis usually take pride in beating a queue. After standing an hour in the queue, I abandoned the effort as I could not beat the heat, noise and the futility of waiting indefinitely as the queue did not seem to be moving at all. However, Haridwar later on, without my knowing about it, got a card prepared for me in Delhi. He had got himself and the other family members registered in Dehra Dun.The claims for property, on prescribed forms, were registered only on production of a refugee rehabilitation card. A certified copy was also to be enclosed with the claim application and the card number was also indicated in the claim application form at a specified place.

Haridwar was among the many who came to Delhi from other places in search of a job. At Delhi, he stayed in a bungalow on Ajmal Khan Road near Rohtak Road. This bungalow was that of a Muslim family who had gone to Pakistan, but at that time it belonged to the people of Kohat, where Kohatis from different places stayed temporarily till their pursuit of their objective ended. I usually went there in the evening to meet Haridwar. About six people were always staying there. Sometimes there were many more. During the daytime there were quite a number of people there. Many Kohatis, having houses of their own or staying at other places, came there to gossip and exchange views about the apathy of the authorities in settling refugees or on schemes under consideration by the Government in the matter.

The refugee problem arose from the two-nation theory of Jinnah and his preaching of the incapability of the Hindus and Muslims to live together. The Muslim League's intransigence and its vitriolic campaign against the Hindus led to communal violence being unleashed in Punjab and the Frontier in March, 1947 and the consequent mass scale killings and destruction which followed. Ultimately by the end of the year, things had scaled down to getting compensation for the property left behind, finding shelter and a chance to earn one one's livelihood.

When the trouble had reached its height in the beginning of September in both parts of Punjab and even engulfed Delhi in its spread, at that time, according to Freedom at Midnight authored by Larry Collins and Dominique Lapierre, Pandit Nehru and Sardar Patel and their advisers lost their nerve and asked Lord Mountbatten to assume charge of the whole affair. So Mountbatten became the head of the emergency committee of the cabinet at Nehru's and Patel's request. It is strange to read that Nehru and Patel found themselves unequal to face a crisis and requested Mountbatten to run the country for them, but it seems they had not managed any worthwhile problem in their life earlier. Nehru, in any case, was an idealist and a dreamer.

So when large-scale killings started on both sides of Punjab and at Delhi, Indian leaders suddenly woke up to realize that a problem of gigantic proportions had arisen before them. On the one hand they had to mobilize their resources to stop killings on their side of the border and on the other they had got to get thousands of people extricated from peril and transported to India as the Government had come to realize, by the beginning of September, that the minorities faced extermination in Pakistan. Many writers have rejected or doubted the veracity of the statement of Collins and Dominique Lapierre that our leaders asked Mountbatten to take over the management of the emergency that had arisen. They, however, have not been able to produce any evidence to the contrary. They also have no answer as to why Mountbatten was made Head of the Emergency Committee of the Cabinet. By right, Nehru should have become the Head of the Committee, being the Prime Minister, and not Mountbatten, who was neither in the Cabinet nor was holding an elective office.

Had Nehru and Patel been good administrators or had believed the intelligence coming to them from different sources or had foresight, they could have anticipated the mass scale slaughter which was going to take place. I, myself, had written to Nehru in May, 1946 that the Hindus of Kohat could not move about in the town, and many had left their houses and were living in safe places. I had even written that Khan Saheb, the premier of N.W.F.P, also could not move out of his house. According to Larry Collins and Dominique Lappiere, Nehru had received a telephone call from Lahore on the night of 15th August that the water supply, to the part of the city where the Hindus lived, had been cut off. Nehru, as usual, gave vent to his impotent rage but did nothing to meet the situation. In 'Freedom at Midnight' the authors' state that Mountbatten had provided 55000 thousand strong Gorkhas as the boundary force, but they were grossly indequate to meet the situation, as trouble was so widespread that it possibly could not cover the whole area involved. Had this force been properly organized, in co-operation with the military on both sides of the border, it could have spread all over the countryside, with reserves in the towns. The units of this force would have been formed of Military on both sides with the personnel of the boundary force constituting the nucleus. Even the police forces could have been organized as effective forces to combat commual trouble. In most of the districts, the Superintendents of the Police were Britishers. They would have insured fair play. But, unfortunately, there was no planning. Our leaders proved unequal to the task. Large-scale bloodshed on communal basis caught them napping, though that should not have been, and they involved the help of Mountbatten only when the trouble spread to Delhi. It was too late however. India's leaders showed more perception and foresight than the Government of Pakistan. They came to the conclusion that the minorities would have to be evacuated enblock from Punjab and the N.W.F.P. The Pakistan Government, in the beginning, hesitated, but later on came to the conclusion that the minorities from both sides of Punjab and the N.W.F.P had to be evacuated. The Hindus and Sikhs, who had come over to the Hindu major area from March to September as temporary migrants, to escape danger to life, thinking they would go back once the situation improved by September, had become refugees, and in due course Indian citizens.

Many authors and historians blamed Mountabatten for showing too much haste in ending British rule in India. I think they do gross injustice to Mountbatten. He knew that the communal situation was worsening rapidly and so he wanted the British to quit as early as possible. He felt that once the partition of the country was achieved through the agreement of the parties concerned, the cause for internecine fighting would end; hence the haste in the formation of the two dominions. I feel any delay in the matter would have resulted in much more bloodshed. The Hindus, in any case, had been dying in West Punjab during the March to August period. Any delay in the formation of the two states would have prolonged the agony and bloodshed of the Hindus there. The slaughter on both sides after the partition would have been there in any case. In the absence of adequate measures it took place after the 15th of August 1947 or after the 31st of March 1948. However there was great danger of a great number of Muslims being killed in other Hindu dominated provinces, as the trouble was bound to spread in case the killing of Hindus in West Punjab had remained uninterrupted for a longer period. However Mounbatten cannot escape responsibility for not providing sufficient safeguard against the probability of atrocities against the minorities in Punjab, and even elsewhere. Mountbatten was a good organizer of men and material, and if he had set his mind on doing a thing, he could do it. For example, even Wavel was of the opinion that Britain could not hold India for long, but he could not find a way to effect transfer of power. Mountbatten did it in a short time. Mountbatten, with his acumen, should have anticipated largescale bloodshed after the partition. He should have known that the hatred generated by Jinnah and other leaders of the Muslim League in their speeches, against the Hindus, would not end by the division of the country between the Hindus and Muslims, especially when a large minority of Muslims was left in India, particularly in East Punjab, and a minority of Hindus in Pakistan.

Chapter Eight

Independence-Before and After

For independence and partition of the country, Muslims, Hindus and Sikhs, mostly of Punjab and the Frontier paid the following price:

In the first wave of pre-partition riots, 3000 people, most of them Sikhs, were killed.

By July 1947, 100,000 Hindus and Sikhs had fled Lahore, when Cyril Radcliffe, the Boundary Commissioner arrived there.

The above figures have been given by Larry Collins and Dominique Lapiere in their book 'Freedom at Midnight'.

In 'Modern India: 1885-1947', Amit Sarkar has given the following statistics about the losses in partition.

By August 1947, 5000 Hindus and Sikhs had been killed at Lahore, Multan, Attock, Amritsar and Rawalpindi. Rural areas of Multan, Attock and Rawalpindi were also involved in large-scale communal riots.

Pendera Moon, who was serving in Pakistan during the pre-partition riots and at the time of partition and until some time later, gives the estimate of Hindus and Sikhs killed as 60,000, while the corresponding figure for Muslims, according to him, was 12,0000.

Larry Collins and Dominique Lappiere, in "Freedom at Midnight", quoted Justice G.D. Khosla's figure as 500,000 killed in his book "Stern Reckoning". The authors have described Justice Khosla as the foremost student of massacres. But none of the other historians or authors quoted by Larry Collins and Dominique Lappiere, in their book, have given a figure of over 250,000 killed. Larry Collins and Dominique Lappiere have quoted Chandu Lal Trivedi, the first Indian Governor, stating that a million migrants crossed the border in a more respectful manner. It means 9.5 million persons crossed the border in not a respectful manner, as Pendera Moon is quoted by Sumit Sarkar, in "Modern India" to have stated that 10.5 million (6 million Muslims and 4.5 million Hindus and Sikhs) people had become refugees. The Muslims had left behind 4.7 million acres of land in East Punjab and the Hindus and the Sikhs left 6.7 million acres in West Punjab. According to Moon, in Bahawalpur State, in southwest Punjab, where he was working, the Muslim population (mostly peasants) was less interested in bloodshed than in the quiet enjoyment of Hindu girls and Hindu property. Physical liquidation was more important in central and east Punjab where opposite communities were evenly matched, and the Sikhs in particular showed a grim determination to wipe out Muslims, so that land could be found for the 2 million Sikhs coming from the West.

Above are some of the grim statistics about the partition. One reason for the lower Hindu and Sikhs mortality can be that quite a number of Hindus and Sikhs had left their homes to come over to East Punjab, Delhi and other places in the March to August period. A lesser reason could be that many Hindus and Sikhs had been converted to Islam on pain of death and all of them were not brought over to the Indian side later on. But, as statistics stand, the Muslims paid a bigger price for the partition of the country. But, the Hindus and the Sikhs were exacted a price for something which they did not get but rather lost. It has been stated by a number of persons that in March trouble started because of Master Tara Singh, a Sikh Akali Leader, taking out his sword and waving it over his shoulders and shouting slogans against the designs of Muslims in forming Pakistan, outside the provincial assembly hall at Lahore. The occasion was the fall of the Unionist Government on 3rd March 1947 as a result of the Muslim League's campaign.

However, the Sikhs did not do much in spreading communal riots in the March to August period in West Punjab and the Frontier Province. It was actually the Rashtriya Sewam Sangh's followers who mostly ran a sort of running duel with the Muslim communalists for sometime at Lahore, where the Hindus and the Sikhs had near parity with the Muslim population, and in Rawalpindi, where the Hindus and the Sikhs had a majority in numbers over the Muslims. But gradually the Hindu position weakened even in these two places mostly due to their own fear complex, as well off Hindus and Sikhs started leaving these cities in increasing numbers from this complex which had its origin in their being over all in the minority. The other reason was the growing militancy of the Muslims in the countryside and other towns. I remember, that the Hindus coming from Rawalpindi to Delhi were very bitter about the Sikhs. So, for the pre-partition riots, one cannot blame the Sikhs.

The genius behind the riots was the same. The one responsible for the partition of the country. However, I admit that the Muslim Leaguers who inflamed the riots did not realize that the consequences of their action would be so great and devastating. The riots were started to make the Hindus and the Sikhs pay in blood for their refusal to agree to Pakistan. When the establishment of Pakistan was made certain because of their action, the idea behind continuing the riots was to get rid of a good number of people of the minorities, through an exodus to India, by use of the instruments of terror and liquidation. One basic element about the use of violence, that the future leaders of Pakistan did not understand, was that violence feeds violence. There is nothing like controlled violence, because once triggered, it goes on increasing in intensity and extent until it is counteracted with a greater and determined force and handled with skill and predetermined planning. On the one hand, violence had acquired a great momentum by the 15th of August and on the other, the Sikhs and the cadres of R.S.S. had got ready to hit back in retaliation. The leaders of Pakistan were not ready for these developments. What they wanted was a controlled exodus of Hindus to India, but what they ultimately got was a two-way traffic. If Jinnah and the Muslim League wanted the riots to subside, it was an easy matter for them to do so in June or even in July. What Jinnah had to do was speak against violence and stress upon the necessity to befriend the Hindus and the Sikhs, as they all would have to live in amity and friendship to build together their country, Pakistan.

But he did not do so, and neither did any other Muslim League leader. I believe, Jinnah's idea was to have a minority of Hindus and Sikhs in Pakistan. Not a large one that would be able to play an effective part in the governance of Pakistan, but one that could be kept as hostage to ensure the safety of the Muslim minority in India. But Jinnah, not being an administrator or a practical man, did not realize that his men, intoxicated by the easy killings of Hindus, would go all out to kill Hindus and Sikhs in areas where they were not in an appreciable number to be of any consequence, and the Hindus and the Sikhs would hit back in East Punjab. One reason for the violence of the Sikh attack in East Pakistan could be that they wanted the Muslims to vacate agricultural land to accommodate two million Sikh refugees, who immigrated from the rural area of West Pakistan. But the other reason was revenge for the humiliation suffered and deaths sustained in West Pakistan.

I can understand Jinnah and the Muslims of the Muslim majority areas of India trying for a formation of a state where Muslims should be in majority. But I cannot understand the Muslims in Hindu dominated provinces like Uttar Pradesh, Bihar and Tamil Nadu striving for Pakistan. As, I have earlier mentioned, actually it was the Muslims of Uttar Pradesh and Bihar who agitated and got Pakistan for the Muslims of Punjab and the Frontier. Though I know in 1947, or even in 1946, the Muslims in the Muslim majority areas had switched over in favour of the Muslim League and Pakistan, but still in the elections held for the legislative assemblies in 1945-46 (According to Sumit Sarkar in Modern History) the Muslim League could form ministries only in Sindh and Bengal and that too they were dependent on official and European support. Perhaps, the Muslims throught that they would be able to hold themselves against the docile and timid Hindus in India, or perhaps they thought that a powerful Pakistan would be at their back to support them if need arose. Whatever may be the reason, it shows fanaticism at its worst. I would not call it idealism. Fanaticism is blind while idealism is based on some logic.

As things stood, the overwhelming majority of Muslims were ready to live under the Hindu Raj. As India was divided on religious basis, it was presumed that India would become a Hindu State and would be named 'Bharat' (an ancient name of India). But when India continued to be called India after partition and independence, the Government of Pakistan and its leaders could not tolerate India continuing as a secular state as before, so they, on their own, started addressing India as Bharat. It was done to cover their own embarrassment, for if India could be a secular state with nearly as much a Muslim population as Pakistan had, then where was the necessity of partition on the two-nation theory. The two-nation theory was created merely by some political leaders, to justify a Muslim majority state where political leaders could have political control, after remaining in wilderness and without any worthwhile following for a considerable period. When the process of constitution making was completed in 1950, the official name of India was adopted as India, that is Bharat. The constitution of India is one of the very few progressive ones, while that of Pakistan ultimately emerged to be very regressive.

As for the two-nation theory, it is based on the contention that the Hindus and Muslims constituted two different nations, meaning thereby that that their origin, their customs and their languages were different. Jawahar Lal Nehru, in his autography published in 1936, has stated that differences between the Hindus and the Muslims were superficial, as the Hindus tied their dhoti one way and the Muslims the other way. Actually, people in South India tied the dhotis the same way. Similarly, the Hindus used for their morning ablutions a lota (a utensil) of one shape and the Muslims of a slightly different shape. The same is the difference in caps of an ordinary Hindu and Muslim. Even in most parts of Northern India, a language is spoken which has arisen from Hindwi. Hindus use more Sanskrit words in it and Muslims Persian. Hindus call it Hindi and the Muslims Urdu. Actually all Hindus and Muslims spoke the same language common to an area. For example, Punjabis spoke Punjabi irrespective of the religion they kept. The same was the case with Bengalis. The same is the case even now in different states. Urdu is Persianised Hindi. The Muslim ruling classes had to perforce speak Hindi or Hindwi in order to converse with their subjects whether Hindus or Muslims. Similarly they had to converse with their subordinates, most of whom were converted from the local population i.e. Hindus, so to speak to them also they had to learn the local language, Hindi. However, the Muslims nobles and rulers went on adding to its vocabulary with the addition of Persian and Arabic words, knowingly or unknowingly. Knowingly, because they wanted the language to become akin to their own language. Unknowingly, as it was a natural process of assimilation, for if a person speaks a language which is not his own, he is bound to add some words of his own language to it, especially if a person is not well versed in the new language he tries to speak. When this new language is spoken by a very large number of persons, and they are not good at it, the rate and extent of addition of foreign words to this language can be considerably large, especially when the ruling class is interested in this transformation.

Every Muslim and every convert is expected to learn Arabic, as the Muslims Holy Book 'Quran' and 'Sunna' (the Prophet's alleged sayings) are in this language. A dedicated Muslim is even expected to learn the 'ayats' (verses) of the Quran by heart. But most of the tribes, who came to India in waves of invasion in the period of Muslim dominance of Central Asia, were not Arabic speaking. However, as they were close to Persia and many of them had been dominated by Persia, they spoke Persian or at least knew something of it, and so the absorption of Persian words was much more than the Arabic words. The Muslim rulers changed the script from the original to Persian. The Persian script itself had undergone a change when the Arabs overran it within a century of Prophet Muhammad's death in 632 A.D. It was formed on Arabic script. As Emperor Humayun, the second king of the Mughal Dynasty, had gone in exile to Persia, after being defeated by an Afghan, Sher Shah Suri, and had remained there for about 16 years and was able to conquer his throne back with the help of then Persian King, the Persian influence in the Mughal court was great. This influence was reflected in the architecture, fine arts and literature. Though the syntax of Urdu, the new language which came up from Persianised Hindi was that of Hindi, its script was Persian and imagery also was mostly Persian, or to a much lesser extent, Arabic. One could read about Firdausi or Harun Rashid in Urdu literature but not of Kali Dass or Ashoka. However, the trend in recent years in the development of Urdu has been reversed. I may mention here that the court language in the Mughal period was Persian; Urdu being the language of smaller functionaries or mostly of the lashker (army). And the name Urdu connotes lashker in some way.

My argument is that the Hindus and the Muslims had a common ancestory in India. Only a small number of Turks, Afghans and a relatively much smaller number of Arabs came with the invaders at different times and settled down in India. They spoke the language of the region they were living in. They had a common culture. Why should a change of religion have created a new nation, and that too when one does not know specifically under what circumstances the change occurred. Arabs changed their religion, but they remained Arabs. They were pagans like Indians before their change of religion. Similarly, Iranians remained Iranians, as did the Afghans, but the Muslims of India had to renounce their cultural and racial identity when they converted to Islam. It is tragic, because it had serious consequences in the past and will have even severer consequences in the future. The Shah of Iran, when he had settled down on his throne, tried to resurrect and glorify the Iranians' pre-Islamic heritage. One day the children of the Muslims who propagated the two nation theory and those who concurred in that theory would like to identify with their ancestors of a bygone age and rejoice in their achievements, but will not be able to do so as their ancestors had renounced India and Hindus and become Pakistanis.

The Indians of today do not belong to a particular race or creed. The India of today has people of nearly all races and hues. India belongs to all of them. However, they have the same culture, with small variations peculiar to various parts. This culture has evolved over a long period of time. Different republics and kingdoms came into being with different names peculiar to the parts they were situated in. However, the geographical unit, later on called India, had no name though the people of that geographical unit had developed a unique culture of their own. The name India was given to that geographical unit by the Greeks, and it came from the river which the Greeks called the Indus.The Indus is a river which originates in Ladakh and then flows down to the N.W.F.P. Punjab, Sindh and ultimately to the Arabian Sea. Ladakh is in India, the other three are in Pakistan.The people of India were called Hindus, again from the Indus, as the Indus was called Sindh by the Aryans. The Persians, because of the difficulty in pronouncing the alphabet 'S' called the river Hind and the people who lived there as Hindus. The Greeks, thus, gave the name of Hindus to those people who were living in the vicinity of the Indus or beyond. And so a people emerged in history known as Hindus, in the area now covering India, Pakistan and Bangla Desh, and this name was given to them by the Greeks and not themselves.

Hinduism was never a religion, nor is it today in the sense Judaism, Christianity or Islam are. Foreigners started called the faith of the people Hinduism, because they called those people Hindus. Hinduism is a way of living, or it is the culture of the people. They believed in the dignity of people. They believed in not harming any animate or inanimate being for self-gratification, or any other purpose except for self-preservation. They were simple people and lived in simplicity. Their sages, over many centuries, evolved and developed a comprehensive philosophy of living or action, the gist of which was the doctrine of karma; a person would be rewarded in the next birth as per his actions in the present birth. Hinduism has evolved from the thinking of human beings; it has not come from God through his prophets. Whatever else is present today in the Hindu religion in the nature of Gods, superstition, idol worship or caste system is due to mythology, acquired from other sources, absorption of different outside people and tribes or selfishness of the priestly class. How could the Hindus, who believe in the equality of men and the doctrine of Karma, indulge in casteism. Casteism must have arisen from the designation of absorbed tribes and conquered uncivilized persons being of the lower castes. Hindus did not have the institution of slavery, but the selfish Brahmins and ruling classes introduced casteism and made it hereditary for selfish gains.

The Buddha's eight fold path (ashtpada) perfectly represents the conduct of a Hindu, as per Hindu scriptures, though the eight fold path was preached by Buddha; the reason being that Hindusim and Buddhism are essentially one. When the Aryans came to India, they believed in various Gods, as the Aryans did in Greece and elsewhere. The Rig Veda, which is the oldest of the Vedas mentions about the existence of the various Gods, but gradually the philosophy of Hinduism emerged in the Upanishads. The Shastras were the latest, in the development of Hindu thought, though many sages later on stressed on the essentials of Hindu thought, in order to make it simpler for the lay man to understand and act upon the essentials. Besides, the other religions and sects, which originated in India and are based on Hindu throught, even the Muslim Sufis are akin to Hindus, as they preach love of man, brotherhood of men and renunciation of desires, as they are the root cause of all suffering in the world.

Judaism, Christianity and Islam are different in conception, doctrine and rituals, as they are primarily based on the conception that their religions are based on divine revelations, and their religious beliefs and practices have come to them as commandments from God through their prophets.

The purpose of writing about various religions is that though there are differences of beliefs between very religions, should these differences be allowed to divide mankind? I believe religion has been created for man and not man for religion. The aim of all religions is to remove suffering and make mankind happy, and not the other way round. The Hindus and the Muslims had a common heritage in India. Their forefathers, a few centuries back, were the same. Then I do not understand why should some of the descendents say they are different and are of a different nation, just because their ancestors had adopted a different faith under certain compulsion, or is it because their forefathers had been defeated by foreign forces, determined and better organized, who were very well versed in the new techniques of waging battles.

I do not think partition was avoidable after 3 March,1947, but earlier, especially before 16th August, 1946, when Jinnah launched his direct action, there was a distinct possibility of keeping India together. Pakistan and India are in confrontation everywhere. Confrontation is across the border, in the U.N.O., in the choice of their friends and in every sphere and every conference. The relations of India and Pakistan and Hindus and Muslims are governed by hatred.

Hindus, not being a monolithic religion nor even a faith in terms of religions, which have a Semitic origin, never had a sense of coming together to fight foreign invaders in the name of religion. Even when nearly the whole of the area now constituting Pakistan was involved in communal violence and Hindus were being plundered and killed everywhere, the Hindus did not react in the Hindu majority areas. Retaliation occurred only in East Punjab and Delhi later on, only when the refugees from West Punjab and N.W.F.P. flocked to those areas in great numbers. Had the communal violence spread to the other parts of India, millions would have died there.

The Hindus were individualistic in nature. Whether it was meditation or having meals, they did it alone. The tolerance of the Hindus is proverbial. Even Greek writers who came with Alexander testified to that. At that time Hindus had more interest in spiritual matters than the desire to get together for material gains. Their empires came later. Whosoever came to the country, settled down here without encountering hostility from the local inhabitants. Whether they were Huns, Kushans, Parsis or other Central Asian tribes, they settled down with the local people, without there being any difficulty in the practice of their beliefs.

Beliefs were a matter of individual choice. A member of a family may become a Buddhist, another a Jain, but they lived together as family members. Any dispute regarding a belief was a matter of discussion or dialectic and not a physical fight or extermination. A couple of months ago, I read that somebody said that Hindus also destroyed Buddhist temples or used them for their purposes. As for destruction of Buddhist temples by Hindus, it is news to me. I have not read about it. I cannot understand why Hindus should destroy Buddhist temples. It is against Indian culture for one, and secondly, Hindus use the temples for discourses and so do Buddhists and so why would Hindus destroy them? Hindus visited Buddhists, Jain and Sikh Temples. They do that even now, because what is taught there is a part of Hinduism. Hinduism allows differences and discussions about their beliefs. I heard Tara Ali Beg on the television the other day. She said, near the Qutab at Delhi, there is a mosque (Quat Ul Islam) built by the Muslims, when they conquered Delhi in the 12th century A.D. This mosque was built from the material of various Hindu and Jain temples, which were destroyed by the invaders. She said in those destroyed temples, was a Jain temple, and that temple was a Jain temple earlier, but later on the Hindus destroyed it and built a Hindu temple instead. The fact is that the motifs on stones and pillars earlier were from

Jainism theology and mythology. When the people of the area switched over to Brahmanism, they sculpted their own religious figures. I am not a votary of Brahminism. On the contrary, after Buddhism, the coming in vogue of Brahminism I treat as a retrograde, or rather a contradiction, or rather worse, an abomination. But I do not think even votaries of Brahminism would destroy any temple belonging to Buddhists or Jains, or even mosques belonging to Muslims. Even Shivaji, who was a product of orthodox and religious teachings and who fought against Muslim kings, who had made his people subjects and made them suffer iniquities and humiliation, never desecrated a mosque or treated a Muslim woman without respect. The only thing could have been that in a certain area, if the popuation became adherents of Brahminism, they used their temples for praying according to their new faith, while earlier they were praying according to Jain or Buddhist traditions. I do not see anything wrong with it. Religious dialogue has been going on from time immemorial. In their quest for truth, they had been experimenting with one belief or another and using the same place for their dialogues or discourses. If people change their faith, naturally they would use the same place, which they had been using earlier, for their prayer and dialogue.

If a person is an idol worshipper, but he turns against it, he might throw away the idols he was worshipping earlier. He would be justified in his action, as keeping idols in his place of worship would be contrary to his new belief. Any person speaking in favour of violence or against the codes of conduct of Buddhism and Jainism cannot be a true Hindu. However, Hindu he would be, if he calls himself a Hindu, because Hinduism is not bound by Gods commandments, it being really a culture. As Hinduism has emerged from the deliberations and interactions of human beings, there could be further developments in its concept. The concept can even change if mens' reasoning so demands. So far Hindu philosophy and conduct has survived scientific and philosophical inquiry, but what can one say for the future. I can say one thing for myself, and that is that if any religion preaches violence against the followers of another religion because of their religious beliefs that religion is not worth having. Religion was created for the good of men, and so it should preach love and brotherhood of men and not hate against others. A person is good or bad because of his deeds and not religion.

Islam has contributed a great deal to Indian culture. And rightly so, as Muslims have been in India for over seven centuries, and they remained dominant in India for about five and a half centuries. Islam affected Indians in various ways.

The first effect was one of shock. It was due to the fierce fighting spirit of the Muslims and their zeal in propagating their religion. Indians had seen invaders earlier, but their effect was very limited. Either they went away or settled down and got assimilated in the local population. The new invaders not only stayed on in India to rule over it, but they carried with them a new religion and culture, which they very vigorously wanted to spread in India, and they did.

The first invasion in this connection occurred in 712 A.D. It occurred in Sindh. It was led by Muhammad Bin Qasim. He was sent by the Governor of Khalifa in the Persian Gulf. Because of this attack, the Muslim rule spread to Sindh and Multan. The second was Mahmood Ghaznavi, if we leave Subuktagin's small raid. Mahmood Ghazni led 17 raids into India from 1000 A.D. to 1026 into Northern, Western and Central India, primarily for plunder, but he called his battles against Hindu princes as 'Jihad', battles of Muslim believers against non- believers. He, however, was a religious fanatic and destroyed temples wherever he went. As a result of Mahmood's raids, Lahore and area beyond it had come under the rule of Ghazni or later under the rulers of Kabul or independent Muslim rulers, until Maharaja Ranjit Singh conquered back Lahore and the area.

The real occupation of India started in 1193, when Muhammad Ghori defeated the King of Delhi and Ajmer, Prithvi Raj Chauhan. After that gradually the extent of Muslim domination in India increased until Malik Kafur, a general of Allaudin Khilji, captured Rameshwaram in 1311. After Allaudin's death, the Muslim empire never reached that extent. After Malik Kafur's exploits, only a small kingdom in the southwest corner of South India had remained independent of Muslim domination. Because of Allaudin's cruelty and lust for power and riches, the Hindus suffered. Otherwise he did not persecute them. Feroz Shah Tughlaq, Sikander Lodhi, Shah Jahan and Aurangzeb were the real bigots. They demolished temples and harassed Hindus in various ways. It was kings like these who kept the spirit of rebellion and the spirit of their identity alive among Hindus.

During the Sultanate (the rule of the Sultans before the Mughal rule), Hindu rulers went on fighting individually against the invaders. A strong king could maintain his rule in a vast area of the country but during the reign of a weak King, the Hindu Rajas and Muslim Subedars exerted their independence. The Hindus were not entirely subdued. Actually, when Babar came to India, the ruler at Delhi controlled a small part of the country; the rest of the country was under different rulers. Among the Hindu Rajas, the most powerful was Rana Sanga of Mewar. In the south of South India was the prosperous and great kingdom of Vijaynagaram, while in the north of South India there were five Muslim kingdoms. Ibrahim Lodhi, the last Lodhi king, was defeated by Babar easily. But the real battle for the control for North India, he had to fight with Rana Sangha. It was only after his defeat of Rana Sanga that the foundation of Mughal rule in India was laid. Similarly, when Humayun, the second ruler of the Mughal dynasty died, immediately after his enforced exile of fifteen years in Persia, his young son, Akbar, under the tutelage of Bairam Khan, had to fight a fierce battle at the famous battlefield of Panipat with Hemu Baqal, a Hindu, to gain the throne of India.

Akbar was the first Muslim ruler who consolidated his empire in India. He laid the solid foundation of his rule by making the Hindus and the Muslims work together. He removed all disabilities against Hindus from which they had suffered till then. This angered the orthodox Ulema and they raised their voice against Akbar and his reforms, but Akbar continued on his path. He removed the tax jezia, which all Hindus had to pay. He also removed the pilgrim tax on Hindus, which all Hindus had to pay while visiting places, which were sacred to them. These two taxes were not only a great burden on the poor Hindu peasants and artisans, but also had implicit in them a design to make it difficult for poor Hindus to keep their religion.

Islam was a great religion. It appealed to people for its message of Islamic brotherhood and its simplicity. While the Hindus, when the Muslims came to India, discriminated against each other on the basis of caste.

Islam was very simple to understand and follow while the philosophy of Hinduism was difficult to follow and practice, as the Brahmins had made a mockery of rituals and had added numerous spurious books and perverted interpretations to old texts. This may have helped in the conversion of many Hindus to Islam, but other causes of conversion were political patronage of the Kings and the Government to Islam and the persecution of Hindus by many kings. Some kings even offered monetary benefits for conversions as inducements. In this connection the jezia hurt Hindus greatly. During the Sultanate and even the Mughal period, Muslim amirs and generals were rich and lived in great luxury. However, the population in general was very poor. Peasants and artisans had very low income and famines were frequent. Under such circumstances, the payment of jezia for a common peasant was too much. The pilgrim tax also hurt the people, as going to sacred places was a thing of great cultural and religious importance. Personally, I do not think pilgrimage can be of religious significance. But the Hindus of old perhaps had introduced this practice to promote national unity and religious fervour.

It is to be noted that when only nobles and upper classes were educated and a foreign language, Persian, was being promoted, the masses suffered. But the ordinary people tried to compensate in their own way. They started teaching their children orally. Knowledge learnt from ancestors and contemporaries was, thus, passed on to a succession of future generations. Knowledge of Hindi and Sanskrit was also passed on by generations of pandits to their successive progenies. Hindi, of course, was taught and learnt by Hindus in various pockets in the cities, in the kingdoms of Hindu rajas and other places, which were untouched by foreign influence. The oral learning tradition has been so strong that even now parents follow this in villages where education has not reached. It is a marvel of this education that even today a peasant in a village, though illiterate, knows more about his profession, religion, traditions and country that villagers in some places in an advance country may not know.

In the time of Akbar, Indian literature and arts were also patronised because his courtiers were all learned people and Akbar though illiterate, was interested in them. Akbar was very liberal in his views. Babar and Humayun, the first and the second emperors of the Mughal dynasty, perhaps, were also of liberal views and had a broad vision. They both were scholars and were of a tender heart. It is said that once Humayun fell ill. His condition must have been serious, because it is stated that Babar prayed for his son's recovery in exchange of his own life. Hamayun got well and Babar died. Humayun also treated his brothers very well. When Hamayun ascended the throne, he distributed his empire between his brothers and himself. When later on his brothers turned against him, he did not bodily harm them. This was in stark contrast to Shah Jahan and Aurangzeb, who walked through the corpses of their brothers to ascend the throne. Unfortunately, both Babar and Hamayun did not rule long enough to do much.

It was left to Akbar, the grandson of Babar, to consolidate the Mughal Empire by his wise policies. Akbar extended his inheritance, consolidated his gains and worked at the grass root level to give his empire permanence. He knew that the Mughal Empire or Muslim rule in India would not last long until the hostility of the Hindus could somehow be eliminated. He knew all conquered people in due course overcome their weaknesses and learn the new techniques of organization, fighting and training from the conquerors and drive them away. He must have realized that one day the Hindus of India, or Hindustan, as it was called in the Muslim period, and later by the common people, would gather together and fight against the rulers under one common leader, instead of singly as they had been doing earlier. The danger was there, as in no time all of India was firmly or even less firmly held together by one single ruler. Akbar, therefore, went all out to conciliate the Hindus. He knew that the empire could last only if the Hindus and the Muslims worked jointly together. He, accordingly, integrated the Hindus in civil administration. He inducted the Rajput princes and soldiers in his army, so that they fought for him rather than against him. Taking of slaves from the defeated enemy's armies had been a common custom of the Turkish and the Afghan kings. Akbar discontinued it. Actually, in many ways Akbar did what the English did two and three centuries later.

Babar, in his person combined the finest qualities of the Turks, which he inherited from his father'side and the Mongols, which he inherited from his mother's side. But the strange thing is that, as it is stated by Muslims now, Babar had demolished a temple, which was located at the site of the birth place of Rama, the incarnation of the God of preservation, Vishnu, in Hindu mythology, and built a mosque in that place. Babar could not have caused that much damage by demolishing a dozen or more temples at other places than he did by demolishing this temple and constructing a mosque in its place. Today, this site is in dispute. The Hindus claim it as a temple and the Muslims proclaim it to be a mosque. It has caused more trouble between the Hindus and the Muslims than all other causes taken together. Many people have died in riots and more will die in due course, as it does not seem probable that Hindus would leave the birth place of Lord Rama, who Hindus believe combined in himself the finest qualities of an ideal man; an obedient son, a faithful and loving husband, devoted brother, a warrior, a fighter for justice and right causes, a chivalrous foe and a just and kind king, who listened to the public and had their interest at heart all the time. It is because of this that Hindus, even now when they talk of Utopia call it by the name of Ram Raj, the rule of Ram. I do not know why Babar did what he did in building a mosque at the site of the birthplace of Rama at Ayodhia. This aberration I can explain only by stating that in the generous heart of Babar lurked a streak of fanatacism, of which history did not see much because of his short rule in India; that is only if he did build a mosque at the site of Rama's birth place, of which, I understand, still there is no historical proof.

It was left only to Akbar to conciliate Hindus and extend and consolidate the Mughal Empire. Jahangir followed the policy of his father. It is said he abolished cow slaughter to please Hindu Rajas. Anyhow, the public was happy with him, and when Shah Jahan came to the throne, he inherited the legacy at a time when Mughal power was at its zenith, and the Muslim power was firmly established. During the Khilji and the Tughlaq period, the empire had extended right down to the south, but the area was loosely held and succession of rightful heirs was doubtful. During the Lodhi period, the empire had greatly shrunk and had an area covering Punjab, Uttar Pradesh and Bihar only. During the Mughal period, as Hindus and local Muslims were also employed in the governance of the empire, the administration was good and the empire was firmly held. Earlier mostly foreign nobles held positions of importance in the court. For three generations, the succession to the throne, during the Mughal rule, had been orderly. With Shahjahan, came fratricide, and each succession thereafter was accompanied by fratricide. So, firmly was the empire established that succession passed on in the Mughal line down to Bahadur Shah Zafar, the last nominal Mughal king, irrespective of the fratricide in the Mughal dynasty. No noble had the courage to usurp the throne, as they frequently did during the rule of earlier dynasties. The ancestors of Shahjahan had given that respectability to the empire in the minds of the public that the people could not think of a king outside the Mughal dynasty. Shahjahan, when he died, left for his heir an empty treasury and a resentful Hindu population.

Aurangzeb really started the downhill journey of the Mughal Empire and the end of the Muslim rule. Because of his bigotry, Aurangzeb provoked the Bundela rebellion. He could not suppress it. He enraged the Hindus by demolishing a temple in Mathura, at the site of the birthplace of Lord Krishna, an incarnation of Vishnu, the preserver. As Rama, the earlier incarnation of Vishnu, played the chief role in the epic Ramayana, Krishna did the same in the epic, the Mahabharta. But their rules were different. Ram is known as 'karam yogi', while Krishna was 'gyani'. Ram did what a perfect man should do. Krishna was a philosopher. He knew the secret of the universe and of life and death. He is stated to have preached the doctrine of the Upanishads in the Mahabharta. His discourse to Arjun, the chief warrior of the Mahabhartha, at the battlefield, just before the great battle of the Mahabharta, which lasted for 18 days, ensued, is contained in a book called the'Gita'. The philosophy contained in the Gita is known to be a gist of the teachings of all the Upanishads. In the place of the temple, Aurangzeb constructed the Jama-i-Masjid. The Jats, who lived in the surrounding area of Mathura, rose against the Emperor's bigotry. This rebellion was suppressed with the help of the Rajputs. However, the Jats remained recalcitrant and some years later, the Jats under Churaman founded a kingdom of their own around their capital, Bharatpur, 240 kilometers from Delhi.

His fanaticism led him to trouble with the princes of Jodhpur and Mewar as well. The Rajputs' struggle against the Mughal rule continued beyond Aurangzeb's life. But, the Mughals lost the service of the Rajputs, which they had been rendering as soldiers to the Mughal Kings, since the time of Akbar. Against the Emperor rose followers of Satnamis as well, for the same reason as the other Hindu sects and Hindu groups did.

In Punjab, a sect came into being from the preachings of Guru Nanak in the 16th century. Guru Nanak preached against the caste system and the exploitation of the people by the priests. He stressed on the importance of Karma, good conduct and good deeds. Guru Nanak was born in 1469. By the end of the 16th century a definite sect had emerged with their sacred book, Granth Saheb, and a sort of self-government, based at Amritsar. The Granth Saheb contained the teachings of Guru Nanak, and his followers were called Sikhs.The Sikhs had become very perturbed by Aurangzeb's policy of the persecution of the Hindus. The ninth guru of the Sikhs, Guru Tegh Bahadur, was called to Delhi by Aurangzeb for his resistance to Aurangzeb's efforts to suppress the Hindus. He was asked to become a Muslim. On his refusal, he was beheaded. This event led to the militarisation of the Sikhs under their 10th guru, Gobind Singh, and the Sikhs' persistent armed clashes with Mughal and Afghan forces, which ultimately climaxed into the formation of a Sikh state, comprising by 1923 of all the Punjab upto the right bank of Sutlej, N.W.F.P. and Jammu and Kashmir.

The Marhattas became the unbeatable enemy Aurangzeb faced. The Marhattas had not appeared in Indian history until the advent of Shivaji. Shivaji, brought up by his mother in the glorious traditions and past achievements of the Hindus, grew up among the people who were searching for their true path, having been influenced by the teachings of various saints, such as Tuka Ram and Ramanand. Shivaji, however, came under the influence of Ram Dass. The impetus for Shivaji came from the tyranny of the Deccan Sultans, and the persecution of the Hindus by Shahjahan and later by Aurangzeb. He started his fight at the age of 19, by capturing some forts. He spent his whole career in the achievement of his mission to overthrow the Muslim power in India. He died in 1680, after having been crowned king in 1674, having quite a substantial area under his control. Sometime before he died, he wrote to Aurangzeb, pointing out to him the dangers of the policy of intolerance. Aurangzeb was a Suni fanatic. The Suni sect is the dominant sect in Islam. The Sultan of Bijapur was a Shia so he wanted him to be dispossessed as much as he wanted to annihilate the Marhatta power. He also covetted the wealth of the Sultan of Golkanda. In 1685, Aurangzeb set out for the Deccan, South India, to finish off the business of the Marhattas and the two Sultanates once and for all. He first attacked Bijapur to punish the heretic. After the take over of Bijapur in 1686, he advanced on Golkanda. He took over the place in 1687. He proceeded against the heirs of Shivaji in 1689. The rest of his life, until 1705 when he died, he spent in fighting the Marhattas, but he could not beat the Marhattas, in their hilly terain and with the guerilla type of warfare they fought, they were unbeatable.

Aurangzeb had, in his own lifetime, done everything to destroy his empire. His narrow vision and bigotted approach to every action of his had nearly turned every section of the populace, except hardcore Suni Muslims, against him. The Rajputs, who since Akbar's time, had formed an important part of the Mughal fighting forces, had been alienated for ever. So were the Pathans, against whom he had carried on a campaign in the northwest. The Shias felt isolated. By his actions, he had made the Sikhs a fighting force. He finished off Bijapur and Golkanda, and, thus, extended his empire into the deep south. But what was the use of extending an empire when it could not be held within a few years of his death. The Marhattas controlled nearly all south directly or indirectly. The kingdoms of Bijapur and Golkanda had kept the Marhattas in check. Once they were eliminated, it was too difficult for the Emperor sitting far off in Delhi to prevent them from having sway all over the Deccan. Aurangzeb's successor did not have even that much strength to prevent the establishment of a Jat kingdom nearer home. The Mughal Empire went on disintegrating after the death of Aurangzeb. About fifty years after the death of Aurangzeb, the Marhattas nearly controlled the whole of India directly or indirectly. The Marhattas were defeated by Ahmed Shah Abdali in the third battle of Panipat, but still they were the most powerful force in the country and remained so until the British subdued them and others.

The above narrative would show that during the Turkish and Afghan rule, Hindus remained subdued, but there was no unity between the two communities wherever they were in touch. During the Mughal period the social intercourse between the two communities increased and the Hindus found a stake in the government. But Shahjahan and Aurangzeb destroyed whatever rapport had been built between the two communities. So, by the end of the effective rule of the Mughals in the beginning of the eighteenth century the Hindu and Muslim communities had come to accepting each other, but a sense of unity was lacking. The acceptance was for the following reasons.

The rising fact of the overwhelming majority of the Muslims being of Indian origin helped in due course to bring about a feeling of understanding between the members of the two communities, as neo-Muslims were after all the descendents of Hindu parents one or a few generations earlier and they constituted the overwhelming majority of Muslims in India. In the beginning there might have been hostility between Hindus and neo-Muslims, as it is stated that neo-Muslims are more hostile to Hindus than an ordinary Muslim. It can be that neo-muslims only reacted to the hostility and anger of the Hindus because of the pain it caused them. But living together promotes, ultimately, friendship and induces good neighbourly relations, in case there is no outside influence. In out of the way towns and villages such peaceful conditions prevailed until modern times. However, in cities and big towns the animosities acquired a sharper edge, because of the interventions of nobles, government officials and ulemas.

Two, the influence of saints and sufis also helped a great deal in improving the relations between the members of the two communities. Kabir and Nanak were two such saints amongst the Hindus, who preached the equality of all men, irrespective of religion, caste and status before God. Among the Muslims there were Sufis like Moin-ud-din Chishti, Salim Chishti and Nizam-ud-din. Sufism originated from Iran. But their message is unique in that it is the same as that of Hindu saints, which is derived from the Hindu philosophy of Karma. I understand in Iran, Sufis were even persecuted for their sayings being heretic, but, ultimately, the message of human brotherhood prevailed. In India it flourished, as it found a fertile ground in this land of karma.

In the greater part of the 19th century, the Marhattas dominated the Indian scene, though there were certain other independent Muslim and Hindu kingdoms as well. In the first half of the nineteenth century, the Sikhs dominated the scene in the Northwest of India. The Marhattas were not subdued until 1818. Haider Ali and Tipu were powerful kings of Mysore, but their kingdom did not last for more than 35 years and ended when Tipu fell before the British in 1799. Both were just kings and treated Hindu and Muslims alike. The Nizams of Hyderabad also controlled a large area in the Deccan, but they were weak kings and the Marhattas would have incorporated their Kingdom into their empire, had the British not descended on the Indian scene.

In the 18th century, the Muslims had lost the feeling that they belonged to a ruling class or race, except for some descendents of the Muslims Kings or Nawabs, but that was so in the case of the Hindus as well. In the 18th century and half of the 19th century, Hindus and Muslims shared their joys and sorrows either together or at least in equal measure: For example, if Nader Shah indulged in carnage in Delhi in 1739, the Hindus and the Muslims were both his victims. If in the attack of Ahmed Shah Abdali on Delhi, the Hindus suffered greatly, the Muslims also suffered from the Marhattas attack on Muslim kingdoms. From the depredations of Pidares in the beginning of the 19th century, they suffered together. So they died from famine and poverty. The Hindu kings employed Muslims in their armies and civil administration, and they were given high positions. Similarly, Hindus were employed by Muslim kings. In the third battle of Panipat, which the Marhattas fought against Ahmed Shah Abdali, in 1761, the officer incharge of their artillery was a Muslim: Abrahim. Actually most of the Hindu kings had Muslims as their artillery officers. Artillery was something of a new thing for them. They did not seem to have mastered it. Artillery was first introduced to India by Babar in 1526. But, the Marhattas, who became a force to be reckoned with about 150 years later, in the reign of Aurangzeb, neither mastered artillery nor did they learn the modern methods of warfare. After the eclipse of the Vijaynagaram Empire in 1565, in the beginning of the reign of

Akbar the Great, no possible challenger to Muslim power, amongst the Hindus, remained.

The Rajput princes remained, but they were weak personally as well as collectively. Personally, because they were chivalrous. They fought not to win, but to demonstrate their chivalry and to avenge insult to their honour. They were vain and generous, while to win a battle they were required to fight for their side rather than for personal glory, and had to be ruthless to win at all costs. It is because of their vanity that all the Rajputs could not join together to fight the invaders. The House of Mewar produced Rana Partap, and songs of his bravery are still sung by Hindus all over the country. But what could one Rana Partap do against Akbar the Great, while other Rajput princes were fighting against him as part of the imperial army. Rana Partap did not submit to the Mughal power all his life, but primarily his fight had been all along that of survival.

The Vijaynagaram kingdom was destroyed by four of the Deccan Sultanates combining together to beat the Hind Raja at Kalikota. They completely destroyed the capital city of Vijaynagaram. One can today only see heaps of stones all around and a few walls and a gateway in a broken down condition at Hampi on the bank of the Tungbhadra river, near Hospet railway station.

The Marhattas definitely mounted a challenge to the Muslim domination, and succeeded in establishing their paramountcy in India, and most probably would have firmly established their position but for the intervention of the East Indian Company. The Company's troops were well-trained, marched in easily maneuverable formations and were led by competent officers. The Company's commanders and officers had been given well-defined objectives and their armament was of the latest in design. Against this the Marhattas troops were composed of untrained soldiers; they were more a rabble than an organized formation. Their officers did not have the knowledge and training of contemporary European officers to lead their men capably. The Marhattas never seemed to have either local or long range well-defined objectives in their fights against the company. As for weapons, they neither had the weapons of the latest in contemporary designs nor had they the know-how to use those weapons. The worst feature of their backwardness was that they had not mastered the techniques of surprise, mobility and the concentration of forces at a point in the shortest possible time. Changez Khan had used these maneuvers very effectively in the 14th century. Many Turkish and Afghan Kings used them in India in varying degrees.

Napoleon mastered them and used them with great success at the end of the 18th and the beginning of the 19th century. He combined the concentrated artillery bombardment in conjunction with maneuvers to achieve preponderance of forces at a point of his choosing. German commanders achieved even better results in World War II, because of the use of tanks, armored vehicles and troops carriers to achieve mobility and surprise and used aeroplanes and heavy artillery to add to the efforts of tank corps and infantry to get the preponderance of force at the point of their choosing. I think, my point would be better explained if I gave here an example about Napoleon. Napoleon's first campaign was against Austria in Italy. He met with great success there. The Austrian strength in Italy was more than three times that of the French. He defeated Austrians in a series of battles, the most famous of which was at Merengo, and drove the Austrians out of Italy. He, even, in pursuit of the retreating Austrian army, had reached the gates of Vienna, the capital of the Austrian empire. While Napoleon was sent by the Directory, which was governing the French Republic, to deal with the Austrian menace, it had sent general Moreau against the Prussians, who had attacked France. Moreau was an experienced and a reputed general while Napoleon was about 26 years of age. During a conversation, after his return from the Austrian campaign, someone remarked to him that Moreau was suffering reverses in the Western front against the Prussians. Napoleon replied, it was not his fault, as he was outnumbered by the Prussians. That person stated on this that he, Napoleon, had also been outnumbered in Italy. Napoleon replied that he was never outnumbered. Whenever he attacked, he made sure that at the point of attack, his soldiers outnumbered his enemies. This principle, great conquerors and generals have always observed, but Indian princes never seemed to observe this principle, at least after 7th century A.D. Maybe it was because of the fact that Indians were peace loving people and they had generally discarded war as an instrument of the states' policy. India was not alone in it. The people in South America and Africa also fell easily before unscrupulous and vigorous invaders, but the only difference is that the Indian civilization was much more advanced than other civilizations anywhere in Africa, the Americas, Europe, Central Asia and South West Asia when it was overrun by barbarians.

The Marhattas, under Shivaji, applied this technique in fighting against Aurangzeb and the Deccan Sultanates. He attacked his enemies suddenly at a point of his choosing, with a maximum of force to achieve superiority of numbers, by using guerilla technique, but the Marhattas could not do so at the Third Battle of Panipat in 1761 against Ahmed Shah Abdali. They were beaten by Abdali inspite of the fact that they enjoyed a superiority in numbers of 5 to 1. Abdali beat them by using horses to gain mobility to achieve advantage of numbers at the point of choosing and to execute an enveloping movement. The Marhattas used elephants, which had been the bane of Indians against the earlier invaders, but the Manhattas of those days, it seems, never studied contemporary warfare techniques. The Marhattas, to further encumber themselves, had taken their ladies with them. The Marhatta generals led disorganized rabble while Abdali led a well-organized army. There were other faults also in the organization of the Marhatta army, but the fact was that the Marhatta did not have a Shivaji at that time. Shivaji was a capable general. He capably led his men. He knew the capability of his men, and so attempted what he could achieve. He also made the best use of the terrain he fought on.

One remarkable feature of Indian history has been that many a time a same single factor turned the tide at a crucial time in a crucial battle.

This singular factor was the death or incapacitation of the leader when on the verge of his army's victory. This happened first in the battle of Mahmood Ghaznavi against Anandpala, the King of Lahore in 1008. This was the crucial battle for Hindus, as it was their first serious attempt to stop the Muslim advance from the northwest. Mahmood Ghaznavi's raids, 17 in number into India, he called Jihad. Local Rajas had gathered round Anandpal to stop Mahmood from advancing further after crossing the Indus. In the battle, Mahmood lost thousands of his soldiers. While he was thinking of fleeing, Anandpala's elephant took fright and fled away. Seeing Anandpala running away, others in his camp also followed suit. This battle opened the gates of India for Mahmood Ghaznavi and Punjab was lost to the Muslims until the 19th century.

The second time, it was in the second battle of Panipat between Akbar and Hemu Baqal. When Hemu Baqal was on the verge of winning the battle, an arrow struck him, and this arrow cost him the throne of India and his life.

The third time it was in the Third Battle of Panipat in 1771, between the Marhattas and Ahmed Shah Abdali. When the battle was being fought fiercely, Sadashiv Rao Bhave, the Marhatta commander, got killed, and this brought about the rout of the Marhatta army.

This was the fatal flaw in the command structure of an Indian Army of yore. There was no chain of command, which could enable the second-in-command to succeed to the command in case of the death or the incapacitation of the leaders.

This all shows that the Hindus of those days were not inclined towards the martial art of soldiering while all the Muslim commanders who invaded India were capable generals well versed in the art of war, such as Mahmood Ghaznavi, Mohammed Ghori, Babar, Nadar Shah and Ahmed Shah Abdali.

In the beginning of the 19th century, the Hindu and the Muslim empires were something in the past. The slate was clean. The struggle was for survival, in which the Hindus and the Muslims were equally involved. They had to survive in the present and think of the future. The past was in History books, but the Hindus did not know much of their past. Most of the Hindus knew what they had learnt only by word of mouth from the previous generation. The Hindus and the Muslims lived together, shared the same climate, same food, same environment, same culture, same pedigree and the same problems. After survival, their main problem was to live happily and honourably in the changed circumstances in which a foreign power, Britain, had become the paramount power in the country, which within a short period of time had brought the whole country under its firm control. This they could do because they belonged to a very advanced civilization and had the education, training, conceptual goals, efficient organization, well trained army and highly organized administrative set up. Their army and administrative services were not only well organized but had available with them the latest and the very advance techniques. The best thing they had was that they were the representatives of a government which ran on democratic lines, and this gave the officers in the field pride in their job, dedication to what they were doing, initiative and a lot of latitude to do their job in a way they thought was in conformity with the principles of good government or in the best interest of the empire. The fact is that in at least the last 2000 years of its history, India had not been ever governed in such a democratic way, where everything was done in accordance with the law. The common man in the street may have suffered at the hands of a corrupt and sadistic officer, but earlier an autocratic officer could do anything to a poor individual. India had never been so well knitted together as under the British rule. In adverse circumstances such as during a foreign rule or under a cruel king, lose administration or concentration of administration in the major cities of the provinces was a boon, as people in the villages or far-flung places escaped the cruelties on injustices of the tyrant.

India had been very rarely united under the earlier kings inspite of the fact that a sense of unity prevailed all over the land from earlier times and every strong king tried to bring the whole country under his rule. The British Government, by their efficient administration, better communications, through institution of different services such as army and other civil services and in their policy in the spread of literacy had helped in bringing people together. The British government had done everything in the interest of running an efficient government, and by doing so they had brought people together. By their interaction, the people had evolved a composite culture in the evolution of which every section of the people had contributed.

Before the coming of the Muslims, India had evolved a very advanced culture. But a culture, which does not grow with time, becomes a dead culture. The Muslims brought with them a culture of their own. It was a rich colour. It was also composite of Arabic, Persian and Turkish cultures. The culture of the Muslim invaders enriched the Indian culture greatly, and so did the culture of the British invaders. The Muslims influenced greatly the eating habits and dress of the people. They actually introduced a new cuisine altogether. They introduced new languages like Persian and Arabic. A new language, Urdu, came up with interaction of Arabic and, especially, Persian with Hindi. Socially also the Hindus were affected by the Muslims. Hindus were individualistic in their entire outlook. They normally did not mix. They ate alone. They meditated alone and their social functions mostly were limited to within the family or immediate groups, while in the case of Muslims, they spent most of their life together. They ate together, rather from the same plate. This was the result of the nomadic life of Arabs, Turks and others, which they led. Muslims are enjoined to pray (nimaj) together by their religious precepts. Hindus were affected, mostly in the north, by becoming more social. I believe, Hindus had even imperceptibly changed the concept of God. Hindus believe God is all pervasive and without any form. They also believe that he is just. Muslims believe God to be a very powerful identity. They believe God in his kindness can overlook some one's sin or punish him if that person makes him angry. The Hindus do not believe God to be like that. They believe that in the universe, everything is in accordance with certain given rules and they cannot be changed. But now when an ordinary man in the street talks of God, he talks of him in terms of the Mohammedans 'concept'.

The greatest visible impact of Muslim invaders has been in architecture, fine tracery work, carpets, pottery and gardening. The arch was unknown in India. It came with the Muslim conquerors and so did the dome. The Persian impact had been the most. The Mughals built their buildings on Persian designs. The painted tracery on marble walls also came from the Persian. The Mughal gardens were also patterned on the Persian model. Islam brought with it innumerable artefacts and knowledge of various advancements made in other civilization. For example, though India had evolved a good system of medicine of their own, the Muslims brought with them a system of Greek medicine. Similarly, though peitra dura was original to Italy, Muslims introduced it into India. Similarly, ghazal' and 'qawali' became popular means of entertainment in North India. The Muslim religion does not permit any entertainment for its followers, and singing and dancing are taboo, but interaction of Urdu and Persian romantic poetry led to a formulation of a vocal music, known by its generic name ghazal. It is a popular music in North India. Qawali is another popular item. Qawali has its origin in sophism (Muslim). Qawali is led by a lead singer but then many others, who are accompanying musicians, either join him or follow him. It is mostly about the singer's love for God. The theme of the song recurs frequently in singing and with it the accompanying musicians join in with full gusto, singing and playing their instruments.

It is a historical process of levelling that conquerors take away much from the conquered but give away also much in return. Conquerors are ultimately absorbed among the conquered or are defeated and return to their homelands. The British also gained much from India. They got wealth and goods from India to make their island prosper, and men and bases to build and protect their empire. But with them came their religions and zeal to convert pagan Hindus to their religions. The Muslims came as conquerors. They spread their religion in the beginning by sword but later on when they settled drown, they used financial inducements, lure of office and their ulemas. Christians came later in more civilized times, but in the beginning they also used their priests for the job. The latter are still at it. The Hindus and followers of Judaism did not believe in converting others to their religion, as in the case of Judaism, its followers considered themselves a special people, and others could not be what they were. In the case of

Hinduism, the question of conversion did not come, as Hindu beliefs took time, hundreds of years, to crystalise, and so whosoever believed in them was a Hindu and the question of conversion did not realize. However, in due course of time, different people and tribes merged in Hinduism as well as in Judaism. However, when decadence set in and other civilized people emerged in their environs, Hindus as well as Jews did not admit them in their folds to show them that they were inferior to them. This was all due to the vanity, conceit and selfish interests that prompted them to refuse admittance to outsiders to their fold.

When Islam emerged in Arabia, its followers, conscious of their strength in their new found unity under the flag of Islam, gushed forth from their frontiers and in a short time they had overrun Iran and the middle eastern countries. Within a century of the death of Prophet Mohammed in 632 A.D, the middle-eastern countries, Iran, Sindh and Multan in India, North Africa, Spain and a part of south of France had come under the domination of Islam. It was not only the geographical extent of the Muslim power that was so overwhelming, but more so were the demographics of those area. The overwhelming majority of people of those areas had become Muslim. The Khalifa of all Muslims was not only the temporal head of Muslims but also their spiritual head. So, the armies of the Khalifa on one hand overran other countries for sake of plunder, but on the other, to spread Islam. But these two aims were not contradictory, as future history showed. The physical control of a country is not permanent, it is usually overthrown after some time, but by putting people into spiritual submission, everlasting control is ensured. The Khalifa got wealth, the resources of other countries to exploit and near total submission of people. This pattern remained, and religion accompanied the sword in every battle against the non-believers until the present times.

When the Christian Spain and Portugal started their expansion overseas, they did the same as Muslim monarchs. Christianity spread in the West Indies, Central America, South America, North America and Africa. Everywhere religion went with the sword. When the Europeans first came to India, the Mughal power had not yet made its inroad into the country. In Delhi, the Lodhis controlled a sizeable empire and in the rest of the country there were small to large kingdoms. In the Christian era, the Europeans first entered India, when Vasco da Gama came to Calicut with the Portuguese fleet. They came as traders, but started establishing their empire. They were given concessions and allowed to establish themselves at Calicut. Almeida was their first governor. Albuquerque was the second. He had designs to increase his territory and spread his religion. He captured Goa and forcibly converted the local people to Christianity. After this period of pioneering, I do not think that Europeans resorted to largescale forcible conversions. However, the Christian priests accompanied the army, wherever it went, and the priests enjoyed great prestige in the British regime.

Conversion of people in famine stricken areas or selling of a child for a seer of grains or a little money had been a common affair. Lure of higher education or education of even upto school level was another ruse in getting people converted. Establishment of convent schools in the British period was another measure for the propagation of Christianity. Even colleges were opened later on to inform the students about the righteousness of Christianity and show them the backwardness of their own religions and inequity of their rituals. The worst was and still is to indulge in proselytisation in the garb of charity. Whether one bribes a person or provides economic gains or makes his life miserable, in order to convert that person to another faith, it is a crime against humanity. But when one is a ruler or in a position of responsibility over that person whose conversion is effected by any of the above means, then it is or rather should be a capital offence. When theft of property and cash can be a serious offence, then to keep a person under personal captivity is even a more serious offence. What can be the punishment for an offence when a person's mind is kept in captivity for perpetuity, because the conversion of one person usually means conversion of all his future generations.

Convent schools and other missionary institutions are doing excellent work now and I do not have any complaint against them, but when in the past missionaries indulged in the work of converting poor people, or even now indulge in it, then it is reprehensible work. After all, whom did they convert, a simple, honest and docile man who does not tell a lie, who considers it a sin to kill any living being, who thinks that his deeds in the present birth would determine his fate in the next birth. Perhaps his only fault is or was that he is or was an idolator. But who is not? At least the followers of all major religions are, in one shape or another. Some worship an image, some a relic, some a building, some a book and so on. The peculiar part is that Hindus do not consider an image as God. An image only represents a manifestation of God. Actually Hindus see God in everything, even in oneself. A person, because of habit, ignorance and weakness of mind may pray in front of an image, but all Hindus know and believe that 'Karma', knowledge and renunciation of desires constitute the basis of Hinduism. For them prophets are not important and nor are they divine, because God is impersonal.

At the time of the partition, in 1947, India had about 25% of its population belonging to alien religions, about 2% were Christians and nearly all the rest were Muslims. Religions might have been alien, but people were not. People were nearly all Indians. Muslims here were not like Arabs or Persians or Turks. They had their own identity, which was Indian. Religion might have superficially imposed a certain code of conduct, but underneath they were Indians or Punjabis or Gujaratis or Biharis, depending upon their places of residence. It has been noticed abroad that Pakistanis like to befriend Indians rather than Arabs or Iranians. Arabs, somehow, they do not like at all. I would not say religion is not important. It is important in the making of the mind of a person, and especially because the Muslim religion prescribes a strict code of conduct, even lays down its own personal and criminal law and then their religious Quran, which the Muslims believed to have come to them from God in the shape of commandments through their prophet, Hazrat Mohammed, is written in Arabic. But the effect of Indian culture on all those whose forefathers were nurtured in the ambience of Hindu culture cannot be minimised.

The Hindus may have been exposed to the Muslim religious teaching for over seven centuries but conversion of all Hindus to Islam did not take place seven centuries ago. This conversion was a gradual process. At the time of the partition, for a good many Muslims, their religion may have been only a few generations old. So the general Indian culture could not have lost its appeal and effect for the Indian Muslims. Inspite of the efforts of the kings and the nobles to transform Hindi or Hindwi into an Arabo-Persianized language, they could not change the basic structure of the language. The only change they could affect was in the script and the vocabulary. The Persian script, which was adopted for Urdu, was itself based on Arabic. Even areas which comprise Pakistan, have retained their original languages, which were derived from Sanskrit, the classical language of India. Punjabi, Pushto, Baloch, Sindhi and Bengali are derived from Sanskrit.

As I mentioned earlier, in the 18th and a great part of 19th century, cultural unity, common interest, common experience of poverty, deprivation, famines and exploitation by a foreign government had welded nearly all Indians into a nation. The education, efficient means of communication and transportation also helped in this process. In the Mutiny of 1857, while every leader fought for self-interest, Hindu and Muslim soldiers fought together shoulder to shoulder to throw away the foreign power. I do not consider the Mutiny of 1857 as a war of independence, as every leader fought for his or her self-interest. Bahadur Shah Zafar was not the emperor as it was claimed he did not even rule Delhi and the Mutiny did not cover the whole of India or even the greater part of India. But it was the finest hour in the history of the people of India because in that year the Hindus and the Muslims fought together to throw away the yoke of domination of a foreign power.

But only twelve years later, Sir Syed Ahmed Khan said that Hindus and Muslims were two different nations and could not live together. He might have been prompted to say that because of the advance Hindus were making in the social and educational fields. The Hindus creative faculties had remained dormant in every field since the advent of Muslim rule in India. Foreign rule kills initiative pressure because of lack of state's patronage and fear of attracting adverse reactions. Even before the advent of Islam, schism had set in the faith of Hindu society. With the coming of the foreign rule, their attitudes became rigid, the discussions ended and religious debates became things of the past. It was as if the true spirit of Hinduism, which found expression in inquiry, self-criticism and religious debates had become dead. Hinduism had frozen in time. Hindus adopted a defensive strategy in order to save what they had, and not only lost its philosophy but the past itself. In due course they guarded the shell only, the spirit having left it. This frozen state remained until the beginning of the 19th century.

Al Beruni, who came to India in the time of Mahmood Ghazni and stayed in the country for some time and studied philosophy, astronomy and other disciplines, found Indians believing in one God but worshipping images. The caste system then existed, but the members of various castes lived in the same towns and villages and mixed together in the same houses and lodgings. It means that the caste system was not rigid. Under the Muslim rule, Hindus became secluded, as a defensive stratagem, and well-to-do Hindus kept their women folk confined to their houses like the Muslims' 'purda'. Gradually, the caste system became rigid; another self-preserving, but a religious and political evil custom. Al-Beruni also stated that the Hindus were haughty and conceited persons who looked down upon foreigners and called them Mlecchas and avoided contact with them. The above stated behaviour of the Hindus comes true to type. A person in a high position, when he falls down from that position, what does he normally do? He poses as a superior being but he does not deceive anybody, except himself, by doing that. They called foreigners Mlecchas for the same reason I think, but there are two other reasons. The Muslims called the Hindus 'kafirs', so the Hindus called them Mlecchas derogatively. But there is another reason and that seems to be more potent and that is that Muslims ate meat, and especially beef and they otherwise also did not come upto the Hindu code of conduct, while the Hindus generally did not take meat and abhorred those who ate cow (their sacred animal). The Hindus otherwise also are very clean people. Cleanliness has been interwoven with all their religious rituals. Even the poorest try to do everything hygienically.

Poverty and hygiene generally do not go together. Dominique Lapierre, writing about the Hindu residents of slums areas of Calcutta, in his book 'City of Joy', states that they were the cleanest people in the world.

It was only in the beginning of the 19th century that a thaw of the frozen Hindu society started. Hindus, until then, were creatures of customs and rituals. It was only the study of Sanskrit by Western scholars that revealed to the Hindus that they were descendents of a great civilization. Many Hindu reformers, who spoke against the evil customs and their eradication, also came up during this time, A number of Sanskrit scholars and researchers, especially in Bengal and Gujarat, during this century, gave Hindu thought a new vigour which had been lacking till then. They interpreted the old texts and threw out the erroneous interpretations. Many of the beliefs and practices were challenged in the light of a new learning of the Vedas, the Upanishads and the Shastras, which had been overlooked and forgotten because of the dross accumulated over the knowledge of the past, the motivated interpretation of old texts, the publication of spurious religious books and adulteration of old literature by doctoring it. The Hindus in the cities, large towns, being relatively better off financially and advanced in outlook, took to education earnestly.

Foreign archeologists also dug up many sites to discover stupas, pieces of sculpture, paintings and pottery dating back to thousands of years. Previously there was not much evidence to show that the Hindus were builders or had any claim to artistic achievements. In North India, no temple claiming any title to antiquity was left. Foreign rulers had destroyed all old temples or other structures of any significance. Only two groups of temples escaped; one at Khajuraho and the other at Bhubaneshwar. The temples at those places escaped destruction because they were at out of the way places, not being near any main route. Bhubaneshwar was in far away Orissa. Khajuraho's temples dated back only from the 10th to 12th centuries A.D. So were those of Puri. In the south also the oldest temples were of that period. The shore temple at Mahabalipuram beach, which is a small temple of stone blocks, is stated to date back to 6th century A.D. The Kailash temple at Kanchi Puram is a proper stone temple, belonging to the 7th or the 8th century A.D.

All these developments did give the Hindus a sense of pride in their beliefs and history, and provided them impetus to learn about their past, and the developments taking place in their vicinity and elsewhere in the world. Some writers state that it was the age of reformation for the Hindus. If it was, it is not complete yet. The Hindus still have to get rid of many religious practices which are contrary to the thinking of the philosophers of yore; such as casteism and social practices like dowry, superstition and belief in astrology.

Muslims by the middle of the 19th century slid back in education, social and cultural pursuits and started suffering from an inferiority complex from the new found confidence of the Hindus. They came to feel that while once they had ruled over whole of India, the Hindus were forging ahead in every field. This was a mistaken belief, because the rule in India was that of foreigners. The forefathers of the Muslims suffered as much as the forefathers of the Hindus, as many Muslims after all are converts from Hindus. After the Mutiny of 1857, the Muslims felt aggrieved because of British discrimination against the people of Agra and Audh, the whole area which is known as Uttar Pradesh. This came about because over the years, in the past, Delhi and this area came to be the stronghold of the Muslim power. The nobility was generally from this area. The imperial army was also mostly recruited from this area, apart from the Pathans who constituted an important part of this army. Later on Akbar, being a very shrewd man, had a wing of his army composed of Rajputs. Akbar achieved two objectives from this move. By honouring Rajput nobles and recruiting Rajputs in his army, he won over a greater number of Rajput states to his side, and this eliminated perpetual hostility of Rajputs to a great extent. He used his Rajput soldiers and Raja Man Singh of Jaipur, a great general, to fight and defeat Maharana Partap of Mewar, a great Rajput warrior who never submitted to the Mughals. The Rajputs were very reliable, as they could not rebel against their king or leader, it being against their honour.

The second objective, which he achieved, was to ensure that the army remained loyal to him, as no general could subvert the army, as long as the army's constituents were of disparate elements. The British followed the same policy. The British had also recruited a large number of Indians in their army, and they came from different areas and people. They used this army to beat the Indian princes. During the Mutiny, the soldiers from Delhi and Uttar Pradesh revolted and they formed the core and the largest element of the Indian army but the British brought soldiers from other areas to suppress the Mutiny in Delhi, Uttar Pradesh and a part of Bihar.

After the Mutiny was over, the British stopped recruitment of the army from this area of Delh and Uttar Pradesh, as their loyalty had come under doubt. Though the Hindus were also recruited in the army from this area, the Muslims had constituted a major part of that army. This became a big grievance because the Muslims of this area, had in the past, provided the ruling class and the nobility and in the 19th century provided the leaders of the community, the thinkers and the muscle power in the shape of soldiers of the Company, Nawab of Audh and the ruler at Delhi, though the ruler of Delhi did not have much of an Army. So when the British stopped recruitment from among this area and also denied patronage to the Muslims from here, it naturally became a major grievance of the Muslims as the previous army formations from this area stood disbanded after the mutiny.

To relieve the backwardness of the Muslims, Sir Sayyid Ahmed Khan led a movement, called the Aligarh movement for education of the Muslims. Sir Sayyid was responsible for the establishment of Aligarh University. He was the best-known Muslim leader of his time. Though he did say that Hindus and Muslims could not live together, but once he also said that Hindus and Muslims were like the two eyes of India. So I do not attach much significance to what he said at different times, but the fact remains that the Muslim leaders felt resentment at being left behind by the Hindus in nearly every field.

In 1885, the Indian National Congress was formed. Gradually more and more Indians, through it or other forums, demanded independence for the country. Many writers like the Bengali writer, Bankim Chandra Chatterjee wrote in a patriotic vein. Swami Dayanand, the founder of the Arya Samaj, was the first Indian of his time to have stated, even before the establishment of the Indian National Conference, that bad rule of our own is better than a good foreign rule.

This upsurge among Indians, made the British Indian Government sit up and take notice. In order to alienate the Muslims and the Sikhs from the Hindus, it started creating dissension between them and the Hindus. The Hindus and the Sikhs politically, socially, culturally and in religious beliefs had always been one. But the Government, through influential Sikh leaders sowed the seed of dissent between the two by making their own organizations independent of the Hindus to look after their interests. In a colonial set up, it is always easy for the government to manage the people through some influential leaders. In the case of India, upto World War I, the British could manipulate the community leaders easily, through patronage like award of titles, contracts and nominations to position of authority, recruitment of kith and kin at government jobs, grant of agricultural lands and such like other favours, and even after the war it retained a lot of maneuvering power, and exercised it upto the independence of the country to a varying, but declining, degree of success.

In the beginning of the twentieth century, the Sikhs formed Singh Sabhas to look after their interests. In 1911, the Muslim leaders, under the leadership of Agha Khan, met the viceroy to ask him for the protection of Muslim interests. This was prompted by the government, otherwise there was neither a political forum of Muslims nor was Agha Khan a political person.

The British introduced communalism in India and separate electorates for Muslims to strengthen it, in order to keep the Muslims separate from the Hindus, so that they would not unite together against the British to overthrow the foreign yoke.

Mahatma Gandhi was responsible in glorifying Muslim communalism and bringing it into the mainstream of national politics. The allies, after the conclusion of World War I, decided to do away with the Sultanate in Turkey. The Sultan of Turkey styled himself the Khalifa of all Muslims, and the Muslims all over the world recognized him as such, though Turkey for a long time had been considered the sickman of Europe. If Turkey's political setup had survived till then, it was because of the rivalries amongst the major European powers. The Ottomon Turks had established a vast empire in Turkey in the fourteenth and fifteen centuries. Once the Turkish Empire extended from the Balkans to Western Asia, including all the Arabian countries in Asia and Egypt. However, in the 19th century it was a weak power. Its territorial possessions, it lost one by one. Greece became an independent state in its war of independence, 1921-1931. Actually,

Turkey got involved quite often in open insurrections or wars in the 19th century in connection with the independence of certain subjugated Balkan countries and the territorial claims of Russia and others. Because of these causes, Russia and Turkey got involved in war in 1854. Great Britain and France intervened on behalf of Turkey, in order to stop Russian expansion in southeast Europe and West Asia. This was called the Crimean War and it lasted upto 1856. Russia and Turkey were again involved in war in 1877 and 1878. Because of this war, Bulgaria became an autonomous province of Turkey. Bulgaria was declared independent of Turkey in 1908. Egypt became independent of Turkey in 1879, except for the nominal suzerainty of Turkey. That suzerainty, British ended in 1914. Albania became independent of Turkey in 1912, after an uprising. Turkey faced the combined attack from Serbia, Greece and Bulgaria in 1912.

In World War I, the Arabs revolted against Turkey's domination, and became independent with the help of the British. The modern Arab states in Asia, were the result of the dismemberment of Turkey in World War I.

The Arabs revolted against Turkey and they did not recognize the Sultan of Turkey as the Khalifa, but when the allies after the World War decided to remove the Sultan, Indian Muslims got agitated and demonstrated against that decision and 20,000 of them from Sindh and N.W.F.P. even migrated to Afghanistan against the decision. Mahatma Gandhi saw his opportunity in the resentment of the Muslims. He launched an agitation, in co-operation with the Muslim leaders. The agitation was based on non co-operation, and had the dual purpose of self-determination and maintenance of status quo ante in the matter of the Khilafat. Gandhi's idea was to bring Muslims into the mainstream of political agitation against the British; otherwise what interest in the survival of the Khilafit could he have. He could neither be interested in Turkey nor in the survival of the Khilafat. On the contrary, as a democrat, he would be against the survival of a King, and the Khalifa who would command extraterritorial allegiance of the Muslims of India. Such an allegiance meant extraterritorial loyalties of the Indian Muslims, which was a direct threat to Indian nationalism then and to the Indian nation subsequently. However, for the first time in history, Hindus and Muslims had joined together, on an all India level, for a cause, and that too against a foreign power. But at what cost? In Malabar, on the west coast of India, the Moplas (Muslims) rose against the British. Their uprising was political, but they killed some Hindus and converted a large number to Islam in their misguided zeal.

Perhaps, this occurrence would not have caused much damage, if the converted Hindus had been reconverted immediately from Islam to Hinduism, but the problem was that Hindus did not believe in proselytism. As I have mentioned earlier, tribes and people have gradually got absorbed in Hinduism, but Hindu casteism has been so strict for the last one thousand years that no person belonging to another religion could be admitted into Hinduism until recently. A Hindu was born a Hindu. A change of faith from another religion to Hinduism did not mean acceptance into the Hindu fold. Actually this restriction was valid only in case of semitic religions who believed in an all powerful God and trace all their religious commandments to him. Buddhists, Jains, Sikhs and such like other religions did not come under such restriction, as in their case, the difference is only in nuance, and emphasis on dialectics; otherwise the basic faith remained the same, and hence no change in the faith is involved.

There was a great hue and cry among the Hindus at their impotence in not being able to do anything about the outrage perpetrated by the Moplas, not even to bring back within their fold their co-religionists, who had been forcibly snatched from them. At this, the followers of Arya Samaj came to the forefront. The Arya Samaj, a Hindu reformist movement urged the Hindus to go back to the Vedas and discard idol worshipping, rituals, injunctions of the Purans and the caste system, which were contrary to Vedic teaching. They believed that anybody who believed in the basic Hindu thought and philosophy could be a Hindu. Arya Samaj, at that time, was mostly confined to Punjab. However, they got mobilized and sent workers to Malabar to reconvert the Hindus forcibly converted to Islam. They achieved some success in this mission. But this Mopla rebellion had great effect on the Hindu Muslim relationship. The Arya Samaj started the 'shuddhi' movement to bring back into Hindu fold all those who had been converted to other religions as well as to convert others who wanted to be converted to Hinduism from other religions. This led to a reaction from the Muslims. The Arya Samaj leader, Swami Shraddha Nand, who started the Shuddhi movement, but was a great national leader, was killed by a Muslim fanatic. The Khilafat movement died down, as in 1922, in Turkey, Mustafa Kamam Pasha, later known as Ata Turk came to power and he abolished the Sultanate, and along with it the Khilafat. The relations between the Hindus and the Muslim in the cities had their ups and down, but in general, were never very cordial. Mutual interest occasionally made them friendly, but ultimately, the state of uncertainty returned.

In 1906, a separate electorate for Muslims at the request of the Muslim leaders, under the leadership of Sir Agha Khan, and its acceptance by the then Viceroy, Lord Minto, had put the two communities on the antagonistic path. It was in line with the British policy of divide and rule, but the Mopla rebellion and the Muslim religion upsurge generated by the Khilafat agitation had dealt a severe blow to the national movement and the integrity of the country, as they had evoked a reaction among the Hindus. The Shuddhi movement was one manifestation of it, but the arousal of communal feeling in a section of the Hindus was another and the most important. The reaction was more noticeable in Punjab, Maharashtra and Uttar Pradesh. The religious conflict had led to communal violence of the Muslims against the Hindus in Kohat in September 1924. Even the revolutionary leaders like Savankar and Bhai Parma Nand who had been deported to the Andamans to undergo long sentences of imprisonment there, became communal in outlook and founded a Hindu communal party, the Hindu Mahasabha.

Lala Lajpat Rai, another revolutionary, who had undergone a prison sentence along with Sardar Ajit Singh, another revolutionary, in the Andamans, and was called the Lion of Punjab, had developed mixed feelings about the political and communal situation in the country. He, however, died from injuries suffered from lathi (thick stick) blows from Seargent Saunders, while leading a procession against the Simon Commission in 1927 at Lahore. The Simon Commission was entirely composed of Britishers, with Sir John Simon at its head. The Commission had come to India to examine constitutional reforms. The Indian National Congress boycotted the commission, as it wanted a firm commitment of the British Government to Dominion Status of India. In revenge for Lala Lajpat Rai's death, Bhagat Singh, a Marxist revolutionary, along with a colleague, shot dead Saunders a few days later. The Ahrar party came into being during the Khilafat movement, but it remained in existence even later. It was controlled by pro-Congress religious Muslim leaders, but its following remained very limited. Another violence prone party, 'Khaksar', came into being in the thirties. It was trained on military lines, and it operated like the military. This party had really worried the Hindus and the Sikhs of the Punjab and N.W.F.P. It remained a source of anxiety for them until Sir Sikandar Hayat Khan, the then Premier of the Punjab, in the early forties, forcibly crushed this party after the incident when the Khaksars, in strength, were marching to forcibly occupy the Shaheed Ganj Gurdwara, in Lahore, and the police fired at them to disperse them. Quite a number of Khaksars were killed in this firing.

However communal relations continued to deteriorate and the Muslim League increasingly became very popular and was the vocal party among the Muslims. Its propagation of the two nation theory and the revilement of the Hindus and the Congress by its leaders had created the right atmosphere for its leaders in 1940 to raise the demand for Pakistan, the Muslim homeland, by integrating the Muslim majority areas into one unit. This, followed by vituperative campaign by the Muslim League leaders against the Hindus, led to so much blood and violence that in 1947, the Congress leaders, who were vehemently opposed to any partition plan of the country had to tell Lord Mountbatten, through Jawahar Lal Nehru, that the Congress would be agreeable to partition if Bengal and the Punjab were also partitioned. Hindus, who considered their country a sacred land, which had been inhabited by them since time immemorial, and were not willing to part earlier with even an inch of its land, had ultimately got reconciled to part with a substantial part of it. This partition, as far as the Hindus were concerned, was forever. They did not want to face the type of trauma they faced in 1947 again, which an aggressive and numerous minority could always bring about. The circumstances and the situation was such that a union government of all the Indian territory, as it existed before 15th August, 1947, could not have held, after the lapse of British authority, the Muslim majority areas against the will of the Muslims of those areas. The fact is, that after the acceptance of the two-nation theory by the Muslims of the country and their nascent hostility towards the Congress and the Hindus, the partition of the country had become inevitable for getting independence as well as peace on the subcontinent.

History had made Hindus and Muslims antagonistic to each other, but in the 18th and the 19th centuries they had come to accept one another. They lived in harmony with each other. They worked together. If they fought against each other, they also fought together as well. The Bhagti movement had also helped to bring them together. After the death of Aurangzeb, the dominance of Muslims in this country had ended. The decline of the Mughal power and the rise of the Marhattas and other Hindu kingdoms restored Hindus morale and self respect. This fact had proved to be a big leveller. The fact is that the intercourse and cooperation between the Hindus and the Muslims had greatly increased. In the second half of the 18th century, people of India were one nation in every sense of the word. By descent they already were, but history and religion had separated them. But by the second half of the 18th century, history had taken a full circle and united them. The surge of forces released by nascent Islam had been moderated by time and the spread of this faith to a vast area of the world. Hindus also had come to see Muslims as their brethren. Inspite of political differences arising later, nobody thought, at least seriously, that the country would have to be divided to provide a separate homeland for the Muslims, especially when nearly half the population of Muslims lived in the Hindu majority areas, until the beginning of the fourth decade of the century.

First the idea of a separate electorate was mooted by the then Muslim leaders in 1911, at the instigation of the British Indian Government; then came the communal award in 1932. Then was an idea floated of the formation of the federation of Muslim areas under one unit, within the Federal Government of India. In natural progression of this idea, after the Muslim League had consolidated its position among Muslims, came the suggestion of a separate country. Once the Muslim League officially adopted in 1940 this suggestion and demanded the formation of an independent Pakistan, a separate independent state comprising all the Muslim majority areas, there was no looking back. The demand gained increasing momentum with the passage of each year, until in 1947 it became a reality.

As I mentioned earlier, it was a good thing that Hindus are mild and politically never a monolithic community as Muslims are, otherwise one shudders to think what would have happened to the Muslims in the Hindu majority areas. While all the Muslim majority areas were involved in communal violence immediately before the partition, at the time of the partition or immediately after the partition, on the Indian side violence did not take place beyond Delhi and Punjab. Even Uttar Pradesh, Rajasthan, Madhya Pradesh and Bihar, which are called the heartland of India, did not get involved. Uttar Pradesh is, and was before the partition, the largest state in India population-wise. It is adjacent to Delhi and Punjab and had a history of communal trouble (actually it still has) but it remained aloof and did not face any communal problem those days.

Apart from the physical and emotional damage, which the minorities suffered in the northwest corner of the country, and to a much slighter extent in Bengal, because of the partition of the country, the national Muslims suffered a great loss emotionally and otherwise. The greatest sufferers in this respect were the Khan Brothers; Khan Abdul Ghafar Khan and Dr. Khan Sahed and their kith and kin and followers.

The nationalist Muslims in the Indian part suffered loss of prestige, expectations of rewards and respect in the Indian National Congress. Nationalist Muslims occupied an important and enviable position, as the Congress used them to counter balance the Muslim League's influence amongst the Muslims. When the League's threat was removed in the Indian Union because of the Congress leaders conceding the partition of the country, the loss of prestige of Indian Muslims was inevitable. Similarly, if India had not been partitioned, but had become independent as a whole, the national Muslims definitely would have occupied a position of importance in the new setup, especially when the Congress was prepared to offer the Muslims a much greater proportion of the share of power than their population justified. Immediately after the partition of the country, Muslims became suspect in India, as the partition was decided on the basis of religion, and Muslims overwhelmingly were in favour of it.

The loss of the Khan brothers was much greater, as they lost their identity. Instead of being patriots, they had become suspect in their new country. They lost everything: their identity, their ideal for which they had spent their whole lives and their hope for the future. Abdul Ghafar Khan told Indian leaders that he and his people had been deserted and thrown to the wolves. He was right; but there was no alternative for Gandhi and his followers. If they had not done as they did, the whole of India would have witnessed a blood bath, as Punjab witnessed, in due course. Dr. Khan Saheb was murdered a few years after partition in Lahore. But Dr. Abdul Ghafar Khan suffered incarceration in Pakistan's jails, for a greater portion of his long life, though in stretches, spreading over various periods, as he never got reconciled to the idea of Pakistan. He felt that if Muslims could not live with the Hindus under one government, in one country, so could not the Pathans with Punjabis and Bengalis in one country. He, therefore, demanded a separate country for the Pathans, Phakhtoonistan. Later, he advocated the idea of the merger of Afghanistan and the North West Frontier Province, so that the Pathans and the Afghans could live together, as after all they were from the same ethnic group, and the majority of Afghans spoke the same language, Pushto, as did the Pathans. According to his wish, he was buried in Jalalabad in Afghanistan, where he had spent a few years in the later stages of his life. His love for India was everlasting. He visited India at least twice, after partition, for treatment. The last time he was in India for treatment was in 1987. The treatment was of no use. His days were numbered. He was taken back to his native place Utman Zam, where he died after about a couple of months at the ripe old age of over ninety. He was a fighter; he kept fighting his whole life. He never submitted, even in the most adverse period of his life. At the height of his popularity, he dominated the political scene completely in N.W.F.P.

In 1930, Bengal sent the highest number of people to jail for political agitation: 15,000. While the N.W.F.P. sent 5000, but the population of the latter was less than 3 million, while that of Bengal about 14 times higher. In the second disobedience movement (at that period) between January 1932 and March 1933, the United Provinces had 14,659 convictions, 0.030 %; N.W.F.P. had the highest percentage of convictions: 6,053 and 0.25%and the Bombay presidency had the second highest percentage of convictions 14,101 and 0.064%. Madras had the lowest percentage of convictions and the Punjab the second lowest from the bottom. (The figures have been quoted from Modern India; 1885-1947 by Sumit Sarkar)

Abdul Ghafar Khan knew that Pakistan would be dominated by Punjabis, and so the Pathans would never be able to have much say in the administration of the country. Even otherwise, population wise, the Pathans would have the fourth position after the Bengalis, the Punjabis and the Sindhis. They all were from different ethnic stocks. Ghafar Khan knew that in a large India, the Pathans would be able to do what they liked, but in a small Pakistan, where ethnic disparities are very clearly marked, the Pathans would not have much scope for development. India being a large mosaic, where ethnic groups are nicely blended but have retained their individual identity, no group has any scope of domination over other groups; none being so strong as to dominate other groups spread over that vast and populous land.

Abdul Ghafar Khan's misgivings came true when East Bengal's representatives were not given the chance to form the Government in the centre inspite of they being in majority in Pakistan's parliament, and eventually East Bengal broke away to form an independent state of Bangladesh. It is to be seen whether Pakistan can retain its identity as such and hold together N.W.F.P, Punjab, Sindh and Baluchistan. It still seems that the provinces of Sindh, Baluchistan and N. W. F.P. are not reconciled to the domination of Punjab in the political life of the country though in the military, Punjab and N.W.F.P. both together have the dominant position.

Before the partition, Hindus and Muslims both were of the same ethnic stock in Punjab.The same was the situation in Sindh. Therefore, there were no differences because of language or identity in these two provinces. The only divisive force was religion, and that proved decisive. In the N.W.F.P. and Baluchistan, the Hindus were a very small minority. The Muslims had no fear of competition from the Hindus in the matter of political power. The Muslims there had a feeling in general that they were not good in commerce and accountancy, and that the job was done mostly by the Hindus and to a smaller extent by a section of the Punjabi Muslims like the Parachas, who spoke Punjabi. The Hindus, therefore, filled a need there. The Hindus in villages spoke Pushto and in such a rustic manner that the Muslims could converse with them. The Muslim small farmers and peasants trusted the Hindus more than the Muslims. They knew that an article kept for safe keeping with a Hindu would be returned on demand but they were not sure of their Muslim brothers in such a case. Similarly, they knew an article kept with a Hindu for mortgage would be returned even though the interest for the loan might be heavy. However, moneylenders and usurers were the bane of the Hindu community in Punjab, and to a small extent in the N. W.F.P. They gave a very bad name to the whole community. The Hindus in the Frontier had got integrated in the lives of the people. It may look strange, but nevertheless it is a fact, that Muslims there resented the presence of Punjabi and Kashmiri Muslim workers and businessmen but not the presence of Hindus, whom they had got used to and accepted. It was only the propaganda of hatred against the Hindus, based on religious differences between the two communities, which originated and was directed from the Hindu majority areas that not only gradually brought about a feeling of animosity against the Hindus in the minds of the Muslims, but nearly finished the Red Shirt Organization, headed by Abdul Ghafar Khan, which was well entrenched and once fully dominated the political scene in the N. W.F.P.

In the Pakistan of today the different ethnic groups are still not integrated, as one hears the news occasionally from Sindh or Baluchistan of demand for an independent state. I feel, after the settlement of the Afghanistan problem, one would hear about the N.W.F.P. as well. Actually, when India was partitioned, the

Imperialistic press and experts on India had not only expressed their fears but also gave their positive opinion that India would be further divided into a number of parts. They had based their opinions mostly on linguistic and ethnic differences and to some extent on statements and opinions expressed by regional leaders, who were inspired by the British rulers. The ethnic and linguistic differences in Pakistan were even sharper but they thought their religion, Islam, would keep them together. They had not realized the strength of India's culture and it's binding power. Its resilience has been tested for over twenty centuries. Western experts had not been realized that ethnic differences in India were not vast, as I have explained earlier. India's adoption of a faith of 'Karma' and self-realization much earlier in history (Modern scholars date it to about 800 B.C). had produced a very gentle and tolerant society. It had helped in the smooth mingling of people and the prevalence of a culture, which was based on tolerance, and absorbed, over a period of time, essential characteristics of all regions and groups. There was a breach in this cultural unity with the Muslim onslaught from across the border. The Muslims who invaded India represented a different religious philosophy and were from different cultural groups, like the Arabs, the Turks, the Pathans and the Persian. The violence of the Muslim onslaught had very badly shaken India's cultural unity and its faith.

I feel, India's greatest challenge to its integrity is still its large Muslim population. India's Muslims are Indians, but instead of rejoicing in its traditions and tolerant and secular culture, Muslims generally look to Iran and Arab countries for help and guidance. Unfortunately, Muslims in general are obscurantists, as they always interpret every doctrine or reform in the light of what the Prophet had said or what was obtained in the 7th century of the Christian era in the Muslim holy land, without taking into consideration the conditions of the present age. Indian Muslims are worse, as the interpreters are 'Mullahs', who are ignorant and selfish. To keep their leadership, they will block any reform affecting the Muslims socially or otherwise. So, on the one hand they keep the Muslims backward, and on the other they keep the Muslims away from the Hindus. To integrate the Muslims in the main stream, therefore, is a very difficult job, and would require quite some time to accomplish. The tragedy is that the Muslims of India cannot get integrated with the Arabians and the Iranians, and they know it, because religious affinity is not enough to override economic and geographical differences. The example of happenings nearer home is illustrative of this point.

At the time of the partition, because of riots or otherwise, many Muslims migrated to the Sindh province of Pakistan. Even after more than forty years of partition, riots occur frequently between the emigrant Muslims from India and the other people inhabiting the cities and towns of Sindh, where these emigrants have settled down. As I have already mentioned, the nationalist Muslims suffered a great deal because of the partition. Apart from the prestige and leverage they enjoyed, being the representative of a powerful and numerous minority, they nearly lost their identity altogether after the partition, as the basis of partition was religion. They were in a wilderness. Some of them adjusted to the new reality and adjusted accordingly, like Rafi Ahmed Qidwai who was a dynamic person and had established his position on the basis of his work in the field. He carved a niche for himself even after the partition and proved to be a very effective cabinet minister in the State of Uttar Pradesh as well as in the Union cabinet. Others like Maulana Abul Kalam Azad had gained importance because they were Muslims but were with the Congress. I understand, Maulana Azad was well read and especially in Muslim scriptures and Hadis (traditions relating to and sayings of the Prophet Mohommed) his knowledge was very deep. He came in contact with the Congress during the Khilafat movement, but while others like the leaders of the movement, Muhammad Ali and Shaukat Ali, drifted away from the Congress eventually, Maulana Azad stayed with it. He used to lead the Muslims of Calcutta in Id prayers, but he was removed from that prestigious position in the Islamic hierarchy by the Muslims of Calcutta, after retaining this position for a number of years, when the Muslim League had achieved ascendancy amongst the Muslims during the second part of the forties.

Maulana Azad remained a national leader, and an important one, in the Congress, because he was the most known, in general, among the Muslim Congress leaders. For the same reason, he was consulted about nearly every policy decision by the Congress high command, especially Pandit Jawahar Lal Nehru. However, he was never a true national leader. He was a Muslim leader in the Congress. His appeal to the Muslims was that he was a religious man and a master of Muslim theology. He had no appeal for Hindus. He could not stir Hindus by his rhetorics. Neither did he appeal to them as a nationalist, nor did one ever hear him talking of the glorious traditions of India pertaining to the pre-Islamic period and nor did he preach as a socialist. He was a Muslim leader in the beginning and he remained as such until the end, but his usefulness to the Congress diminished considerably when a non-practising Muslim, Muhammed Ali Jinnáh, who never claimed to be in the know of Muslim theology, led Muslims away from cow worshipping Hindus. That became the basis of the two-nation theory and led to the demand for Pakistan in 1940. Maulana Azad had rhetorics, but did not have the biting sarcasm of Jinnah. He could have attacked Jinnah on the basis of the desertion of the Muslims in the Hindu dominated India on the formation of Pakistan in the North West and in the East. He could also have put forward a socialist system acceptable to the Hindus and the Muslims both. Similarly he could have carried on a countrywide campaign against the Muslim League, rebutting its arguments, attacking vigorously its very concept of Pakistan and the two-nation theory on which it was based and mobilising the Muslims against it on the basis of self-interest. But, unfortunately, he proved to be inadequate to meet the League's challenge. As a leader of the nationalist Muslims, he failed miserably. He was neither a revolutionary nor a missionary. An ailing Jinnah had more fire and vitriol in his words than the robust Maulana. The fact remains that he did not bite, he did not fight and the worst was that he did not even exert. His rhetorics were staid and colourless, and too infrequent. Things came to such a sorry state of affairs that when the Viiceroy's Executive Council was formed in 1946, Maulana Azad had to be accommodated against the quota of seats allotted to Hindus, as Jinnah asserted that nationalist Muslims had no following amongst the Muslims, and so they could not present Muslims in the Council. The fact is that, except for Khan Abdul Ghafar Khan, who dominated the political life of N.W.F.P. until the middle of forties, and had a sizable following in N.W.F.P., even at the time that the partition of the country took place in 1947, no other nationalist Muslim had much of a following in the forties.

I understand, Maulana Azad has written in his biography that Rajinder Prasad was mediocre; having not the intellectual capability to reach the position he reached in the Congress hierarchy and the Government. According to the Maulana, Rajinder Prasad's rise was only due to his devotion to Mahatma Gandhi. That is not entirely true. He had organized the farmers of Bihar in 1921 at the time Mahatma Gandhi launched his first non co-operation movement and he remained the leader of Bihar until he died. He also carried out his duty diligently as Agricultural Minister. He was conservative in his outlook, but so was the Maulana. The Maulana's name was not even linked up with any reform, social or otherwise.

It is said that the Maulana has stated in his sealed papers, which are to be released 30 years after his death, that the partition of the country could have been avoided if Nehru had agreed to give one more seat to the Muslims in the Central Cabinet. I think what he means to say is that there should have been parity amongst Hindus and Muslims. He further states that Nehru had agreed to the partition after a month of the arrival of Lord Mountbatten and Mahatma Gandhi did the same sometime later. It seems to me that the Maulana wanted India to remain united at any cost, because the Maulana's own identity was involved. Without a united India, the Maulana had no relevance in India's politics.

He was a conservative leader of nationalist Muslims; and nationalist Muslims had much more importance than their number justified, because their very presence in the Congress ranks helped the Congress to meet the Muslim League and Jinnah's claim that they alone represented the Muslims of the country. Not that they were not sincere; that they were. Besides, the Redshirts of the Frontier, under the leadership of Khan Abdul Ghafar Khan, played a significant part in the Civil disobedience movements, between 1930-34. Due to them the contribution of the N.W.F.P. became much more than that of any other state in the country, taking the ratio of persons imprisoned to the population in each state. The Ahrars and other nationalist Muslims played an important part in the various activities connected with the Freedom movement, but, unfortunately, their contribution gradually diminished after 1934. The Ahrars were the product of the Khilafat movement, but even after that movement had lapsed, the Ahrars stayed on with Congress. The Ahrars wore red shirts and shorts. They were controlled by the Maulanas of Deoband School. Maulana Azad, however, had no relationship with the Red Shirts of the Frontier, nor was he the leader of all nationalist Muslims, as all provinces had their own leaders; besides some were liberal with a socialist bent of mind. Maulana Azad, however, was the most prestigious Muslim leader at the centre.

But the Maulana did not fight. Actually, he did not have in him the spirit to fight to maintain his position. The fact is, he was a phlegmatic person and had neither appeal for the educated nor for the man in the street; his strong point was that he was a Muslim who was a religious leader and a scholar in Islamic studies, having studied in Al Hazar at Cairo (Egypt, the famous seat of learning of Islamic studies.) Having failed to fight Jinnah and the Muslim League in defence of his principles and position, he accused Nehru and Gandhi in his papers for acceding to the partition of the country. The Maulana was unmindful of the killings in West Punjab and nor had he the sagacity to realize how many more lives would be lost in the future if the partition was not acceded to and neither did he care that India would be an unstable country if not divided on religious basis.

Epilogue

Dewan Jagdish Dass Sehgal completed a B.Sc. in Agriculture and then worked in the Agricultural Department in Lucknow for a short time before he joined the Indian Navy, which he served for ten years. He then went on to join the Department of Tourism, Government of India and retired as a Deputy Director General in 1983. It was during the early years of the retirement, in the eighties, that he wrote this book, which he had wanted to write all his life.

In this story of his early life, which he interweaves with the birth of a new India, he gives expression for the first time to the emotions, which he had kept hidden even from his family throughout his life. For the first time we, his family, learnt how he felt while growing up and for the first time realized that he, whom we considered our pillar and our inspiration, gained his spirit and strength through a constant trial by fire.

Jagdish Sehgal did not finish the book nor did he get it published. The reasons for both are unkown but maybe he felt the canvas of his thoughts was too vast to be put down on paper. When he passed away in July 2000, we found the book amongst his papers and in its reading, the man, as he was, came so much more alive for us than when we had seen him only as our father, and maybe for the first time the pre-partition age became a reality rather than a story in a book, which it always seems to our generation.

He did not fulfill many of his dreams. Maybe the time was never right to accommodate his strict principles and upright nature. But he lived upto his ideals at the expense of his ambitions and the fulfillment of his goals. He was known at work, amongst friends and family as a "satyavadi" and one who had the courage and zeal to live according to his ideals in his official and personal life.

We have always tried very hard to live upto the example he has set for us and feel the most important monument we can make to his memory is to share his thought and views, which are too precious to keep to ourselves. For in his story is the story of our country, and in his hopes and dreams lie those that we are too scared sometimes to envisage ourselves.

Sarita Bhatheja Vanita Sehgal Amita Sehgal Field